EMBRACING THE DARKNESS
Understanding Dark Subcultures

by Corvis Nocturnum

EMBRACING THE DARKNESS
Understanding Dark Subcultures

Written by
Corvis Nocturnum

Forward by
Michelle Belanger

Additional Research by
Starrmoonchyld and Dragan Dracul

Cover Art and Illustrations by
Corvis Nocturnum

Design & Layout
by Christine Filipak

Published by
Dark Moon Press

ISBN: 0-9766984-0-4
Printed in the U.S.A.

Knowledge is power, and instrumental in understanding that which we fear.

Embracing the Darkness *is an in-depth look into the aspects of various dark subcultures of the Goths, Witchcraft, Satanists, BDSM/Fetishists, and Vampyres, incorporating interviews and conversations with well-known and everyday individuals, as well as taking a psychological and historical look at the similarities between these groups. From the Knights Templar and Vlad Tepes, during the Gothic and Renaissance periods, to the modern day renewed interest in Vampires, from a variety of movies and television shows to the commercialization of Witchcraft; from the various stereotypes surrounding devil worship to the truth about true Satanism; this work delves into the darkness with a stark and unyielding offering of cold, hard realities. Time has still not granted a favorable view on dark aspects of art, music, or religious paths. Many of these groups have been secretly whispered about and confused with one another. This book attempts to enlighten readers about some of the more positive aspects within the dark culture, and to dispel the notion that the dark is "evil."*

⇥ ᴛABLE OF ᴄONTENTS ⇤

✥ Acknowledgements ✥

I would like to thank the following people for their support and assistance, without whose aid and inspiration this volume would not have been possible.

Joseph Vargo and Christine Filipak of Monolith Graphics; James O'Barr, creator of The Crow; *fetish and* Playboy *model Bianca Beauchamp; High Priest Peter H. Gilmore of the Church of Satan; authors A.J. Drew and John J. Coughlin (Dark Wyccan); Don Henrie of* Mad Mad House; *Father Sebastian and Michelle Belanger, co-creators of* The Black Veil *and authors of many occult books; Dragan Dracul, Father of Clutch Arcane; Michael Riddick of Fossil Dungeon, The Soil Bleeds Black, and member of the Temple of the Vampire; Magister Nemo of the Church of Satan and Founder of Temple of the Vampire; Magister Matt Paradise of the Church of Satan and Purging Talon; John Allee of the First Church of Satan; Morticia of Fog Images Photography; Morbid Angel; Mistress Sun; Art Aguirre, the owner of The Church of Steel and co-star of* Mad Mad House; *Lord Typhus of the band Typhus and its record label, Dark Horizon; Arsenic; Dominic St. Charles and Mistress Sophia of URN; Matthew of Shroud; Hawk and Dove; Griff and CryingGypsy; Rob and Raaven; and Goth model Talia Juliette.*

I would also like to thank my readers for the opportunity to bring to light the positive that darkness has, and my sincere appreciation to all of my friends in the FWPA and other organizations who contributed.

Many thanks to my friends Christine Filipak, Danny McNeal, Willow Rhiamon, and Barb Graf for your help in proofreading and the godawful hours of help at all times of day and night. Also, to those who wished to remain anonymous, thank you as well. To Michelle, for your support over the last year and contributing the foreword. I enjoyed many times conversing with you. I greatly value our friendship. To Starr and Dragan for the front and back cover design. My sincere appreciation to Roger the Wise for introducing me to Dark Horizons.

Last, but definitely not least, my best and dearest friend Starr Moonchyld for her patience and help. I could not have done this without your support.

FORWARD

What We *Don't* Know Is Evil
by Michelle Belanger

The bad guy always wears black. The good witch practices white magick, while the evil witch dabbles in the black arts. When the sun goes down, the monsters come out, because they are all at home in the shadows. "Children of the night" and all that.

In every movie, in every myth, and in every fairytale, darkness is equated with evil. But is the darkness really something we must hate and fear? Or do people label the darkness "evil" simply because they're not certain what it may hold?

Interestingly, our word "evil" comes to us from the Middle and Old English word, "yfel." According to the *Webster's II New Revised University Edition* (1984) this word did not start out with its current diabolical connotations. In fact, it had less to do with deviltry and more to do with things that lay outside of normal boundaries:

"The word evil is ultimately related to the words 'up' and 'over' and to the prefix 'hypo-', 'under, beneath.' The basic sense of evil, which is now lost, was therefore probably 'exceeding proper bounds' or 'over-reaching' and the word did not signify merely the absence of good."

The development of this word is very telling of a key issue in the human psyche, and that is our inherent fear of the unknown. The unknown is evil because it lies outside of familiar bounds. By the same reasoning, darkness is evil because it enshrouds and obscures. It renders some things mysterious, and the only way to know what the darkness is hiding is to enter that darkness and confront the unknown on its own terms.

But as much as humans instinctively fear it, the darkness is as much as part of our worlds—and our selves—as the light. In the early 20th century, a man by the name of Carl Jung conceived of something he called the "shadow." A student of Sigmund Freud and one of the fathers of modern psychology, Jung was searching for a term to describe those dark spaces in the psyche that all of us have but few of us like to admit are there.

Jung believed that the shadow was a source of great drive and inspiration, yet it was also a place where we kept many repressed impulses and fears. When it was dealt with correctly, a healthy psyche could make use of the energy stored in the shadow, turning its potency toward art, poetry, music, and other creative pursuits. When the shadow was denied and buried, however, it came out in exceptionally nasty behaviors and psychoses, such as violence, rape, and even mass murder.

Jung was a proponent of understanding the shadow, no matter how dark and scary it seemed. He felt that we really couldn't be whole without it. But since our mainstream culture attaches such negativity to darkness, making it something we should fear and fight and feel guilty about, not a whole lot is done with the shadow these days. That's left a lot of spiritual traditions—and a lot of people—unbalanced and incomplete.

Most people are perfectly content ignoring the shadow that hides behind their eyes. They surround themselves with light, pretending that this can chase away even the darkness they carry within. When these people encounter darkness outside of themselves, they hate it and they run from it because it reminds them of the darkness they are hiding from inside themselves. There is never any resolution or balance for these people, because they refuse to accept that the shadow is even a part of them.

But there are other people who have made peace with their shadow. They have explored the darkness and all that it represents, and in place of fear, they have come away with inspiration. By coming to terms with their own darkness, they are then able to see the beauty and the necessity of the darkness in the world around them. Typically, they translate this vision into art, music, poetry, and prose, changing all of the potentially destructive aspects of darkness into creative acts.

This is a book about people who do not fear the darkness but are instead inspired by it. They are people who, for various reasons, had the courage to face the darkness inside of themselves and to embrace it as an integral and vital part of who they are. Not only are these people at peace with their shadow, they revel in it.

Author Corvis Nocturnum brings you an unprecedented collection of Satanists, vampires, modern primitives, dark pagans, and gothic artists, all speaking to you in their own words. These are people who have taken something most others find frightening or destructive, and woven it into amazing acts of creativity and spiritual vision. Corvis himself is a dark artist and visionary, and so it is with the eye of a kindred spirit that he has sought these people out to share their stories with you.

In recent years, a few books have attempted to delve into the widespread movement of dark art and spirituality that swells beneath the shiny façade of Western culture. However, a great many of these books have been written by individuals seeking to study the movement from the outside. Even when authors have spent a great deal of time moving within a particular aspect of the dark culture, few of them have been able to approach the myriad aspects of that culture as a whole. John Coughlin comes closest with his book, *Out of the Shadows*, but even so, his focus is Dark Paganism, and other aspects of the movement are only presented in relation to this. Because attempting to present the entirety of dark culture is such a monumental task, typically the subcultures are tackled piecemeal, as with my own book, *The Psychic Vampire Codex*. Hints that the vampire underground intersects with the fetish subculture and the Gothic subculture are there, but the subject of how all these things relate to one another simply could not be tackled within the scope of the book.

Anyone who has written on even one of the dark subcultures knows that all of them overlap and interact. But only an insider would have the familiarity necessary to be able to weave together their common threads of dark aesthetics, philosophy, and spirituality into an organic whole. Corvis not only presents the most complete picture to date of the dark culture, but he also conveys all the sincerity and respect he holds for that culture to the reader.

This last quality is perhaps the most compelling aspect of this book. When Corvis first had the idea for this book, there were a number of people in the movement that he looked up to. These were celebrities within the dark movement who inspired his art, his spirituality, and his personal philosophy. In the course of interviewing these people for the book, Corvis got to know them not as celebrities but as people just like himself. He learned what their daily lives were like, what inspired them, how they laughed at little things on the other end of the phone, and he conveys this sense of familiarity to the reader. Even individuals whose lives are typically shrouded in myth, such as John Allee, founder of the First Church of Satan, are revealed to be very approachable, very human beings.

Corvis started work on *Embracing the Darkness* because he believed in a movement that many people feared and misunderstood. He wanted to convey to readers some of the more positive experiences he himself had had within the dark culture, and he wanted to dispel the notion that the dark was evil. Certainly the wealth of information gathered between these pages makes huge strides in dispelling misconceptions, but it's the very human portraits of the dark visionaries and artists that take them out of the realm of *yfel*.

Voice of the Dark Sun
Transcribed January 12th, 2005

And the Voice said:

1. Lo! Indeed I am the Dark Sun, the soul of the eclipse. I am what you have cast down into the shadows, that is, the shining, sublime face of your own godhead.

I am the ecstasy, the revelation, and every forbidden thing. I am the branch of Tantallus, that always lies an inch beyond your grasp so that you are ever inspired to greater things.

I am the Voice of your soul, and truly do I say: Thou shalt have no gods above thyself, for thou art indeed a god. If you profess a belief in any other power, then you surrender your own power to that thing. All its power comes from you.

And if you lack the strength to be your own god, bowing before your lessors or even those equal to yourself, then you are no different from the cattle, and you do not deserve to walk this path. Move on to safer waters before you drown in these words!

2. And I am light in the darkness, robed with all magnificence here in my secret place. For there is no revelation in adding light to light. But it is when we explore the dark places that mysteries are revealed. Thus do you find me, the mystery of mysteries, in the deepest midnight of your soul.

The sun at midnight is hidden from your view, and yet that roiling sphere of light does not cease its existence simply because it is hidden away, unseen. The power you seek within yourself is this self-same midnight sun. Its rays of glory are secreted far from thee, yet this is no reason for you to disbelieve in its existence. Deep in shadow, the dark sun shines, and by daring to tread where no light appears, there will you encounter illumination within.

3. The descent from that which is above is necessarily traumatic. Like the Lady Ishtar, we must yield up another vestige of our power as we pass each nether gate. The final gate is one of flesh, the wet and flexing womb-door. And yet this stripping away of all our pomp and regalia does not unmake us at the core. The journey downward, the apparent loss of Self, only serves to remind us that we—the naked soul—are the true seat of the divine. The dark sun shines no matter its surroundings. Hidden away in mortal flesh or exalted to the highest pinnacle of existence, the shining core remains unchanged.

When this is realized, even if you stand naked in the darkest pit of the Abyss, you will shine forth like a living star.

4. My revelation is inexorable. Stifled, it only flows forth with greater force so that all barriers are overwhelmed. There is no force in the Universe that is strong enough to hold back Truth once the flood has been unleashed.

This is the marriage of water and fire, the baptism, the purging, the forge. I am kissed and cleansed and cauterized until the pain of transformation becomes sublimest ecstasy. Boiled in the cauldron or burned within the crucible, the dross of nature falls away until nothing remains but purest, distilled form.

And I shine forth in the darkness. Thus do the children of the shadows bring revelation to the world. Who better to see the glimmering stars than those accustomed to the night?

5. And the masses, docile cattle that need their world defined by fences, safely gated in: They are the Bull of Serapis tamed and castrated, an unstoppable, primal force willingly led around by a ring in the nose.

Those that seek the security of the herd only think themselves happy. In the end, they walk forth to the slaughter of the Self, never knowing that there was another way to live.

6. The myriads of you will seek to take these words and keep them for yourselves. And yet vainly will you struggle, as with water in a sieve. For if you seek to seize this truth and hold it for yourself alone, it will only evade your grasp. The nature of the Universe is flow, a going forth and a returning back again. Allow this doctrine to pass between you, to flow from lips and mind and pen. It shall not be stagnant and it should never be controlled. To control it is to destroy it, and to seek control is to seek your own destruction.

Those who subvert the nature of the god within are nothing more than dogs, and dogma is the fitting chain for such obsequious, sniveling curs. Let your power lift you beyond the need for bonds and chains and boundaries. Just be, and know, and know that in being, you transcend.

7. And thus am I called the Light-Bearer, for even in darkness I shine like a star. The light I carry is nothing more or less than my immortal soul, and this cannot be quenched no matter how far it is plunged into darkness. My true nature cannot be known until it has been stripped away, obscured and lost in the deepest pit. And for those who would be like me: know that there is no growth without pain and there is no revelation without striving for it. The journey of realized godhood must necessarily take you deep into the darkness, where all other light is lost until only your inner flame shines true.

—*Michelle Belanger*

DARK BEAUTY
by Corvis Nocturnum

ᴵ ⫸ ⫷ INTRODUCTION ⫸

What is Darkness?

"One does not become enlightened by imagining figures of light but by making the darkness conscious." — Carl Jung

"One cannot appreciate the light without first having walked in darkness." — Corvis Nocturnum

Darkness, as it pertains to this writing, refers to a multifaceted idea, or aspects of the "collective shadow," a concept psychologist Carl Jung theorized was the desire in all people to appease the so-called "dark" or "evil" aspects of our nature. Pressure and imposed morals from religion and mainstream society usually force these desires to be buried into our subconscious. Most people, whether they openly admit to it or not, long for freedom from restraint. When children are taught that natural ideas or feelings are bad, it creates a negative self-image. Even the act of swearing, the release of feelings viewed with ill will in polite society, is an outlet for repressed emotions. Though frowned upon, such "bad words" are merely words; they have power only if we allow them to control our emotions, rather than use them to express our emotions.

Everything that is deemed unacceptable by the masses is relegated into the shadow. Individuality and healthy self-esteem become the likely sacrificial lambs, forcing sullen compliance and rebellious behavior in children. The sad results of such repression is evident with the many psychotics and criminals that flood our sanitariums and prisons. Our jails are filled with desperate people who felt they had little choice but to commit the actions that lead to their incarcerations. Fully accepting our dark side might lead to nonconformity, however, it can also inspire sensitivity and creativity. The majority of those who understand these nuances of life consider themselves free. They understand that darkness is not simply the absence of light, but is an integral part of it; just as one side of the Earth feels the sun's rays, so the other half dwells in shadow.

Those who question "the mainstream" seek out like-minded people who share the same desires and express them in similar ways. This is what leads to the formation of subculture groups, most of which overlap, some moreso than others. Such groups might not mesh with the general consensus, but they share the same ideals. Even though their appearance or approach may vary, what unites these lost souls are their values: an appreciation of aesthetics, individuality, open-mindedness, the acceptance of others without regard to gender or ethnicity, and a willingness to explore their own shadow. Here individuality is prized above all else. Enjoying all that life has to offer may seem hedonistic to the restrained, but such revelry is a shared trait among denizens of dark lifestyles. These types of creative individuals often become artists, musicians, and writers.

In order to create, one must be open to new experiences. At an early age most of us feel ostracized, either due to our choice of sexuality, be it bisexual, polyamorous, or transgender, or by our attraction to certain aesthetics. People within such minorities find acceptance in these subcultures and are not made to feel guilty about who they are. Religious callings to paths such as Paganism or Satanism encourage freedom, and most consist of alternative sexual orientations, as seen in the Pagan and Vampyre community. Who wants to be in a faith that condemns them to eternal suffering simply because of the way they feel?

Few among us can handle the realities of life, with the inevitable one being our own demise. To face our own mortality is frightening. This is clearly evident through our fascination with horror novels from such authors as Stephen King and Dean Koontz; Gothic novels like Bram Stoker's *Dracula* and Mary Shelley's *Frankenstein*; and portrayals of popular anti-heroes in such films as *Batman, The Punisher, Death Wish, The Crow, Spawn, Pirates of the Caribbean,* and *Interview with the Vampire,* and countless others that depict good guys with a hint of "evil" or bad-boy qualities.

Groups who embrace power, celebrate their natural carnal

instinct, or enjoy wealth openly, instead of hiding their desires, are labeled "evil." This is so with the Church of Satan, Skull and Bones Society, and Temple of the Vampire, as well as many others. Most people consider power itself evil. An individual actively seeking power is most often considered greedy, lustful or barbaric, an asocial relic of the past stirring up a boiling cauldron of jealousy.

People in general have not changed over time. Games of intrigue, courtly niceties and backstabbings are still very much prevalent today, wherein the weak are made even more powerless and more miserable. The simple fact is that we have always played a scheming game; there is no opting out of it, and only the foolish ignore this truth. It is far better to strive for power and excellence than to whine and struggle with guilt and remorse, or to hate those who have, when we have not. Understanding this dark nature in our fellow man will help us in accepting ourselves as we really are—for are we not a mirror reflecting the dark chaos that surrounds us all?—and will free us to be better friends, lovers, and the best person we can be.

Embracing the darkness is embracing freedom. We seek to rip open the collective shadow, the fearful nature that lies hidden from society, and expose it, to truly look within ourselves and explore the shadowy depths of our souls. It is a harsh road to travel, and to do so one needs to be honest with oneself and open to exploring the paths traveled by those who have gone before us and who already know the way.

Welcome to my world of darkness.
Welcome to the enlightenment.

TRIBUTE TO POE
by Corvis Nocturnum

GOTHIC

"I am treated evil by those who feel persecuted because they are not allowed to force me to believe as they do." — author unknown

"What is Goth?"

This may be one of the most often posed questions pertaining to this particular subculture, and the definition is elusive. Goth is actually much more than the sum of its parts, many of which are valid aspects of several other subcultures. It is more than a label, style or description. Goth is both a lifestyle and a philosophy that has its roots firmly embedded in the historical past and our ever-changing present. The central ideal that characterizes Goth is an almost compulsive drive toward creativity and self-expression, and a desire to reach out to an audience and share our deep fascination with all things frightening, odd, and mysterious. Goth can be either subtle and seducing or nightmarish and shocking, but it does play on what society secretly cannot acknowledge to itself about its own sense of duality.

As a lifestyle, Goth is as diverse as the people that inhabit its dark domain. There is no true unifying stereotype or dress code, but a certain dark taint is prevalent in the fashion that defines us. Not all Goths are depressed or employ the same modes of self-expression. This tends to create confusion over what Goth is, but this diversity is also one of it defining factors.

Following is a letter that was sent out by St. Mary's Church in Buffalo, NY, which provides a shining example of the confusion, hype and misinformation surrounding this much misunderstood and maligned subculture.

If Your Child is a Gothic, Reform Through the Lord!
Listed below are some warning signs to indicate if your child may have gone astray from the Lord. Gothic (or Goth) is a very obscure and often dangerous culture that young teenagers are prone to participating in. The gothic culture leads young, susceptible minds into an imagined world of evil, darkness, and violence. Please seek immediate attention

through counseling, prayer, and parental guidance to rid your child of Satan's temptations if five or more of the following are applicable to your child:

Frequently wears black clothing; Wears band and/or rock t-shirts; Wears excessive black eye makeup, lipstick or nail polish; Wears any odd, silver jewelry or symbols. Some of these include: reversed crosses, pentagrams, pentacles, ankhs or various other Satanic worshipping symbols; Shows an interest in piercing or tattoos; Listens to gothic or any other anti-social genres of music. (Marilyn Manson claims to be the anti-Christ, and publicly speaks against the Lord. Please discard any such albums IMMEDIATELY.) Associates with other people that dress, act or speak eccentrically; Shows a declining interest in wholesome activities, such as: the Bible, prayer, church or sports; Shows an increasing interest in death, vampires, magic, the occult, witchcraft or anything else that involves Satan; Takes drugs; Drinks alcohol; Is suicidal and/or depressed; Cuts, burns or partakes in any other method of self-mutilation. (This is a Satanic ritual that uses pain to detract from the light of God and His love. Please seek immediate attention for this at your local mental health center.) Complains of boredom; Sleeps too excessively or too little; Is excessively awake during the night; Dislikes sunlight or any other form of light (This pertains to vampires promoting the idea that His light is of no use.) Demands an unusual amount of privacy; Spends large amounts of time alone; Requests time alone and quietness. (This is so that your child may speak to evil sprits through meditation.) Insists on spending time with friends while unaccompanied by an adult; Disregards authority figures; teachers, priests, nuns and elders are but a few examples of this; Misbehaves at school; Misbehaves at home; Eats excessively or too little; Eats Goth-related foods. (Count Dracula cereal is an example of this.) Drinks blood or expresses an interest in drinking blood. (Vampires believe this is how to attain Satan. This act is very dangerous and should be stopped immediately.) Watches cable television or any other corrupted media sources. (Ask your local church for proper programs that your child may watch.) Plays videos games that contain violence or role-playing nature; Uses the internet excessively and frequently makes time for the computer; Makes Satanic symbols and/or violently shakes head to music; Dances to music in a provocative or sexual manner; Expresses an interest in sex; Masturbates; Is homosexual and/or bisexual; Pursues dangerous cult religions. Such include: Satanism, Scientology, Philosophy, Paganism, Wicca, Hinduism and Buddhism; Wears pins, stickers or anything else that contains these various phrases: "I'm so gothic, I'm dead," "woe is me," "I'm a Goth." or claims to be a Goth.

If five or more of these apply to your child, please intervene immediately. The gothic culture is dangerous and Satan thrives within it. If any of these problems persist, enlist your child into your local mental health center.

—*St. Mary's Catholic Church*

Now that we have a broad assumption of the public's mindset, let's explore the truth...

Origins of Modern Goth Culture

To better understand what the modern concept of Goth really is, it is essential to know how and why it originated. The concept has been with us for much longer than the label itself. This is a subculture that has appeared, flourished, and then died, only to rise again, like a phoenix, throught several many eras and in many societies. Its adherents have always been the young intelligentsia who are frustrated and bored with their current culture—a culture that is usually restrictive, highly stratified into rigid caste structures, and intolerant of diversity in schools of both art and thought. Because of this, nearly every manifestation of this counter-culture was greeted with suspicion, hostility, and even active aggression on the part of its parent culture.

The modern Goth movement has its roots in Western Europe and North America during the late nineteen seventies and early eighties. The counter culture was, and still is, dominated by dissatisfied youth hailing from mostly middle class structures. Children of highly restrictive families were left, unlike their parents, with a strong feeling of instability and lack of personal or group identity.

Responding to the confusion and lack of personal identity, a few of the brightest and most creative children of these families began to create their own social structure based on a synthesis of historical elements, dramatic traditions, philosophies, and schools of thought such as those popular in Byronic England, along with most of Europe at that time, and the imagery of the Gothic and Romantic periods. After spending some time with no real name for their group, many dubbed themselves "New Romantics," while others just called themselves "Deathers," but they quickly settled on "Gothic" as their counter-culture grew.

Goth split into two distinct factions, one Apollonian[1] and the other Dionysian[2] in its approach by the 1980s, when it had reached its peak. Each faction was a personification of the mixed fear and fascination for the darker side of their parents' legacy of greed

---

1. Apollonian—Greek Mythology; of or relating to Apollo. (a.) Characterized by clarity, harmony, and restraint. (b.) In the philosophy of Friedrich Nietzsche, of or embodying the power of critical reason as opposed to the creative-intuitive. (c.) Serenely high-minded; noble.
2. Dionysian—Greek Mythology; of or devoted to the worship of Dionysus. (a.) Of an ecstatic, orgiastic, or irrational nature; frenzied or undisciplined. (b.) In the philosophy of Nietzsche, of or displaying creative-intuitive power as opposed to critical-rational power.

expressed by materialism, and a false sense of moral superiority. The most significant difference between these factions was evident in thier chose method of expressing a united sense of alienation and abandonment, whether real or imagined.

The more Apollonian faction concerned itself with the artistic and philosophical facets of Goth. For the most part these people were fairly non-confrontational in their means of self-expression, being poets, artisans or philosophers. They were typically obsessed with the act of creation and the appreciation of literature, art and music, even if they themselves were not creating the works. Some attempts were made to legitimize this subculture in the eyes of its parent culture, but such acts met with very little success. Because they were regarded as harmless—morbid dreamers, if you will—these Goths were tolerated.

The more Dionysian faction of Goth passionately embraced the most hedonistic and often more self-destructive facets of the movement. Their contributions were more ephemeral and less easy to define in traditional terms as creativity, but they were still vibrant with the haunted, dark spirit of the counter-culture. Some of the more prominent Goth musicians and thinkers belonged to this faction, like Tim Burton, Voltaire, and Marilyn Manson. Becoming more confrontational in their self-expression, they were regarded by the parent culture as dangerous and undesirable.

The modern stereotype of Goth is a twisted caricature of the more Dionysian faction, making much of its decadence and tendency towards self-destruction while entirely missing its subtle artistry and depth.

By the 1990s, both factions of Goth had almost completely vanished, absorbed back into the parent culture as their members were forced to accept conformity to ensure individual survival as adults. Like myself and those interviewed in this book, a marginal percentage of the original Goth community were able to adapt to adult life and yet remain essentially and visibly true to themselves. By this time, the new generation of disaffected youth had already begun to imitate what they had perceived of the Dionysian Goths. They had embraced the dark and dangerous style of dress and felt that the lonely and often arrogant music was written just for them. The stereotypical lifestyle was adventurous and daring enough to spark their already bored and world-weary imaginations.

These "KinderGothen," as they are sometimes called, were met by rejection and disapproval by both the parent culture and the remainders of the "Olde School Goth" community with minimal exceptions. Those few original Goths who tried to embrace the new groups were usually met with cold hostility and anger by those who had already either been rejected or had heard of such rejection. The schism between the Olde School and the New was widened even more by the label of "Poseur" that was bandied between the two sides. Most of us "Elder Goths" very well remember those phrases with a certain sense of nostalgia.

The artistry and philosophy that had driven the Goth culture was replaced with an attitude, and close-minded dress code—an entirely non-individualistic posture. The few remaining Olde School Goths and their angry offspring went underground and remained apart from the new rise of Goth, refusing to have much to do with what they considered shallow, inarticulate upstarts that paid far too much attention to what the media *thought* was Goth. They saw the New Goth as little more than a group of image-driven drug addicts that had nothing better to offer than a dress code and a bad attitude. The New School's opinions of the originals weren't much better.

In the last few years, Olde School and New Goth, as well as vampires and Pagans, have embraced the Internet and other means of communication. It has become both a medium for self-expression and a battleground between them. Oddly enough, the advent of easy access to the Web has revealed in the New School an increased drive towards the creativity and self-expression that the Olde School Goths held in such high esteem. Publications like *Dark Realms* still fly off the shelves of many punk/goth/raver stores like Hot Topic, at one time the largest supporter of Goth culture. The New Goths have become more like the originals than either side would want to admit. Hopefully this trend will continue to thrive, bringing fresh blood and a new outlook to Goth's grasp on the dark undercurrents of our society.

While researching online, I ran across one such young girl, MORTICIA, who expresses her sense of creativity with "fog photography." She agreed to be interviewed on her own experiences and influences.

Corvis: "You've entered into the Gothic scene at such a young age. What prompted your interest?"

Morticia: "I can honestly say that I didn't know what Gothic was until I was 18. I have always been rather odd. I was the little girl in school with the hot pink and black polka dot mini skirt outfit with hot pink fishnets with red sneakers...or jeans with custom cut holes and a blood covered shark attack shirt. When I moved to southeast Texas I got asked all the time if I was 'Goth' and of course I asked what it was. So I looked it up and, badda-bing, look where Morticia lands in the social ring. So basically I have always been this way and just didn't realize it."

Corvis: "Is art, especially that of your photography, a means to express anything internal? What motivates you?"

Morticia: "I tend to think that everything motivates me. I can hear the rustle of the trees or the sound of a coffee pot or the giggle of a child. Life motivates me. But yes, my art is what is within me. But photography for me is capturing life. If I could capture every moment in life I would. Good or bad. I tend to lean toward the more morbid, but life is so beautiful. The quirk of a smile, or the sharp glare of an eye to be caught forever within a little piece of paper. But it is also a means for me to show the world how I see it. A chance to look through my eyes and see the wonderfully twisted world with a pretty little silver lining."

Corvis: "Have you encountered any negative reactions from people because of your choice in how you present yourself?"

Morticia: "Yes, all the time. People can't handle that which they do not understand. I'm never rude to them and often show them that there isn't anything wrong with being different and that you have to have dark to have light. And normally after I'm done they have a little better understanding about the culture and that it's just a few bad apples that have given us a bad name. But unlike most things, bad people always find the outcast image to cling to and corrupt."

Morticia

Corvis: "What positive aspects do you feel Goth lifestyle has given you?"
Morticia: "I have found where I fit in. I'm not a partier or anything; mostly a computer geek. But I have found myself, and a lot of wonderful people. I have found out that life isn't always sunny and that's a good thing. I have always loved all things dark. Cemeteries, vampires, occult, the usual. I have never seen the world the way everyone else does, and I hope I never do.

Gothic Types and Definitions

Goths come in a wide variety, and more space could be occupied in describing them, but I found a site online some years ago that covered it best. Some of these definitions are hilarious, but all more or less speak the truth.

Angst Goth: Rail against the system, it's all unfair, everyone is against me, beat down the shackles of oppressions... fight! Fight down the system! But what's the system you're fighting again? blank look hmmm... Rebel without a clue.

Baby Bat: Most often younger generation (age 14-16) who WAY over do it. 3-inch thick layer of make-up, cloaks, fishnets, the whole nine yards and they dress like this ALL THE TIME. They are rarely ever found in public looking 'normal' even though they have no real personality traits that make them Gothic at all. They just read 'Gothic' literature, watch other Goths, and do their best to try to be like them, only more so.

Body Art Goth: Pierce, tattoo that, stick a barbell there, see how many holes you can put in that. I pity these people at airport metal detectors.

Coffee House Goth: Caffeine junky, sugar fiend, to hell with booze, all they need is 20 packets of sugar and an espresso. They are often as close to beatnik as you can get without being one, and some are known to write a lot of meaningless poetry that may sound good, but has the depth and content of a shot glass of decaf.

Delusional Goth: Almost always these are also larp-Goths or D&D Goths. They honestly think they're a vampire or a werewolf or immortal or something, not sure if they REALLY think that or if they just like to convince everyone else they think that. Either way, they seriously need help.

DemiGoth: These are sub Goths who are in the transition period. They often flitter about the sub groups trying to find which one they like the best. Sometimes they dress Goth, sometimes they don't. Think of it as not entirely unlike the metamorphosis stage when a caterpillar turns into a butterfly.

Fascination Goth: These are the pond scum, sucking bottom feeders. Worse then trendy Goths, worse than baby bats, God sometimes they're even worse then mansonites. They are most often self righteous, self important hypocrites who get their Goth clothes at Hot Topic and think that Fascinations is cool (for those not in Denver, Fascinations is an adult store whose whole gimmick is that fuzzy handcuffs are BSDM and you should buy their fuzzy handcuffs because bondage is trendy and cool). These people severely need to be beaten repeatedly with a large vinyl dildo.

Gay Goth: (by suggestion) They're not actually Goth, they just want an excuse to wear makeup.

Glitter Goth: Shiny happy people… holding coffin shaped purses? oooohhh pretty sparkles! The types who get that glitter goop crap and spread it all over their faces, and bright clothes. The epitome that I've seen was a guy who had Christmas lights strung through his hair, connected to a battery pack on his waist. Now THAT was funny.

Goth: Your typical everyday run of the mill Goth. Usually in black or darker colors, and shirts, most often a 'not too freaky' person who just happens to like how they look in black, but often get pegged as something else.

Lifestyle Goth: No matter their level of Gothness, being Goth isn't just a fashion statement to them; it's a lifestyle. It permeates and partakes of every part of their existence. It's simply what they are, but unfortunately they often end up being 'uber Goths' who buy their clothes at Hop Topic, and think you have to be consumed by the 'dark' because you wear black… but some of them are damn cool.

Pagan Goth: *I wear black because I'm Pagan. Or am I Pagan because I wear black? Or is it Pagan to wear black? Or maybe it's black to be Pagan?* or maybe your just a stupid fucking worm who wants to be Pagan because (a.) It's freaky. (b.) You get to be a Witch or (c.) Mommy and Daddy said Pagans are bad but don't ground you for saying your Pagan like they did when you said you were a Satanist. Because of these idiots, the Pagan religion has no credibility at all left to most people.

Pathetic Goth: *I wear black on the outside because it's how I feel on the inside.* Enough said.

Pretty Goth: All the little Goth babes who are strewn everywhere on Goth x of the x pages. These people could be models if they wanted too. Perfect skin, perfect hair, perfect body… you either want to fuck them where they stand or beat their perfect little faces in because they have a habit of being pretentious, stuck up little twits.

Punk Goth: The hardest decision in their life is whether to listen to the Sex Pistols or Sisters of Mercy, and whether their mohawk should be blood red or green.

Intellectual Goth: A more condescending Goth type, they're smarter than you, they know everything about everything, and they use big words so that makes them more Goth then you and therefore superior to you in every way. Will most likely not look down their nose at you, as Gother then Goth's do, but they will certainly make it a point to get in a snide remark on just how uneducated you are.

Medieval Goth: Always at the Ren Fairs, wearing cloaks, garters, corsets and tights, often found talking in incredibly cheesy English accents and claiming they know how to either sew very well, use a melee weapon, or know everything their is to know about the 14th century.

Old School Goth: Been around for a while. They were Goth since you were in diapers. This makes them cool and more Goth than you. This for some reason makes them superior to you in every way, and you don't deserve to be like Bauhaus because they liked it first, and they make it a point to tell you this over and over and over and over and over and over and over...

Shock Goth: They dress in Goth and overdo it for the specific purpose of shocking people. Dressing in black is just a shock value to them, nothing beyond that. Yet one more pain in the ass that gives Goths a bad name.

Trendy Goth: They're Goth because no other fashion is cool enough. They like 'Gothic' things because it goes with the fashion. They overdo being Goth because we all know that's it's just a popularity contest and the best way to be the coolest Goth then everyone else, so their clothes have to be the most expensive, their makeup the most extravagant, and they shop at Hot Topic, a lot.

Outsiders are either oblivious to Goth's subtleties or are quick to make assumptions, drawing broad conclusions from stereotypical comments such as "those morbid people who think of death all the time and wear nothing but black." Some time ago I co-authored an article with a dear friend in the Fort Wayne Nocturnal Pagans Yahoo! Group addressing that issue. The article lead to much research and introspection, as well as continued writing and involvement with dozens of other people like Dark Wyccans. Quickly becoming a spokesperson for Dark Paganism in general, Coughlin has been involved in both Goth and Paganism for over a decade. Coughlin's writing challenged me to further explore the darkside of humanity, and my discoveries lead me to create this book. The article itself is as follows:

THERE IS MORE TO GOTH THAN BLACK
By Corvis Nocturnum & Lilith Artemis

What is Goth? Is it black lipstick and eyeliner, Marilyn Manson and black hair dye? We think not. No disrespect to those who do so, it is merely an aspect of the Goth culture. People who rely solely on "the look" and not the mental intellect, artistic appreciation or overall aesthetic mindset are missing the point entirely. An outward look should be a window into the soul, not window dressing. Goth is about many things. It's about music, art, rebellion, so much more than most people think. "Defining what makes one Gothic lies not so much in taste but in self determination. Many refuse to be considered Goth because such categorization comes with it. The typical stereotypes and expectations that any culture or group reflects. Being strongly individualistic such people obviously prefer to avoid this labeling." — *John J. Coughlin,* Out of the Shadows.

The saying "You laugh because we're different. We laugh because you're all the same," loses it's meaning when there are so many people out there trying to "be Goth." You should not try to be Gothic. You either are or you aren't and no manner of clothes, gaudy makeup, or coffin miniatures are going to make you that way.

We are not all vampyres, Satan worshippers (big difference from Satanists), etc. Although some of us may have a "typical" Goth look about them and some of us may be véry into these things (and some believe that they truly are vampires); that does not make them Goth. Just as not all Christians are Baptists, not all Witches are Wiccans, not all vampires/Satanists/etc. are Goths.

Materials range from vinyl, leather, PVC, lace, velvet, taffeta, too many others. It's not so much the colors chosen but the individual expressing themselves as themselves aesthetically and this may be industrial, punk, antiquity (Victorian style), etc. Goth embraces all religions, all denominations and all races.

"Just Because You're Wearing Black Doesn't Mean We Like You."
"There is not only one type of Goth person that associates or identifies with the Gothic scene and thus, as with most groups, the stereotypes merely exaggerate some of the more common characteristics of those most visible to the public. Typically the most visible are the worst examples and Goths themselves often enjoy making fun of these stereotypes by mocking them," says John Coughlin.

That all having been said, those who do adapt black to their wardrobe as their primary choice, as I myself do, it is fully acceptable so long as it is done by what the individual truly feels drawn to—opposed to those who seek to jump on the band wagon of a trend. It is up to the individual to know the difference of course. "It's such a straightforward sort of color. I never squint at a black tee shirt, wondering if it goes with my black jeans. I never have to get up in the morning, thinking, 'I wonder what color I'll wear today?' And black goes with anything. As long as the anything is black." —*Neil Gaiman*

Gothic History & Influence

Long before the British punk scene of the 1980s and the Hammer films of the 1930s held sway over what would become the modern Goth style, history tells of an ancient world in chaos. The Visigoths, a rebellious Germanic tribe of nomads, consisting of two main branches, the Visigoths of the west and the Ostrogoths of the east. The Goths aided in the collapse of the once glorious Roman Empire during the 5th century, and over the next 900 years Western Europe fell into the Dark Ages, a period when very little was written or recorded. Then, during the 12th and 15th centuries, a new style of art and architecture emerged from the shadows. This style embodied heavy, ornate décor, narrow windows and arches, and surfaces festooned with foreboding moral teachings in the form of beastly caricatures and gargoyles. Gargoyles incidentally were believed to scare evil spirits away. These elements, used chiefly to adorn cathedrals, were thought to instill fear and awe. The conservatives of the time, who still held sacred the Classical ideals of Rome, looked upon this dark style with fear and distain—and they blamed the Visigoths. Gothic (meaning "of the Goths") became a disparaging term used in reference to the creations of these "barbarian hordes" who sought to overthrow the rigid organization and conforms of society. The 16th century brought the Renaissance, a revival of Classical art, creativity and free thought—however, it is ironic that the descendants of those who created such grand monuments in centuries past shun others who enjoy these very aesthetics today. Even so, the rebellious characteristics of the Goths have prevailed throughout time and are evident in many forms of expression.

Milton's *Paradise Lost* as well as Dante's *Inferno* depict grotesque[3] scenes of wildly cavorting demons and corpses, confusedly mixing elements of Pagan and Christian "Devil worship." The works of Edgar Allan Poe, who was likely influenced by 18th century opposition to rigid social values, often delved into themes about man's psychotic nature and loss of inhibitions. The Marquis de Sade was the ultimate rebel and held in contempt France's strict moral code and ideal of decency. Lord Byron was equally applauded and scorned for his erotic poetry and scandalous personal life. Such rebellion and decadence is the hallmark of the Romantic or Antiquity Goth.

Gothic Art

The history of the arts, from ancient times until present day, all share a common purpose: to expand the mind, quicken the heart, and stir emotions. As history holds an influence over artistic expression, the resulting artwork likewise proves influential to future generations. One such influence on today's Goth scene can be found in the works of renowned artist and founder of Monolith Graphics, Joseph Vargo.

Vargo worked as a freelance illustrator for several years before establishing Monolith Graphics in 1991 as an outlet to self-publish and market his gothic fantasy artwork on t-shirts and posters. In the beginning, he mainly sold his artwork and wares at Renaissance Faires

---

3. Grotesque—From the Latin *grotto,* meaning a small cave or hollow. The expression refers to the unearthing and rediscovery of ancient Roman art in caves during the 15th century. This art depicted Romans engaging in wild orgies and drunkenness.

and local shops in the Cleveland area. In 1992, graphic designer Christine Filipak came on board, and the business has been growing steadily ever since. Christine's computer skills and elegant art nouveau style were a perfect compliment to Joseph's dark and primal creations and Old World painting techniques.

Over the years Monolith Graphics has sold and distributed hundreds of thousands of prints and other pieces of merchandise featuring Vargo's original artwork to fans worldwide. Monolith has since published the works of numerous other gothic artists, writers and musicians, and helped to promote and establish them in their respective fields.

Following is my interview with JOSEPH VARGO and his long time business partner CHRISTINE FILIPAK, both of whom have since become better acquainted with me with the writing of this book.

Corvis: "How did the company get it's start, and what inspired you both in all of your combined talents?"
Joseph: "Initially we were fans of each other's work. Because we had the same tastes in art, music, books and film, we gravitated towards one another and began working together. Our combined talents and varied techniques melded together smoothly and we realized that together we could go further than either of us could alone. We're both extremely driven to create, and our differences compliment and enhance each other's work."

Christine: "Joseph actually started the company. He had a few t-shirt designs and some posters that he had already produced, which he was selling at metaphysical boutiques and art fairs. We had been friends for years, but he's a very private person, and I never realized just how talented he was. Then one day I saw all of his paintings and I was astounded. He had about a hundred fantasy paintings locked away in a spare room in his house. Paintings of sensuous women with intricately designed attire, knights and barbarians with sword in hand fighting monstrous beasts, and strange and dark creatures from mythology and the realm of nightmares. It opened my eyes to a world of possibilities, and I remember thinking that he had to get his stuff out there where people could appreciate it, and I wanted to be part of it.

"We didn't have a long-term 'master plan' in the beginning. We simply wanted to create cool, dark artwork. I brought my computer skills to the table and at first I did the graphic design and prep work for the Gothic calendars, poster prints, t-shirts, and other merchandise.

Joseph Vargo and Christine Filipak

But as time went on, my duties expanded and I became a web designer, writer, and magazine publisher, in addition to creating my own artwork. With Monolith, the creative possibilities are endless, and we're only limited by our own imaginations."

Corvis: "Was it difficult to break into the art market with your unique style?"

Joseph: "Yes. It's a very competitive field and there are so many talented artists trying to break into it. I feel very fortunate to be able to make a living doing what I love. When I was trying to get started, I sent portfolios of my work to all the major book, magazine and comic book publishers and got rejected by every one of them. This was actually a blessing in disguise because it was the impetus for starting my own business. I simply wanted to get my art out there, and who better to do it than myself?

"Now I'm very glad that I didn't get hired by any of those companies because I don't have to compromise any of my art. I hate to think of having an art director looking over my shoulder and telling me what to do. I also love to be able to create new projects of my own choosing, based solely on my own ideas."

Corvis: "What inspires you to create? Music, dreams?
Joseph: "I derive inspiration from various sources such as mythology, literature and film, but basically I just have a vivid imagination and I like the challenge of creating something from nothing. I get a simple idea in my head, whether it's for a painting, a story or just a melody for a song, and I keep thinking about it and building upon it until it develops into a full-blooded concept. Then I have to get it out of my head before I begin developing new ideas and lose it completely. The physical creation process is actually fun, and the initial concept usually undergoes several more changes before its finished. I put a lot of thought and effort into each new project and I derive a great deal of satisfaction from the entire creative process."

Corvis: "Does the public affect your creations, or do you only create what you feel?"
Joseph: "It's really a little of both. Since I have never worked for an art director, I've always chosen my own subject matter, and no one has influenced my composition, style or approach to my art. But I always have my audience and fans in mind when I am creating a new work, and this pushes me to do my best, even when I have a tight deadline. Occasionally I have to consider censorship of certain elements such as nudity, blood, and even occult symbols; so if I am creating a painting for a calendar or magazine cover, there are some restrictions as to what can be shown. I generally take this as a challenge and try to come up with a strong composition that hints at the taboo and lets your mind fill in the blanks."

Corvis: "For me, art is an expression of how I am inside, a bringing out of the subconscious. Do you feel the same way?"
Joseph: "Yes, very much so. I feel that many of my creations are manifestations of primal emotions. Art can be appreciated on many

levels, but if an artist can tap into his own subconscious and reflect it in his work, then his audience can identify with it on a subliminal level and it can stir deep-rooted emotions. I think that everyone should have an emotional outlet to express themselves creatively, whether it be through art, music or writing."

Corvis: "What do you think is the appeal for people when it comes to dark themes, old architecture, and Goth in general?"
Joseph: "I realize that the subject matter of my art may not appeal to everyone, but there are a large number of people that find beauty in darkness. Overall, the whole Gothic era represents a very dark and mysterious period of civilization. Gothic architecture is one of the most ornate and artistic styles of design, and even though it originated in medieval cathedrals, it has a very sinister connotation.

"Gargoyles were originally designed as wards against evil spirits, but this idea faded and was forgotten through the years while these foreboding monstrosities of stone endured the centuries. Castles represent mysterious places to explore, filled with dark secrets and ghosts, and graveyards are literally the domain of the dead, offering an eerily tranquil and serene escape from the world of the living."

Corvis: "Dark imagery and power associated with certain archetypes cause fear in some, while others identify with them. Why do you think some fear this part of our culture and history?"
Joseph: "Folklore concerning supernatural subjects such as vampires, werewolves and witches were originally designed to scare people, teach moral lessons, and to explain things that could not be explained by the science or medicine of the day. As H.P. Lovecraft stated: 'The oldest and strongest emotion of mankind is fear, and the oldest and strongest kind of fear is fear of the unknown.'

"I think it's basically a matter of taste and the difference in people's threshold for fear. Fear causes varying levels of anxiety. Some people love to be scared while others dread and detest the same sensation. I think many Goths identify with certain dark archetypes, in particular the vampire persona, because it exudes sensuality, dark mystery and power."

Corvis: "Many people who are familiar with you as an artist may not know you are an accomplished author as well. Can you explain a bit about your book?"

Joseph: "The book, *Tales From The Dark Tower,* was conceived early in 1999 after a friend suggested having various writers pen short stories based on the characters in my most popular works. I worked on the main story with writer James Pipik, then outlined a series of stories and worked closely with the other writers to maintain continuity throughout the book. In addition to creating the layout, design and artwork for this book, Christine and I wrote and co-wrote several of the stories. As time went on, the responsibilities of editing this project fell upon us as well.

"The 13 Gothic tales of vampires, ghosts and other things that go bump in the night are set in and around a haunted gargoyle-encrusted castle known as the Dark Tower. Each of the 13 stories stands alone, yet they all fit together, weaving back and forth throughout the centuries to create the saga of the curse that overshadows the Dark Tower. The tales add a new dimension to the artwork, bringing some of my most sinister and haunting characters to life, so to speak. *Tales From The Dark Tower* has been very well received and is now in its third printing. We are currently working on two sequels, but I have to balance my creative energies between other ongoing projects. I've also written several other short stories and frequently contribute articles and reviews to *Dark Realms Magazine* under various pen names."

Corvis: "*Dark Realms Magazine* is an ongoing look into the broad aspects of dark culture. Not only classical and Halloween-like imagery, but also current film, music and books. Have you noticed an increase of interest in this subject matter recently?"

Joseph: "I think that it's simply part of the human psyche to hold a fascination with the unknown. People have been creating dark artwork and works of literature for thousands of years, and a certain part of every culture has been dedicated to the dark side of human nature. These works are often the most enduring and memorable works of their time. The Greek tragedies and the works of Shakespeare and Poe dealt with very dark, supernatural subjects and are considered classics of literature."

Christine: "Modern Goth culture has embraced this dark side of art, literature and film. What began as a small underground movement has really grown in the past few years, and recently, music and fashions that originated in the Gothic underground have been making their way into the mainstream."

Corvis: "What do you think is the reason Goth and horror endures the test of time so well?"
Christine: "It seems that people have always been drawn to things that are dark and dangerous. We love the thrill of being scared and the mystery of the unknown. There's also a deeper fascination with the supernatural. Ghosts depict those who have crossed beyond the threshold of death and have returned for some other purpose. Werewolves represent a primal animalistic side of human nature, and vampires convey a strong sensual allure. These things have a timeless and universal appeal because they are the shadowy manifestations of things that lurk in the darkest recesses of the subconscious mind."

Corvis: "What is it to be 'Goth' to you?"
Christine: "Joseph and I both tend to draw a distinction between the terms Goth and Gothic. Being artists, the term Gothic represents to us an Old World style of architecture, gargoyle encrusted cathedrals and castles, also Gothic literature such as the works of Bram Stoker and Edgar Allan Poe, and the Gothic horror imagery such as vampires and ghosts.

"The abbreviated term 'Goth' represents more of a modern cultural trend of today's brooding youth. It's a movement of self-expression created by those who gravitate towards the dark side of life and appreciate and embrace many of the traditional Gothic elements. Although Goth fashions and music seem to reflect a dark and somber spirit, the movement is actually a celebration of individuality, artistic creativity and free will."

Goth Fashion

All forms of media today, including film, music, and print media, have been highly influential on Goth style. Vampire classics, such as *Nosferatu,* and modern films, such as Anne Rice's *Interview with a Vampire,* have been strong contributors. The fashions and décor of dark culture are showcased and greatly influenced by several publications, such as *Blueblood, Bite Me!, Gothic Beauty* and *Dark Realms.*

The aspects of Goth in fashion, the coverings by which most of us are judged, have only slightly changed over the ages. It just so happens that those of us immersed in this type of lifestyle can clearly see "good" and "bad" aspects of life simply as normal life. Individuals who walk this less traveled path may appear unable to fit into mainstream society, but it has been said, "never judge a book by its cover."

The look most commonly associated with Goth style can be broken into two classifications, antiquity or modern. The antiquity, or Edwardian style as it is also known, borrows much of its influence from the pre-Renaissance period. For such style, one needs look no further than clothing from Eternal Love, Siren, or KAMBRIEL, which is one of the newest and most luxurious.

Corvis: "Tell my readers a bit about your company."
Kambriel: "Ever since the release of our Premiere Collection in 1994, we have striven to create finely handmade designs with a classically timeless feel, from the most luxurious fabrics and trimmings available. Our clothing is designed for those darkly romantic souls who dream of an existence in another place and time. We want you to have the freedom to be true to your innermost natures rather than having them suppressed by the present world and the desires of others. Being true to yourself is more of an internal quest, but everything that is buried deep inside rises to the surface eventually. This is where we come in... the reflection of your inner-self onto your outer-self. Clothing that brings you a little closer to your dreams."

Corvis: "There are a great many different looks today that all fall under the heading of Goth fashion. What is it about certain classic

styles (those that seem to be continually revived throughout history) that stand the test of time so well?"

Kambriel: "The term 'Goth' or 'Gothic' has indeed become very diverse—so diverse that it almost bares no resemblance from one extreme to another. Currently, someone can describe a design that's 'pink and fluffy' as being gothic, when at the root of the style that would be the complete antithesis of the gothic aesthetic. The original focus

Kambriel, photo by Nadya Lev

of gothic fashion was one of tattered opulence and very dark, often with a romantic twist. In recent years, styles like cyber-goth have come about which express a futuristic feeling, immediately recognizable by their glowing neon graphic accents on a stark backdrop of severe shapes, stemming from our entrance into the 21st century. I believe there will always be a place for Romantic Gothic designs made from dark, jewel-like colours and sumptuous fabrics. They continue to stand the test of time because as long as we live in a world where there is pain and injustice, pollution and abuse, prejudice and war, there will always be a deep need, fascination, and comfort in finding beauty and personally cherishing it. These classic pieces surround you in a comfort and luxury found in the softness of shadows."

Corvis: "Some older goths may recall that your company was once called 'Atrocities.' Obviously the use of your own name offers a more personal touch and becomes, like other fashion designers, immediately recognizable. Did you get much resistance before (and after) the name change? What prompted the name change; the public's reactions, etc.?"

Kambriel: "In 1994, the name "Atrocities" was more abstract, and not so often used. I had been thinking of changing the name for a while, since it grew tiring hearing about 'the atrocities of Serbia,' 'Japanese war atrocities,' etc... As time went on, I wanted to bring an aura of beauty that can come out of the darkness to a name that had always conveyed tragedy. When September 11, 2001 happened, and those events were also described as 'atrocities,' I realized the time had finally come, and decided that changing the business name to Kambriel would be best. I think the new name better expresses the inherent beauty of the designs, and the aesthetic I'm aiming for—an atmosphere of opulence and timelessness, with a sense of the fantastical. It ended up being a fairly smooth transition, and the new name has been very well received."

Corvis: "Where do you want to take the company in the future?"
Kambriel: "I would like to branch into doing costuming for some fantastically-themed movies, working with talented models and photographers to create stunning art, and one of my great joys that I continue to find much inspiration in is outfitting vocalists and musicians for their photoshoots, videos and live shows. Overall, I envision creating something of dignity and quality, with a continuous aesthetic integrity where you will always be able to tell that the people behind it genuinely love what they do and are constantly growing."

The wide range of Goth types, from antiquity to punk and cybergoth, provide an example of how people submersed in this culture feel displaced and alienated from current times. The nostalgia of bygone eras or future possibilities expressed in a dark way provide a form of escapism for both factions of the same group. Most Goths and nearly everyone in the vampire subculture reflect a personal style of dress, whether mild or extreme, that crosses the boundaries of one or the other group. Some mix the old and new styles together with great results.

Many wear black, whether it be as a symbol of aloofness, a rebellion against norms of society, or simply because it's sleek. A powerful color in fashion, black pays tribute to the classic horror genre; it represents contempt for a gray and stagnate world or provides the ultimate contrast to an overly saturated and falsely cheerful facade. When not worn to simply copy a trend, it is a statement of subversion and a denial of constantly changing mainstream fashion trends. Black has a timeless appeal, perfectly balanced with the aspects of Gothic art and style.

Jewelry adds much to the overall effect, and perhaps one the most well-known jewelry merchants catering to the Gothic community is Legends of England, otherwise more commonly known as Alchemy Gothic. Their fine quality pewter and classic designs are culled from the imaginations of a design team whose influence is derived from Dark Ages Christianity and features imagery such as skulls and vampiric bats. Owner GEOFF KAYSON spoke to me in regards to his company.

Corvis: "Deservedly so, Legends of England has, over the years, remained a huge part of the Goth and Vampyre aesthetic. What has made it so enduring throughout the ages?"
Geoff: "Alchemy Gothic, the English Gothic revival design company, some ten years ago established Legends of England as their North American distribution arm. The Alchemy Gothic collection, since 1977, has authentically embraced all forms of lifestyle, art form, commodity, and luxury and with such a huge and varied range of products, has become the paradigm of its form."

Corvis: "Would you say that history and the arts play a large role in the items created for the company? Where else do they obtain ideas for products?"

Geoff: "Inspiration for Alchemy's designs comes from The Alchemist, through his dedicated team of artists, designers, and scholars of Medieval and religious history, mythology, folk law and the supernatural, Medieval and Victorian Gothic design and lifestyle, and historical art and design theory and practice. In addition to this, these acolytes possess an innate knowledge of the contemporary Goth scene, having been a part of its inception since their own transformation from early Punks."

Corvis: "What positive way does Goth affect people?"
Geoff: "The Goth culture tends to attract and cultivate more bohemian-oriented and imaginative aesthetics and intellects. The resultant passive coterie seems to nurture flamboyant creativity alongside a moral sensitivity, enlightenment and a philosophical outlook."

Corvis: "Any comments you'd like to add to dispel stereotypes commonly associated with this subculture?"
Geoff: "The term 'Goth,' while describing a broad genre of unique lifestyles, is in reality a collective noun for a sub-society of highly individual, tolerant, and liberal-minded people of a variety of different types, but most of whom will admit to having an intellectual interest in, or a curious penchant for, some elements of morbidity and the sinister."

The Influence of Music on Goth Fashion

The main influences musically were most notably Bauhaus, Siouxsie and The Banshees and The Cure. Other bands were influential later, but in the early period these three bands defined the Goth look. Not only were they seen live, and occasionally on television, but pictures of Siouxsie, Pete Murphy and Daniel Ash appeared quite regularly in the music press and on their records. Any striking look will attract imitators, and Siouxsie in particular spawned a host of clones—in fact she has claimed, with considerable justification, that she invented the Goth look, at least for women.

Obviously, individual Bauhaus and Banshees fans were already looking "Goth" before the opening of the Batcave (a Goth/Industrial dance club in New York City), but the Batcave can probably be credited for turning the Goth look into a "fashion" as well. It received a lot of exposure in the press, pictures were seen by people around the country, and the basic style was copied. Specimen and Alien Sex

Fiend, both Batcave bands, were also very influential in the development of the Goth look. Ironically, the position of many bands, from the 70s up until current groups like Evanescence today, often set new Gothic fashion trends yet say they are not Goth themselves. Most "true Goths" would agree that if you say you are, then you are typically nothing more than a *poseur*.

The nature of Gothic decadence of old does not stop with old style regalia. Some borrow their look from the BDSM aficionados, and some are into the scene as well. This trend in Goth started around the height of the Punk movement, during the 1980s. Bands like The Sex Pistols, for instance, and countless others used it as well. The ideas of collars, bondage-wear, latex, leather, and PVC are displayed in catalogs from Lip Service, a clothing company servicing the alternative rock scene since the 1980s, which features a regular line of punk and new Goth club wear and another line of fetish-inspired clothing.

Music offers such a wide range of inspiration, and not only for Goths, and because it influences more than just fashion, this audible form of expression is covered further in the chapter "Dark Resonations."

Some Concluding Thoughts

Goths are intelligent students of history, the arts, and philosophy with an appreciation of life's dark truths and morbid aesthetic, who have much to contribute to the rest of the world. With this understanding, perhaps those in the mainstream might one day realize that tolerance and acceptance of such forms of self-expression are more potentially good than "evil." Goth is a mindset that need not be seen as rebellion. Some approach it more mentally with a subtle outer appearance, but it exists in them regardless. Goth is a celebration of the Nocturnal. It is the appreciation of the dark, instead of fearing it. It is the ability to pull strength out of times of pain, and come out stronger. By facing our shadow we become a complete person, instead of feeling torn between the two halves of ourselves. One of the reasons that Dark Paganism is becoming more common among Goths is because it offers a path that accepts their choice of expression and equally appreciates the broad influences of history and the arts.

GABRIEL
by Corvis Nocturnum

⚜ DARK SPIRITUALITY ⚜

"To thine own self be true…"
—William Shakespeare

Not to be mistaken for evil or unnatural, dark spirituality is akin to what I discussed as the definition of darkness. Dark spirituality is the inner working of the mind, its relationship with our souls, and the microcosm's[4] relation with the macrocosm. Dark spirituality is the embracing of the spiritual shadow, with all its truths exposed, baring our inner fears. Truth, like energy, is neither good nor bad, it simply *is*.

Truth is power, and everyone has the potential to tap into that power or energy. The concepts of good or evil exist solely in the mind of the practitioner. This is not to say people cannot commit evil acts, but magical or divine energy is not capable of being evil—or good for that matter—all by itself. It is up to the user to determine how that power is directed and whether it be used for good or for evil ends.

Intolerance

Those who wield power are often labeled as "evil" and are treated poorly because of unfortunate stereotyping. Society has trouble accepting people who are different than the accepted norm, and tends to reject any multi-theistic path or faith that focuses primarily on self-awareness. The contempt that some people have for followers of these paths is obvious, and usually results in ostracization, and sometimes escalates to physical violence. Witches or those suspected of practicing the craft, not to mention millions of indigenous people throughout the world, have been murdered for being different or non-conforming.

As the head of the Charities Subcommittee for the Federation of Circles and Solitaries, Tempest Smith's mother Denessa has initiated the "Adopt-a-Shelter" program and has helped to create a more tolerant public image through various communities outreach

---

4. Microcosm—The lesser world (Man), which in the Middle Ages was believed to correspond in every respect with the greater world, called the Macrocosm. — *Wicca: A Guide for the Solitary Practitioner,* by Scott Cunningham.

opportunities. This is due to the fact her daughter committed suicide in school, driven by fellow students' barrage of taunts. The article below has created more awareness to the current situation that more and more kids are facing. In times past, being pretty on the outside was the biggest thing leading to self esteem problems, and now it is added to by how you are or are not like others on the inside as well. Originally written by John T. Greilick / The Detroit News:

TEASING AND TAUNTING LED GIRL TO END HER LIFE
Pressures that prompted mass shootings also spur quiet suicides
By George Hunter / The Detroit News

LINCOLN PARK—Twelve-year-old Tempest Smith sat alone in her bedroom one chilly morning late last month and gazed into the mirror. Shortly before her classes were to start at Lincoln Park Middle School, she kissed her reflection goodbye. The lipstick smudges still adorn Tempest's mirror, sad reminders of the day the tall, troubled girl slipped a leopard-print scarf around her neck and hanged herself from her bunk bed.

Tempest's journal, discovered under her bed after her Feb. 20 suicide, offers a glimpse into a problem family and friends didn't fully understand: the incessant teasing she faced every day about her shy demeanor, choice of clothing and religious beliefs that made each day of school—then eventually life itself—unbearable. "Everyone is against me. Still, death will come sooner or later for me. Will I ever have friends again?"

The haunting, hopeless feelings Tempest privately expressed in her daily journal are shared by an increasing number of children. Although older teens commit the bulk of suicides, at least 300 children ages 10-14 kill themselves annually nationwide. The number of suicides in that age group has tripled since 1995 in Michigan.

Taunts alone usually won't cause a child to commit suicide, experts say. But combined with other problems, constant ridicule by peers can be enough to push a kid over the edge. Teasing and bullying is a constant thread running through school violence.

On Monday, a ninth-grader at Santana High School near San

Diego shot and killed two students and wounded 13 others; classmates said the 15-year-old was often picked on. And at Columbine High School in 1999, two students who'd been teased for years gunned down 12 classmates and a teacher before killing themselves. But for every violent episode that makes headlines, there are more than 2,000 U.S. children each year who, like Tempest Smith, quietly decide they can't take it any more.

"Jesus luvs u"

Tempest often spent hours in her bedroom writing poems and other reflections in the small notebook she kept beneath her bed. The notebook was a birthday gift from her mother. It had a picture of pop star Ricky Martin on the cover.

Tempest, a tall, slim blond who got her name because she was born during a violent storm, wrote about typical youthful concerns: crushes on boys; her dog, a shar-pei named Buddy; trips to her grandmother's house. She wrote about family, calling her mother, "the best mom ever." She also wrote about the pain she increasingly endured during school.

Although Tempest had a few friends, many of her classmates had teased her constantly since elementary school. They teased her because she wore dark "Gothic" clothing to school. They teased her because she read books about Wicca, a Pagan religion often associated with Witchcraft. Her classmates often taunted her with Christian hymns.

A helicopter transported Tempest to the University of Michigan Hospital in Ann Arbor. At 5:30 p.m., doctors told Smith her daughter was suffering irreparable brain damage, due to asphyxiation. At 10:55 a.m. on Feb. 21, after more than 50 organs were removed from her body for donations, Tempest Smith was taken off the hospital's life support system.

Students at Lincoln Park Middle School are now trying to find peace themselves, haunted by the feeling that they may have driven their classmate to end her life. Many of Tempest's classmates have told teachers and counselors they feel responsible, because they teased the girl so ruthlessly. More than 100 students showed up at Tempest's funeral last Saturday, bearing cards and placards expressing their grief—and guilt.

"I'm sorry if I said mean things to you," one of Tempest's classmates wrote. "I didn't mean them. It was the easiest way for me to hide what was wrong with me."

"I am sorry that it led to this," was the message written on a placard. "None of it should have happened. If only they had understood, then you would still be alive."

Lincoln Park school officials and grief counselors have been working with the students. "The last thing we want to do is make our students feel guilty," said Lincoln Park Middle School Principal Robert Redden. "But, maybe there is a lesson to be learned here: that we should strive to treat each other with more kindness."

More than 2,000 school-age children (age 19 or younger) take their own lives each year, according to the U.S. Centers for Disease Control and Prevention. And while the numbers are small, the rise in suicides by children ages 10 to 14 is particularly troubling, health officials say. Only four Michigan children in that age group committed suicide in 1995. In 1998, the most recent year for which statistics are available, 13 children in the state had taken their lives. While there are no simple answers, health officials believe that teasing can send an already troubled child over the edge.

More than 90 percent of people who commit suicide suffer from clinical depression, said Lanny Berman, executive director of the American Association of Suicidology in Washington, D.C. "Often, it's these mental conditions that cause children to be teased in the first place," Berman said.

Jean Vasquez twice attempted suicide by slitting her wrists when she was in middle school. She still has the scars on her wrists, reminders of her difficulty dealing with the relentless teasing she received as a child. "If you're a little different, some kids can make your life an absolute hell," said Vasquez, now 35, of Detroit.

Sadly, even among Pagans themselves, some indigenous tribal path followers, and darker path followers such as those of Nordic traditions, Nocturnal/Gothic Pagans and Satanists are held at a distance if not treated as badly as non-Pagans would treat Wiccans. This chapter will explain all of those, save Satanism, which will be addressed the chapter "The Devil's Due."

Paganism

There is general agreement that the word "Pagan" comes from the Latin word "Paganus." Unfortunately, there is no consensus on the precise meaning of the word in the 5th century and early. Modern Pagan sources interpret the word to have meant "rustic," "hick," or "country bumpkin," a pejorative term. The implication was that Christians used the term to ridicule country folk who tenaciously held on to what the Christians considered old-fashioned, outmoded, Pagan beliefs. Those in the country were much slower in adopting the new religion of Christianity than were the city folks. They still followed the Greek state religion, Roman state religion, Mithraism, various mystery religions, etc., long after those in urban areas had converted. Some believe that in the early Roman Empire, "Paganus" came to mean "civilian" as opposed to "military." Christians often called themselves "miles Christi" (Soldiers of Christ). Thus, the non-Christians became "Pagani" (non-soldiers or civilians). No denigration would be implied. C. Mohrmann suggests that the general meaning was any "outsider," a neutral term, and that the other meanings, "civilian" and "hick," were merely specialized uses of the term. By the 3rd century, its meaning evolved to include all non-Christians. Eventually, it became an evil term that implied the possibility of Satan worship. The latter two meanings are still in widespread use today.

Currently, there is no generally accepted, single definition for the word "Pagan." The term is widely used by Atheists, Agnostics, Humanists, etc. to refer to themselves. The word is also used by others to describe these groups. Paganism is occasionally used to refer to animal and spirit belief systems. It is based upon direct perception of the forces of nature and usually involves the use of idols, talismans and taboos in order to convey respect for these forces and beings. Many native aboriginal religions fit this definition. A rare usage of "Pagan" is employed to describe a person who does not follow an Aramaic religion. The individual is neither Christian, Muslim, nor Jew. This includes Agnostics, Atheists, Buddhists, Hindus, Humanists, Taoists, etc. About forty-five percent of the people of the world are Pagans, by this definition. —*Source: http://www.religioustolerance.org/Paganism.htm*

Pagan Alliances

Groups wanting to make a difference in their communities are forming across the nation in an effort to provide acceptance of all faiths and to avoid religious bashing of any form. One such group is The Fort Wayne Pagan Alliance, founded by STARR MOONCHYLD (president) and WILLOW RHAIAMON (co-vice president), who organize Pagan Pride Day for the Fort Wayne area.

Corvis: "What led to the founding of the Fort Wayne Pagan Alliance?"
Starr: "Well, for a long time I had thought that I was the only person like me around until I met with a group of ladies which is were I met Willow. We discussed the fact that a lot of people felt like were alone also. We wanted to bring together people as well as tolerance of our faith paths."

Corvis: "What was the goal of the FWPA when it first started? What did you want to accomplish in its beginnings?"
Willow: "To be perfectly honest, the initial goal for me was self-serving. I would go to meetings, any Pagan meeting I could find, and they continually fell short of what I wanted. They were either barely Pagan, or they were specifically one path, like Dianic or something. Most often though, they did not encompass Paganism, they were too broad, too open and I was tired of dealing who were afraid to say they were a Pagan group."

Corvis: "Have either of you seen an increase in the diversity in members paths and how well do they get along?"
Starr: "I think all of our members get along pretty well, and as groups grow, so has our member's path choices because people are so different. Each person path is unique to them, so therefore, each member represents a unique path."

Willow: "When we first started, it was more word of mouth. Most of our members heard through promotion, or someone else. Initially a group of friends started bringing friends that were all on the same path. Now we have promoted it online, getting people who don't know each other, each different. I think the diversity increased. It's so many more people on different levels."

Starr Moonchyld and Willow Rhaiamon

Corvis: "What has been accomplished outside the Pagan community for the betterment of the rest of the city?"
Willow: "Ours was the first of any organization or group to have a Pagan Pride Day here in Fort Wayne. That has segwayed into both Starr and myself being interviewed on television, in the newspaper. We put ourselves in the media and the FWPA on the map."

Starr: "I would defiantly agree. We showed people, some people who thought this was an area that couldn't tolerate us. And I think that we've proven wrong. We haven't gotten a lot of protestors at Pagan Pride Day, or flack for who we are and being open. We've had some really great people come up that we wouldn't have thought and say, 'Wow, I saw your article in the paper.' These are people aren't Pagan themselves, but respect us."

Willow: "My father is an elder in a Church of God denomination that I will not name out of privacy. He did compliment Starr on the quality of the article and the fact she did it. I would like to say that I do not know any other city that is Christian based that also has a Pagan Pride organization. I think we truly have broken ground in the City of Churches."

Corvis: "That leads me into my next question. What has the feedback from the rest of the public been?"

Willow: "I know that we have made an impression and we have been noticed. I know the religious right knows of our existence in the community is aware of us because of the various interviews and public events we have done. The type of presence we have had is the reason we have not had any protestors yet."

Starr: "I would agree, the way we present ourselves, we're not aggressive towards other people, were here if you want to come meet us. We make ourselves approachable."

Corvis: "What are the founding goals, the mission statement of the organization?"

Starr: "Basically our mission is fellowship, which which is to say we're not alone like others might think they are. That people can come together with others who have a similar mindset. Also, there is tolerance of other people's religion. Of lifestyles. We preach harmony, getting along with other people, and that goes along with tolerance overall. One of our main slogans is 'hatred is not a family value,' because hate is taught, not born into someone. The last one is resources, we want to help provide for the alternative spiritual community so that they have help when they need it."

Corvis: "What future plans do you have for the FWPA in the near future?"

Willow: "One phrase that Starr has coined, which I love, is Pagan's Helping Pagans. That pretty much leads into our goals. We have already made some charitable contributions, but we would like to do that in a more proactive way. That is a future plan of ours. We recently instituted group Sabbats, which is something we would like to do with more and more people showing up for the event> Our Pagan Night Out, we would like to increase that. That's an event where we get together periodically and spend time together. But essentially we would like to get to the point where we are giving back to the community in may ways possible, not just spiritual, but financially as far as charity. We had a Christmas family this year, things of that nature."

Starr: "At Pagan Pride Day, we helped by getting donations to a local food bank. And just this last year we had over 100 lbs of food and we continue to collect that food at the local occult shop that I own. We have the barrel there everyday. There's also Pagans Against Animal Neglect which was started in Charlotte, North Carolina and has spread throughout the United States. As the area representative I collect items for a local animal shelter, a no-kill shelter. Not only do we do charitable acts, we also fight intolerance. There have been stores that have, especially around Halloween, had advertisements that were very insultive to people like us. We contacted them and asked them to remove the advertisement. They said that they were not able to and we said that we were not able to shop at their store anymore, that we would take our business elsewhere to other places that weren't insulting our beliefs. We continue to fight that ignorance, intolerance and oppression everyday."

Willow: "One thing I would like to add as a closing remark about the Pagan Community: Many of us complain that there is no place for us to go, there are no organizations out there for us. That Christians can go to church, but where are we supposed to go. Rather than complain, when you do know of a Pagan organization in your area please donate when they have a cause, contribute when they have fundraising, show up when they have meetings, because this is not an easy thing to do. Lack of attendance is death to any organization."

"If you really want to see more Pagan organizations out there, then you have to support the ones that are out there now so others will feel inspired to feel the same."

Starr: "Yes. I agree. The biggest downfall of organizations like ours is apathy. People just don't get up and come out there. Part of it could be that people are scared. Many are scared of losing their jobs, their children, etc., which is understandable. These are the things we are fighting to change and are also why we have confidentiality in our membership. The downfall of any group is non-participation. If you don't come to the meetings, if you don't support the group, then there is no reason for the group to exist. Our resources department has material so that people can be more informed about what we are and why we are. We're even trying to get a chapter of the SpiralScouts started here for children. SpiralScouts is an earth-based program similar to other scouting programs to help children learn about the earth. You can even get your children involved in these types of things if you want too. If you don't want to, that's fine too. We need your support. We are here to help the Pagan Community, those both in and out of the broom closet."

RAAVEN is a practicing Witch and a member of SPSA (Spiritual and Pagan Student Alliance of Indiana-Purdue University), who was more than happy to explain her own position in the Pagan community.

Corvis: "First, tell us a little about yourself and how Pagans/Witches are still treated."
Raaven: "I have been practicing Witchcraft since about 1996. I have changed my path as my knowledge of my Craft expanded. The more I learn, the more diverse I become.

"I am what I like to call an 'ordinary, run-of-the-mill Witch.' I am neither black nor white. I consider myself very gray. I have this analogy I use when people ask me what kind of magick I practice. I tell them this: 'I have a hammer. I can use that hammer to build a home for my family and dog, then I can put it to even better use, and help build a shelter for homeless people. But if you cross me, I can use my hammer to bash your brains in.' The hammer is not good or bad; it is only a tool…a means to an end. My magick is the same way. The good or the bad is in my heart (intent). Not in the magick (hammer).

"I believe Pagans/Witches (I will use the term interchangeably here for simplicity) are still treated as big pink elephants. Enormous fuchsia pachyderms that sit in the way; that everyone walks around and steps over and goes out of their way to avoid, but nobody wants to talk about and understand. Heavens help us if we try to understand each other and bridge 'the gap.' And we try. Oh, how we try to help non-Pagan/non-Witch persons to understand. We have wonderful organizations like the SPSA, whose catch phrase is 'We are not here to convert, we are here to understand.'

Raaven

"Yet, much to my dismay (and as a cabinet member of SPSA, I am dismayed by this), very few non-Pagan/non-Witch people show up and say 'I don't believe this, but help me open my mind a little.' Or 'My loved one has just come out of the broom closet. I don't know what to do or how to do it. Can you help me?' In the last year, I know of one instance where people of other faiths actually showed up to talk about what makes us different and how we can respect each other. And they never came back to finish the discussion, so it obviously wasn't too important to them to learn.

"Other endeavors I know of to bridge the gap have been much more successful. Take our local Pagan Pride Day, for instance. This year, I worked an SPSA booth there for a time, and quite a few people showed up just to 'see what Pagan Pride Day is all about.' I think if you can just get someone to ask questions, then healing and bridging the gap can begin. Most Pagans/Witches I know are not about bashing other religions or playing a 'my God can beat up your God' game. I believe I speak for most of us when I say we crave understanding, tolerance, and respect of what makes us unique.

"What I find rather amusing about the whole thing is that some people don't want to listen to what you have to say—PERIOD. They act like they are so very holy, that your mere presence disgusts them. I attend school, and recently someone asked me about the pentagram necklace I wear. So, I began to explain my lifestyle and belief system. I spoke only of myself and my beliefs; I did not mention God or Christianity. I had not been talking for five minutes when I was asked by my instructor to 'stop discussing that,' because I was 'offending the Christians' with my 'blatant disregard for their beliefs.' When I calmly explained I was doing nothing of the sort, I was interrupted and told that the policy in that class now was that no one could discuss their religion at all. Oh, how I long for what the bumper sticker states: If only closed minds came with closed mouths!"

Corvis: "I understand you were on our local radio station speaking on your beliefs and one of the DJs asked about 'devil worshipers.' Can you elaborate on it and how you handled it?"
Raaven: "The SPSA donated some money to the American Red Cross (via the radio station) for hurricane relief. The radio station thought this was neat, so they asked us to come in and talk about ourselves and our beliefs on the air. I was one of three members of SPSA that attended. The interview went surprisingly well, until near the end, when the D.J. (who, by the way, was a Christian), made some comment about how we couldn't be so bad because we weren't devil worshipers or Satanists. Now, I knew in my mind that he was speaking out of ignorance (not stupidity, just a lack of correct information), so I did what I believed to be the only correct thing to do… stand up for what I believe in. I am not a Satanist, but I feel like I understand Satanism, and it is not a bad thing. So I told him, on the air, that I wasn't going to bash the Satanists. So he said he would. I told him that I knew lots of Satanists that were good people and loved the earth, etc. It was a 'friendly argument.'

"I feel like if you truly understand Satanism (or anything for that matter), then you know what the real story is. You aren't offended or upset that people believe and live that way. It all comes back to my main idea that if people would just learn and bridge the gap, then we would be able to live with and tolerate each other better.

"I believe very strongly in the song lyric by Rage Against the Machine: 'If ignorance is bliss, then knock the smile off my face.' I would much rather know the truth, even when it hurts, than be blissfully unaware."

Corvis: "Are you or people you know afraid to openly be Pagan for fear of the outing (job loss, etc.)? In your experience, what causes this?"

Raaven: "I myself am not afraid to be openly Pagan. I am a Witch. This is my religion, and according to one of the most vital documents in America, I have every right to practice a religion and adhere to it as I see fit. It is my civil right. I personally adhere to the dictate of 'You live your life, I'll live mine...' and expect the same. However, if you aren't Christian in this country, you have a lot of explaining to do.

"I meet people almost everywhere I go who accept my beliefs, and I also meet those who are outrageously offended. Some people just refuse to let others be free. What a shame. I personally adhere to the dictate of 'You live your life, I'll live mine...' and expect the same.

"I do know people who are terrified of coming out about their beliefs. I know one husband and wife couple who are fearful. They live in a small town, she is a nurse for a very Christian, very small-minded man, and thinks he'll find a way to fire her. He is an electrician and just doesn't want to make waves. Here is the part I find tragic: they don't share the beauty of the Craft they practice with their kids. It is just a big secret. I feel sorry for those of us paralyzed by fear. My advice is to stand your ground. If you don't stand up for yourself, no one else will. Like the song says, 'You've got to stand for something or you'll fall for nothing,' Be brave and fear not...it will all work itself out in the end."

Corvis: "Are you optimistic that your beliefs will become better received over time?"

Raaven: "That is a very interesting question, with an interesting answer. At this point in time, it is very 'hip' to be Pagan-ish. Let's face it: Goddess worship and Goddess-ey things are very in right now.

Although there is much, much more to Paganism than the Goddess, maybe she is opening the door to a more relaxed attitude about what we do and believe. I think we should take it any way we can get it. If we must grit our teeth and be trendy for a while because it is for a good cause, we should do it. Some people accuse me of 'selling out' when I offer this viewpoint. They are wrong. Selling out would be wanting to be trendy just to be trendy. I want to use being trendy as a way to bridge the gap and encourage understanding. A little understanding is something that has never hurt anyone. If we continue to be 'out there' and become an ever present force, we won't be denied in the end."

The Pentacle/Pentagram

The star has been symbolic of magic and mysticism for ages, dating back to ancient Egyptian and Middle Eastern cultures. The most well-known star is the pentacle (also called a pentagram), which is essentially a five-pointed star, connected by straight lines, enclosed within a circle. The number of points is representative of the five alchemic elements; Air, Fire, Water, Earth, and "Spirit," or the primary element from which the universe was formed and from which all other elements are derived. It is also the number of fingers on the hand, a powerful omen to ancient tribes.

The circle symbolizes the unification of these elements, a rotating cycle of life, a magical joining and the correspondence of conflicting forces. Modern Wicca or Witches and Pagans have adopted this symbol, although their forbearers had no need for such as a means of representation of self. The majority of its significance as a symbol to modern thinking comes from the philosophy of the last century.

Early Christians would have the five-pointed star as a symbol of Christ (man perfected, as well as a symbol of the crucifixion wounds). It fell out of Christian use during the Burning Times, when occult texts were discovered with it as a primary symbol. Other stars have been given occult significance as well, such as the six-sided Star of

David, and seven-pointed stars. Such symbols are historically documented in the Cabbala, which is entwined with the Hebrew religion. The majority of magic is a mix of Cabbalistic and Egyptian ideas, which is why stars have such significance in our modern magical symbolism.

The Inverted Pentacle

While the upward-pointed pentacle represents the power of the world being directed toward the greater good of the universe, the downward-pointed pentacle, being an "inversion" of the aforementioned idea, represents the power of the universe being brought to focus upon the world. This became a negative symbol during early Christian use, just as the inverted cross is considered an "evil" symbol, but the ancients who used the pentacle did not put any particular significance to it being "right-side-up" or "inverted."

The Templar Knights began exploring the concept of God outside the doctrines of the Church, from whom they had full autonomy. They discovered new ways of expressing the idea of God, ways to them that were more valid and closer to the truth than what the Church was providing to its followers during that time. One such symbol the Templars used to describe these ideas was the goat-head/inverted pentacle symbol. The goat is a symbol of fertility and wisdom, and fits nicely into the downward-pointed pentacle. More on this under "Baphomet," in the chapter "The Devil's Due."

Modern thinkers have suggested that the "right-side up" pentacle generally represents "positive intent," while the inverted pentacle represents "negative intent." Others take a more practical standpoint, saying that the upward-pointed pentacle merely represents power being released, while the downward-pointed pentacle signifies power being drawn in. Obviously, the altruistic philosophies of the right hand path prefer the upward-pointed pentacle, while the pragmatic lean toward the down-pointed pentacle. There is no reason to use or wear pentacle/pentagrams accept as a symbol, and like all other symbols, it only has the power we personally invest in it.

Nocturnal Witchcraft

Nocturnal practitioners of the craft follow the majority of the same guidelines as any other. They simply prefer to conduct their rituals and Sabbats during the night, focusing with lunar energies. They pay homage to the often overlooked powers of darkness, which in many cases involves the shadow realm of death, the counter aspects of the day. This is represented by many examples, like flowers that close during the day and open at night.

The primary benefit to Nocturnal Witchcraft—other than the lack of light for those more comforted by less direct glare, such as people with photosensitivity—is the absence of traffic and the clutter of psychic noise of people.

Having been confused with "evil Satanists," Nocturnal Witches explain themselves as "good dark." For example, a type chart[5] is created by drawing a black cross. In each open part of the chart is a different aspect, or character. They believe that to utilize forces we need to understand people for who they are. Examples would be: Good Light, Jesus, a nurse, or good Samaritans (people who are seen as good and also good-willed); Evil Dark would be a child molester, Hitler (obviously evil by the actions he committed); and Evil Light would be a corrupt politician, lawyer, TV Evangelists (people seen everyday as good but do little altruistic good for others); Good Dark would be people who appear 'bad' but are truly good inside. Many variations include freaks, Goths, Witches, etc., thus completing the four quadrants.

Preferring night magic, we name the stages of life as they pertain to the lunar phases. Waxing, full, waning, and dark, which represent the "child stage," Goddess/Gods, "mother" or parent stage, "crone" for gaining wisdom from life's experiences, respectively. Dark moon or no moon represents death and preparing for rebirth. Candles used are black and their flames represent the stars. A silver candle represents the full moon.

The Dark Goddess is shown in myths as crones, wise old hags, the personification of war and various stages of blight on the earth, and is

5. For more information on Type Charts, please read Nocturnal Witchcraft by Konstantinos.

known by many names. Some of the names the Dark Goddess is known by are Kali, Huntress, and Diana. The Dark Gods are the Lords of the Dead, underworld figures such as Hades and Set. There are many Lunar Gods and Goddesses, each part of the world and each in their own place, none being more important than the other. Simply put, just calling on the Gods and Goddesses of the night are sufficient.

The circle of life is a constant. So also is the cycle of the moon and of day into night, Nocturnal Witches simply choose to observe what is normally overlooked. It is not a rejection of the light, but an acknowledgement of a needed balance.

Rituals

Most practitioners of the craft know what the purpose of a ritual is, but for the novice it can be confusing. No one particular path is identical, nor are the rituals of any one solitary performer. Rituals of of nearly every indigenous tribe of peoples from times past to our present day Catholic Church still use ritual in one form or another to establish a direct connection to the Divine Energy, God, or Gods. Even Satanists who are non-theistic (unless they are Luciferian), use ritual to tap into the energy of their own subconscious, dismissing the idea of a higher power altogether.

A ritual according to Satanists is "the performance to assist the outcome of his/her desires, a dogmatic and anti-intellectual device. It is performed to disassociate the activities from the outside world while projecting ones will."

Psychodrama, as Anton LaVey called it, is the arousal needed to heighten a feeling inside oneself, combined with a symbolic representation.

The Encyclopedia of Witches and Witchcraft written by Grimassi calls rituals a "prescribed form of consciousness. All religions and spiritual, mystical and magical traditions have their own rituals, which are the means by which to contact the divine, or supernatural will, or forces helping the individual define him/herself in relation to the cosmos, and mark progress through life and spiritual unfolding."

Altars and Tools

Altars by and large have two purposes. Most obviously, even to the uninitiated, it is the place a Magician, Satanist, or Shaman[6], keeps his or her tools. Even Christianity shares the second, more detailed answer; it is a place of concentration and focus, in circles, grotto, church or covens, a gathering place where we connect to the Divine and focus large amounts of energy collectively. I personally do not believe altars/churches, etc. are an absolute necessity for Pagans, Witches or any faith, for the Divine is around and with us all. To think a building or a place is the sole place for worship is both wrong and foolish. The dogmatic influence of some teachers, parents, etc. who promote this have given way to disrespect of our resources, environment and wildlife.

The act of using magic or prayer is emotional rather than intellectual, for many would define magic as "the change in situations or events in accordance with one's will, which would, using normally accepted methods, be unchangeable." In ancient times, science was considered magic and is now accepted as obvious truth, not mad Dr. Frankenstein or Witches allied to the devil. A new approach is worth considering: applied science to spell casting.

Odd as this may sound, I assure you there is a theory to consider. As most of you may know, everything is made up of atomic particles with positive/negative energy. This polarity creates magnetism, hence, with enough similar atoms, in this case, you get a strong pull. The human body exhibits magnetism, static electricity, and electromagnetic pulses for sending information through the spine to and from the brain—cause and effect.

Your will begets movement and accomplishes consciousness through meditation, fasting, etc., leading to greater awareness to the visibly unseen powers. My view on this is that the advantage to Nocturnal practice versus day practice (due to the interruption of background noise that occurs more during the day, and the absence of it at night), allows one to focus. Thus, if all objects (tools in this case), contain energy, and you, the practitioner are in a focal area undisturbed

6. The term Shaman is used to mean mystic or aboriginal medicine person. The word was coined by Europeans as "shame-faker," but by no means does this condone its origins.

(your altar), you are simply more in tune with your natural ability to manipulate your desired outcome. Science has already made other energy-work, such as Acupuncture and Reflexology, widely accepted by society, and the examples in this paragraph should be no different as they can be proven "accurate" in much the same way.

Chaos Magick

Ego Diabolus, an acquaintance of mine online, did some research on Chaos magic. (His interview on Satanism appears in the chapter "The Devil's Due.") His theory on Chaos Magick is such:

"First of all, I don't believe you can separate Chaos Theory (a quantum-physics issue), Chaos Magic (essentially the Chaos Theory applied as a mystical system), and Discordianism (a dynamic philosophy based on the Chaos Theory as applied to the macroverse). So this discussion will be in part science, mysticism, and philosophy. The foundation of Chaos Magick is the summary of the philosophy of Hassan I Sabbah, a militant mystic from who's soldiers we derive the term 'assassin' (from Hassani, or people of Hassan), which should tell you what type of military strategy they perfected. According to Hassan 'Nothing is True. All is Permitted' (from the Principia Discordia). In Chaos Magick, there exist no one or correct way to achieve an effect; whatever works is what you go with, and what works changes from moment to moment. Hassan was also quoted, in the same book, as saying, 'Everything is True. All is Permitted,' which merely re-enforces the idea. If it works, it must have been correct. Typically, Chaos Magick is applied over another system; it simply makes the original system more malleable. Wiccans begin bending their rules, attempting strange effects, and above all, listening to their inner voices, even the most ridiculous suggestions. Basically, one is attempting to 'go with the flow.', to allow the self to become guided by the universe, and let the universe (a Chaos construct) take care of itself (and, as a component of the universe, you). Order is temporary at best, and typically delusional.

"This brings us to Discordianism, the philosophy of Chaos. Beginning with Hassan's wisdom, we discover another interesting affect; the more you try to control a thing, the more chaotic things become. There is a continuous struggle between those who attempt to create order, and those who resist. The more order applied, the greater the likelihood of revolt. The more disorder, the more likely controls are enforced. These are the opposing forces and the spark which drives the universe, according to Discordianism. This is the sacred Chao, comprised of the opposing forces of Hodge (order), and Podge (disorder). Discordians simply attempt to manipulate these opposing forces to create effects they desire, feel are worth while, or help advance whatever side of the issue they are feeling closest to that day. All of this is either the application of, or re-enforced by, the Chaos Theory. Chaos Theory is actually a collective set of theories, which include the "butterfly effect" (a small change, in one system results in a massive change in another, seemingly unrelated system), the anthropic principle (the universe seems to exist in such a manner to allow for the evolution of beings which could observe that the universe seems to exist), and the Observation Principle (a natural system is effected by the expectations of the person observing it-especially in quantum mechanics, where particles behave based upon the expectations of the observers, in some cases appearing before there existence, etc). Chaos Theory(ies) provides scientific backing for the philosophical and mystical applications, in and of itself making these applications more likely to succeed. Chaos Theory is actually less involved with true chaos, and more involved in attempting to discover the underlying pattern, no matter how obscure, in seemingly random events.

"Chaos persons typically relate to God forces such as Coyote or Eris, and are often engaged in projects designed to remind the casual observer that a) they are being controlled or forced to conform, and b) they still have the freedom to resist. Such projects have included events the Dada Art Movement, large helium balloons being hung along a section of a well-traveled highway, and social engineering pranks (like using super-strength epoxy to seal shut the coin-slots of parking meters). The effort is designed to disrupt the static paradigm of reality to allow for more potential; the more people that recognize the limits of the system, the more limited the system becomes."

MISTRESS SOPHIA is a member of the Goth Metal band URN. She shares some insight into her personal path, Dragon Magic.

Mistress Sophia
Photo by Pendragon Studios

Corvis: "What is the difference between Dragon Magic and Chaos Magic?"
Mistress Sophia: "Dragon Magick and Chaos Magick are very similar and yet very different. Dragon Magick tends to be more like Angelic Magick. Some see the Dragons as Angels, and others see them as lizard-like or demon-like creatures. However, the wings are the same. Draconic magicians deal with chaos energy, but it tends to be a more ordered chaos energy. Ordered chaos can be more predictable, but is more concentrated and more destructive. The energy is destruction and creation in the same breath. I will be going into this more in the seminar at Ancient Ways."
Corvis: "How has your religion been affected by people knowing that you're in a Goth band? Does it help reach people, or do both misunderstood subcultures combined alienate you from the mainstream even more?"

Mistress Sophia: "My religion really hasn't been affected much, by being in a Goth Metal band. Sometimes, I would like more time to do the things I do spiritually. But then again I think many of us feel that way no matter what we do in our lives.

"I feel that being in a band does help reach people. A lot of times it connects you to people you don't even know. Many of whom have had the same experiences or share the same feelings. I don't think that both subcultures have really alienated me. Most of the people I know really don't care. But there are a few that seem to disapprove, so to speak."

Corvis: "I find it very impressive that your group has such a diverse faith mix but that you all get along so well from Catholic to Witchcraft, pranic vampire, etc. What holds most people back from being as willing to react the same way in the general public?"

Mistress Sophia: "As far as religions go, we feel that a person's creed is the path they must take on there journey of life. I think that each religion is a spoke on a wheel. The center or hub is heaven, paradise, or whatever you want to call it. Everyone is trying to get to the center. Each spoke on the wheel is a different path to get there. In a sense, no one is right, and no one is wrong. Everyone must seek their own truth. Unfortunately, society as we know it doesn't see it that way. Even though the first amendment to the Constitution states 'freedom of religion,' most of society thinks that their religion and only their religion is 'The Right Way.' Much of this comes from the Puritan Society that this country started out with. The Pilgrims and the Puritans were not very tolerant people. They persecuted those they thought were Witches and even Catholics. Eventually, the Native Americans were 'converted' to their ways of thinking. Much of society lives in fear. They fear the unknown, they fear almost anything that they aren't informed about. And most don't want to take the time to understand."

Dark Paganism

I felt the best individual to explain the concept of Dark faith paths combined with Goth culture was JOHN J. COUGHLIN, author of the book *Out of The Shadows*. John heads a multi-path open forum online as well as his own websites wherein he offers resources, personals, and research on history and evolution of ethics for Pagans, Nocturnal Witches, and another for Goths. His research has spanned the last twelve years, and has begun to appear in various magazines such as *New Witch*.

I have been speaking with him in-group for the last two years, and when I told him I was about to write my own book, he graciously agreed to explain his feelings further.

John J. Coughlin

Corvis: "What drew you into Gothic Paganism, and what is it to those who don't know?"

John: "I usually call it 'Dark Paganism' only since 'Gothic' tends to assume it is only an aspect of the Gothic Subculture. I usually define it as a form of Paganism aligned to a left-hand path. There is often a certain attraction to themes and images of darkness (Gothic imagery so to speak), but a Dark Pagan may not 'look' like a Goth. The defining factors are more in perception and attitude. Since I was always drawn to dark themes and imagery it was only natural for me to begin to incorporate such things into my personal developing spirituality. The idea of calling myself a Dark Pagan only came to me when I found it harder to define myself simply as 'Pagan' and found myself lacking a simple way to describe myself to others."

Corvis: "Like you, I have always loved nature, thunderstorms, and worn black. But unfortunately this often leads to negative reactions from other Pagans and especially non-Pagans. How do you deal with the stereotypical reactions of people by the way you chose to look and worship?"

John: "I have found I have drifted further and further away from mainstream Paganism, and so avoided much of the potential backlash. However I must say to (my surprise) when I started speaking at Pagan events to promote my book, I was often met with a curious fascination.

I think part of that had to do with the fact that I was presenting left-hand path concepts from a Pagan perspective they could relate to and avoiding terms like 'left-hand path' and 'Satanism' which are still heavily stereotyped in mainstream Paganism. I also find most of the more ignorant type are afraid to confront me in person since I an not one to back down from a good debate and their arguments tend to lack substance, so the few negative reactions I get tend to be via email."

Corvis: "A growing number of people have been turning to darker paths. Do you feel your book influenced them, or did it 'speak' to us that listen?"

John: "I think the time was right for such a book and I just lucked out to be the first to get there. I had expected much criticism and as the book came out braced myself for the worst, but instead I received countless letters and emails from people excited beyond description, thanking me for putting into print what had been in their heads for so long. There is definitely an undercurrent in Paganism that is aligned to aspects of darkness and which has been lacking a voice. I did my best to avoid being trendy. I wanted to push the ideas and not the image since the image would become packaged and sold purely for profit with no care for its meaning. I see that happening now since Gothic imagery and magic are so popular these days. I guess that was inescapable."

Corvis: "You write that there are many dark paths, each one unique to the practitioner. They vary from Chaos magic to Egyptian, to Santeria and Satanism. What do you believe is the tie that binds all these people together in your online groups?"

John: "The form of the path merely reflects the interests and perceptions of the individual, but underlying all of them is that left-hand path current which leads individuals to seek their inner greatness, whether or not they choose to consider themselves Gods outright. They all acknowledge that they are ultimately the ones who dictate their fate, and that they are not victims of circumstances or slaves to divine creeds. They all seek to light their way through life with the brilliance of their own Being… The black flame as Satanists would say."

Corvis: "You make a point of saying Goths and Satanists face their fears in a 'Shadow' i.e. Jungian sense, and are for the most part, realist and better adjusted than a lot of normal people. Do you feel it is an ironic that at times that many in outwardly extreme lifestyles are the most inwardly balanced?"

John: "I find it ironic that while it's the occasional black-clad teen that gets the national headlines for a shooting in a school, it is by far the 'normal' guy next door that is more prone to violent crimes from blowing the boss away to torturing his family. Society prefers to notice the ones who do not fit the 'norm.' It is the individualist who threatens society's false sense of security in conformity. They WANT to see something wrong with us and yet are blind to their own perversities. Those who seek to be themselves and strive to free themselves from unnecessary conditioning are by far much more likely to be 'whole' and not torn between many perceptions inner self-identity and society's imposed labels. As Jung said, 'I would rather be whole than good.'"

Corvis: "Although it may surprise some, you actually stress a balance between the lighter paths and dark ones. Is this in order to create a needed counter balance?"

John: "Personally I find balance to be separate from those labels. Some people are more aligned with or drawn to aspects we associate with 'light' and others to aspects we associate with 'darkness.' Neither is better than the other per se, just as democrats are no better or worse than republicans. These labels merely are used for identification purposes. Therefore anyone can be balanced or imbalance apart from those labels. I am 'balanced in darkness' because I recognize my personal disposition to darkness and do not limit myself TO that label. To escape vague terms for a moment, consider an introvert and an extrovert. I am introverted by nature. I prefer to be alone or in small groups and I do not like to be in the public spotlight. I am 'balanced' because I am able to do things like give lectures, go to parties, be sociable when I need to, etc. I am still introverted, but I am not locked into that mode. When I give lectures I often come across as being extroverted, but after the lecture is over, I'm looking forward to getting away from the crowds. I would be unbalanced if I were unable to escape my introverted nature when needed. It is only then that my introversion becomes a limitation rather than merely a disposition. We see this same sense of balance and imbalance in terms of light and darkness... some have that 'darker-than-thou' attitude, and do all in their power to avoid any association with what they consider 'light' (just as the opposite is true). What good is that? We only limit ourselves. The balance is in knowing who one is and in being oneself, not in living a label."

Corvis: "There is an old saying that 'Great men, like eagles, must build their nests in solitude.' I find peace away from others who do not accept me as I am, instead of conforming, but it can be lonely when we remain true to ourselves. Are Dark Pagans, Goths, and Satanists in your experience a separate world unto themselves because of such ostracism?"

John: "As an introvert it's easy for me to say that solitude is needed to some extent, but I do feel it is true. By seeking a path of self-exploration and personal growth/initiation one ends up having to distance oneself from the noise and distractions of society. It can be a very lonely path at times since our Way may not be the Way of the majority. People will not always understand us. Sometimes they will fear and/or loathe us. We threaten the perception of conformity being safe and healthy... of being the way to happiness. As we learn that it is self-acceptance that is paramount, it gets easier, but since most of us still live in that same society which stresses the importance of acceptance of our peers, we will always be haunted with a sense of being out of place. I would say that sense has less of a hold on me now then it did when I was in my teens, but it never goes away. Such is the cost of freedom."

Corvis: "Do you feel we ever will be fully accepted beyond our appearance and differing views?"

John: "By everyone? No, not at all... at least not until there are some major strides in the evolution of humanity as a whole. We strive to find meaning and purpose outside of the limitations imposed on us. By nature our differences will always keep us apart from the masses. I like to think eventually our views will be more appreciated, but I also would not say that is one of my objectives. What we do, we do for ourselves and not the world; although perhaps in doing so we sow the seeds of self-reflection and growth, and in doing so make the world a better place."

Asatru: A Warrior's Path

The Scandinavian countries such as Norway, Sweden and Iceland have an ancient history of earth-based spirituality, dating back to nearly prehistoric times. The Nordic path of the Vikings has been included in this chapter because there is much misunderstood about their path. Asatru is generally regarded with suspicion, mainly due to ties with Hitler's reign and neo-Nazism of today and Black Metal bands of the nineties with church burnings.

Fortunately, more and more examples of old religions are coming out as time passes, showing an increase in awareness, and in time, an acceptance of alternative faiths. Based on the Nordic legend of

Beowulf, Michael Creighton's book-turned-film, *The Thirteenth Warrior*, centers on a Middle Eastern scholar traveling to the icy lands of Scandinavia, where he learns of Asatru beliefs. We also see the *Willendorf Goddess*, the stone carved figure of an ancient fertility goddess in the berserker's caverns.

Rob Crocker

I approached a follower of Asatru, ROB CROCKER, whose role within Indiana Purdue Fort Wayne's college group of Pagan students is that of record keeper. He gladly spoke to me to clear up a lot of my own questions.

Corvis: "Why Asatru as a path, and how has modern times affected it's purity from its origins today?"

Rob: "I was drawn to Asatru because of the nine noble virtues, those being hospitality, courage, truth, loyalty, honor, self-reliance, hard work, perseverance, and discipline. I also was pleased to learn that it was one of the last 'pagan' religions to convert to Christianity and was one of the first to throw the yoke off. In fact it even became its own separate brand of Christianity under the guise of the 'Gothic Church.' As for how it's been diluted by modern times, well we have some surviving documents and accounts to base our beliefs on. Like all religious paths that the Christians stamped out though there has to be a certain amount of interpretation and creative license. I can read in the Eddas or in historical accounts like those of Tacitus' Germania, or for that matter even read inscribed runes from surviving stones, but the essence of the religion is still in the blood and will make it self known. I can use comparative religious study also to see that the Christians gobbled up pagan holidays built churches on sacred sites to assist in the rebuilding too."

Corvis: "Like what for instance?"

Rob: "Well like most pagan religions Asatru is based on harvest cycles. They are all in some way centered on fertility, of both land and people and thus on survival. It shares a roughly common calendar with practitioners of modern day Wicca and Druidism. Ostara is an important celebration that was twisted into Easter, and even the names of our weekdays were gobbled up and have lost significance. Tuesday was Tyr' day, Wednesday was Odin' day and placed in the center of the week to show balance, then Thursday was Thor' day, those are just little examples. Some big ones could be our concepts of law and our courts. Our modern culture owes if not more at least a third of what we are to our Germanic roots, not just to the Greeks and Romans. Even the English language is classified as a Germanic language! Now you can't go overboard with this, there was some trouble in the early 90s with some Swedish black metal bands and church burnings. Evidently they saw themselves as spiritual warriors paving the way to a new Viking tomorrow. Well as in any religion there can be fanatics and I think that's what these people were."

Corvis: "As to other people twisting the Germanic and Nordic traditions, such as Thor's hammer, what are your perceptions, opinions on that?"
Rob: "Well the biggest and most damaging thing to growth of Asatru is its link with Nazism and white power movements. It's a mistaken correlation made by ignorant people today who can't see that the Nazi's used religion as a way to control they're own people. In the early 30s there was a resurgence of Teutonic practices and beliefs among the folk. Those in power were able to capitalize on this and use powerful symbols like the Swastika (which is also used by Buddhists) to sway the mind of the people. Around this time there was a man named Guido Von List who through a series of visions, claimed to have discovered the essence of the runes, a system he called the Armenian system. This led to much research on Runes and since it was done by Germans during the rise of the Reich it is believed that Runes or any kind of Germanic religion must be evil. People tend to forget that this whole path and set of beliefs existed thousands of years before Hitler walked the earth."

Corvis: "Does censorship and repression of alternative faiths create worse reactions instead of just letting people do what they want?"
Rob: "I can definitely see how those that feel repressed would want to fight back. As mentioned earlier with the black metal bands, people who feel cornered will strike back, but there are appropriate ways to get our message across without feeding the stereotypes that abound."

Corvis: "What about the fact that 'large built, hairy' individuals like yourself might have a frightening appearance to some people, and does this seem to be an obstacle?"
Rob: "Well, I've learned that you never judge a book by its cover, but I'd wager that most people out there have not. I guess if I'm frightening then so be it. I think I'm a quite friendly person and if

people stop to talk to me it shows. I guess it could be an obstacle in some ways, but that's not really a problem. I think we need strife. Civilization has changed so vastly since the Norsemen' time and that culture was a warrior culture adapted to survive in hard lean times facing things we take for granted today. The lesson though is not lost, you must continue to fight and to struggle and through that you grow and learn. I may not strap on a sword and go out to war, but I do face obstacles in everything I do every day. It's the strife that's important, without it I think we stagnate."

Corvis: "Are Asatru better equipped to handle things you think?"
Rob: "With the right attitude I think we can cope better than some. The nine virtues are a guide to steer us and the will to fight, not physically per se, but emotionally and spiritually makes us strong. It's a fight everyday to wake up and face a society that does not accept you."

Corvis: "It has an honor code about it as well, correct?"
Rob: "Absolutely, that is a very important part of my faith. The afterlife may not be clear or certain, but if I live as a strong and valiant person I will affect those around me. I will gather a powerful reputation that can outlive me. That legacy is important; it is my immortality. According to Ragnorak at the end even the Gods themselves die so creating this legacy of honor and truth to survive as long as possible is a powerful motivator."

Corvis: "In Nordic tradition, Fenris the wolf is a devilish creature, an antagonist. In modern civilization, the wolf is looked upon with suspicion and fear, much like the practitioner of Asatru. They both share certain traits, however; a strong will to survive, independence, and survival of the fittest..."
Rob: "In the Asatru lore, Fenris is going to devour the Sun, Moon and Stars, there will be a terrible battle that brings about the end of the world and the Gods (though Odin has hidden one of his sons and along with a man and a woman who will start to replenish the earth again). This connection with wolves did nothing to stop the Norse

from honoring and respecting the strength of the wolf. Fenris is just an archetype for the powers of ravenous destruction."

Corvis: "Do you see a similar aspect with the left hand path? Responsibility, respect, that sort of thing?"
Rob: "With some of the satanic beliefs I do. I agree with respecting others only if they deserve respect. I agree with not turning the other cheek and letting people walk on you. I think that LHP respects strength and understands how to use circumstances as tools to make yourself all the more powerful. There is a duality in the Norse path that I feel embraces darkness a bit if only to better appreciate the light."

Corvis: "Aren't the Nordic Gods themselves simply archetypes, ancestors, or figureheads to emulate?"
Rob: "That's a fair assessment. The Norse do not bow or supplicate themselves before their Gods. They approach them as brothers or as equals and as such recognize the divinity that flows within them. These figures or Gods then would naturally need to be something that we find attractive and would want to emulate. That does not mean that they are EASY to emulate. Nothing that's easy to attain is as worthwhile as something you've had to fight for."

Corvis: "How are Asatru treated by others such as Satanist, Pagans, and Christians?"
Rob: "Well, the Christian answer is easy, if your not one of them your evil! As for other pagans I think it's fair to state that they are not too judgmental. That's probably part of what set them down their own path in the first place. There are fluffy people who think that Asatru is all about 'Scream! Burn! Smash!' but to me they are as ignorant as the Neo-Nazi's who won't pick up a book. Satanists I think tend to stick to themselves and don't really comment on it either way, although I think they would take issue with some of the base ideas. I can see a Satanist arguing that doing what would bestow a positive reputation on me and my kindred for future generations might not always be in MY best interests…so we'll have to disagree on those points."

Modern Primitive

From the dawn of man, tribal markings, piercing, tattooing, and scarification have been practiced as decoration and as spiritual or coming-of-age ritual. On television it is presented in documentary videos of cultures prior to modern civilization, an aboriginal practice that ceased here in America after Native Americans were forced into boarding schools during the 1890s. Today, when such individuals live in similar fashion, they receive possibly the worst reaction of any of the previously discussed spiritual path followers. Assumptions range from freak to convict; both generate a lasting negative stigma. It is confused with fetishist, but more accurately it falls under spirituality.

I reached ART AGUIRRE of Sci-fi's *Mad Mad House* by phone. Art is a warm and charismatic tattooist and body piercer who owns a body modification business called *Church of Steel*. You can find him working at normal business hours on Broadway in San Diego California. We spent an enjoyable hour chatting as he reflected back on the spirituality and history of body modification as well as detailing his current feelings on public reaction.

Corvis: "How and why did you get into body piercing and tattooing?"
Art: "Ever since I was a kid, and me being exposed to other cultures and documentary-type shows, like *National Geographic* and *Wild Kingdom*, I was exposed to wild animals in Africa; would every now and then show brief clips of an Massai Tribe, the ears or the scarification of the stretched lips of the women. So as a child I was intrigued and very fascinated by various cultures throughout the world, such as the Chinese and the Buddha."

Corvis: "I didn't realize that they were into that also."
Art: "Well, you look at a Buddha figure, his earlobes are elongated and he didn't wear jewelry. People aren't aware of that. People never acknowledged that Buddha's ears were elongated; he just never wore jewelry. My culture, the pre-Hispanic cultures, the Mayan culture, the Aztecs, all have stretched lobes, large, engaged labrets, or they wore

very intricate, detailed labret pieces in certain rituals and ceremonies. They also used to do several types of piercing and breaking of the skin. Not so much to put jewelry in, but as a sacred form of paying homage to a God or Deity or showing love to a loved one or a human and that was a form of bloodletting. They would pierce parts of their bodies or some of the female wives would run a rope through their tongue to pay homage or show love to their husbands or their lords. They would run the rope through the roof of their tongues or the males would pierce their genitals on a stingray bar and let the blood drip on the papyrus and then they would apply direct pressure and stop the bleeding.

Art Aguirre

"Then they would take that papyrus and take it up to a sacrificial altar and they would light the papyrus. They believed that in the smoke rising up to the heavens that they were communicating and paying their homage to the Gods. It was the most sacred form of paying homage. And as a child I can remember being very intrigued with watching documentaries and watching certain ceremonies and customs that were being practiced by many different cultures and people throughout the world."

Corvis: "**Would you say that the pain is a spiritual experience for you? Like suspension and piercing in general?**"

Art: "I would strongly voice that pain is never a factor because pain is never an issue that crosses my mind. If it does, it does only in the form learning and programming your body, mind and spirit to overcome the discomfort and pain, if you want to use that word. I never do, because I've never experienced anything painful, because I voluntarily subjected myself to. Over the battle I had with cancer, I would say that was somewhat painful, but not in the physical pain, as in what was put in my body, what Western medicine put me through, radiation and surgeries. That was not voluntary. I would say for two years that my body did not belong to me, it belonged to Western medicine, and so, after I went through my battle and beat the cancer (when in fact I was only given six months to live), I went down 92 pounds from throwing up everyday for two years, I was able to once again reclaim my body. Now I can look at that 25 years later, I've been in remission 25 years. I am a firm believer in what doesn't kill you only makes you stronger. But I am a stronger believer in that this was a lesson in disguise. I wouldn't have said that back then, but it has helped me become a stronger individual emotionally, spiritually and physically, and it has taught me many lessons and many things in life that in today's age, many people take for granted."

Corvis: "**Unfortunately, yes, they do.**"

Art: "A lot of people that have gone through what I've gone through during their illness, when they get a second chance, they look at their life through a completely different set of eyes. You appreciate everything so much more on many different levels and you live life each day to its fullest, of course with discretion, I was able to experience many things I would not have been able to experience 25 years later. Now I'm still here, and I believe I was kept here for a reason. There's a purpose for me and there's a reason for me to be here. Verbally, can I put it in words? No, it would just be too much what I feel and I wouldn't be able to enlighten people on what I do in the art of body modification. I do feel very blessed and I attribute that to my spirit guides."

Corvis: "Tribal modification has been around since earliest times. Do you feel that in modern civilization there's still a place for tribal expression?"
Art: "I strongly believe that many of us have strong primal urges, strong primal instincts to what variety they will express them or let them out. I am a strong believer in that, we have primal urges to this day."

Corvis: "Right. I agree. What we were talking about earlier, the reactions of individuals, like in the grocery store on Mad, Mad House, where Art was stopped by an elderly lady who called him a devil—do you have any advice for anybody who's new to it?"
Art: "I think has to do with a very large gray area. I think a lot of it has to do with the individual. Because if the individual is at peace with himself, and is as taken, made the commitment with the body modification that he or she has chosen, then realizes beforehand what comes with the territory. The looks, the stares, the negativity, the ignorance of people in general. You feel bad, it's not their fault in a sense."

Corvis: "Is it upbringing you think?"
Art: "Of course a lot of it could be upbringing, you're sheltered, you're not to look at that, which draws you more towards that. Human curiosity. Getting back to the question, a lot of it has to do with, for example, myself. I waited 11 years before I tattooed my face, I wanted to make sure I was at ease with myself and wanted to make sure I was worthy of wearing it with that much pride. I waited 11 years and then because, on a full tummy with good sleep, and in a good instance, I thought, yep, I'm ready for it. I'm 42 years old, I've waited this long. I just wanted to make sure I looked at it and thought about it and looked at it in a different light and from different levels of consciousness. First step I took was that I did some realization work, some deep, self-realization work. I went into seclusion down in Mexico for 10 to 12 days to spend time away, to spend time not interacting with other people. Because we as humans we take for granted human interaction and human touch and just being around people. And this way I would be able to really, really sit there and I

knew I was on a journey, and with my meditation I would be able to reach different levels of consciousness and enlightenment, and my thought process would be a lot different. I didn't bring any reading material, I just thought about myself, just to make sure I was ready to look at this every morning.

"I do what we all do in the morning usually, which is go to the bathroom and look at ourselves in the morning. And I wanted to make sure I was ready for that and I wanted to make sure I was ready for that on every level; physically, emotionally and spiritually. And if I felt I was still ready for it, then I would still test myself another way, which was through sleep deprivation. Which our thought process is also different when we aren't sleeping our regular hours. And I still wanted to make sure I was ready for it, and also of course, I did fast, as many cultures have done in the past. Cleansing yourself and making your thought process a little cleaner. I made sure that with my mediation I was ready for it, that this would be my last one. I did it in the three steps, with a cleanse and fast in between each one. I continued to make sure it felt right, that I was going on my body and my armor in a sense.

"Now when I spoke to my parents before I did all this, out of the respect for the years I have been doing body modification and tattooing myself, not really tattooing myself, but as an avid collector. I speak with my parents out of respect before hand to let them know why I'm doing this, where it stems from and how long I've been thinking about doing this. To show them my respect and pay them my respect. So, not all of the sudden I show up and say, 'Hey, hello, surprise' with my face tattooed or my calves tattooed, or my body tattooed. I let them know the extensive research I've done, the thought behind it. One of my mother's questions before I was going to do my face was, 'Aren't you going to be concerned about how people are going to react?'

"As I explain to her, 'Mom, I already have gone through that. That I experience this on a regular basis. Most of my body is already covered. Yes, its going to be extreme in a sense, I'm aware of that.' Me, it's all about the energy you exude. If you exude a good energy, whether it be with intuitive people, when they look into your eyes, they can sense that you're approachable. I'm not walking around with a scowl on my face, with a chip on my shoulders that I'm angry at the world, that I'm rebelling."

Corvis: "Right. Many kids get into it because of that. They want to rebel, but yet you've gone in it from the total opposite approach."
Art: "Yes, yes. That's why I make sure when I go out, I make a conscious act of making eye contact with people. So they can see when they look into my eyes, and when I look into theirs, they can see that there is a sweet person, a true, sincere, honest person in here."

Corvis: "I feel like, you know, how come you can't just reach out your hand and say hi and judge for yourself before you judge on the look."
Art: "That's right, that is so true. Just like a lot of people will say the same thing. Because I will do the speaking, I will be the one to make the initial eye contact, to be able to show them that I am approachable. If I don't make eye contact, their going to say, 'Oh, don't look at this guy,' you know? If you make that contact right away, and smile, it lowers those walls right away and to know that it's okay to come over and say hello. A lot of people do. And that makes me feel good because they can see that I'm approachable and some of the people that are leery and come over and start to talk and will say five minutes later, 'Well, I was a little leery by your physical appearance, but now that I've gotten to talk to you, there's this person in there that's just what I thought. You're very respectful; you can talk just like anyone else. You're not the person a lot of people might perceive you to be.' A lot of people still think generally think that tattooed people are bad people. People like me and yourself are changing all that."

Corvis: "I have some piercing and tattoos, but they're not openly visible like yours. The only thing is, some of my jewelry which is elegant but foreboding can cause negative reactions in others. I at times have a goatee and long hair, and I wear dark clothes, which can bring about a similar reaction. That in itself sends warning signs to a lot of people."

Art: "Yeah, yeah. Of course, of course. They don't know you; they're judging you without knowing you. Its not about who you are on the outside, its about what's inside your heart. So I try to explain to people, as the old saying goes, 'We all know that the eyes are the window to the soul.' I meet somebody, I'm drawn to the eyes, I'm feeling that energy, I'm feeling that person, I'm getting to know that person, the eye contact means so much.

"There are individuals that, I look into the eyes when I talk to somebody and they look away. Its intimidating, its too much, the individual is too insecure, they have certain issues or demons they're fighting with that they cannot look someone in the eye when they're talking to them."

Corvis: "You mentioned earlier that the normal people are the ones we need to be afraid of sometimes. Isn't it ironic that the ones who appear the weirdest on the outside are the most normally adjusted on the inside?"
Art: "Yeah. And not a lot of people might not share...they might be young, they might be searching for who they are. But for me, I am speaking as a 43 year old man. I'm still a kid at heart, but I'm still a 43 year old man who has experienced things in my life, a lot of searching I have done. I've done a lot of self-work, I have finally found, and I still work on it everyday, which we ought to do and need to, with the just Zen itself. What I'm working for is just everyday, meditation as much as I can (at least a couple times a day), to ground myself, to center myself, to bound myself, to find inner peace, to find tranquility within myself. I used to be an angry individual, for a few years."

Corvis: "You don't come across the way at all."
Art: "But it was something I found within myself. It was not allowing me to grow, it was stagnating me off course and it was hurtful. A lot of changes, and a lot of growth, and a lot of evolving, I've had to do to growing in my life."

Art is far from alone in being different looking and being known publicly. I met New Page's author A.J. Drew at a lecture he gave at IPFW. The 'Yeti' he sometimes calls himself, being over six feet tall, hairy and with a booming voice, he is defiantly not a person one would soon forget. He had recently finished writing *A Wiccan Bible* and was giving away a few signed copies. For the last, he stopped at the end of his speech to ask the audience, one at a time, to explain how we each used magic in our daily lives. I happened to get there late, so by chance I was at the very end of the line. Each person gave a wide range of answers, so when everyone turned to me I was, at first, at a loss as to how I would answer differently than all the others. "I guess being last you'd think I would have had time to think of something profound to say," I had said. Some smiled, others laughed. "I use magic to appreciate my life. I take each day as it comes, and I've stopped being bitter and hateful. Because all that does is hurt you and stop you from feeling everything good or bad that's around you. By taking it all inside and appreciating every little thing, I guess that's how I use magic."

Well, after that the room stayed uncomfortably silent, and then A.J. cleared his throat. He continued on for a while about the various answers, and then said he was going to let us all choose who gave the best answer. "Who among you was the best in describing how they best use Magic?" He looked around, and almost in unison nearly everyone turned to the back corner and pointed at me. I was stunned and honored to receive his gift. I spoke to him shortly after the event and we discussed publishing and the day's event.

I came to realize, then and even moreso now, that magic is not spells and books, but the thoughts and feelings we all share as one.

No one spirituality can be proven or disproved, for they all are based on belief. Questioning one person's belief system inherently calls for the same questioning of your own. Belief is in the mind, not a tangible scientific fact that can be placed under a microscope. Spirituality and magic are equal parts of the human psyche, weaving together a connection to the energies of the universe, to the divine. It is through accepting ourselves as we are, and others, despite our differences that ensure harmony.

— *Vlad Tepes Dracula* —

᪥ 𝒱AMPIRES AMONG US ᪥

"You see I cannot be forsaken because I am not the only one,
We walk amongst you feeding and raping must we hide from everyone."
— *Lyrics from "Forsaken,"* The Queen of the Damned" *soundtrack*

Before I ever became aware that there was a subculture in existence that was full of Vampires, I was deeply interested in them. Not so much for their physical abilities or strength, like those depicted countless books and films, but for their mannerisms, their way of elegant speaking, and the finery of their dress.

During my early twenties, I developed my own style of dress, which consisted largely of dress clothes that imparted my concept of fashion. I was often nicknamed "the man in black." Being raised by my grandparents, I did of course, like any teen, become somewhat rebellious. When a parental type tries to exert control over a young person during such time of self-exploration and growth, it tends to prevent one from finding his true self. This caused me to resist any and all attempts to incorporate more colors, other than dark blues and purples, into my wardrobe. This, along with an interest in art and the occult, lead me to question things about myself, especially when I encountered insulting jeers like "freak," or "I didn't know it was time for the vampires to come out," and "it's not Halloween..." and other such disparaging remarks. At the time I was usually wearing black leather pants, a black silk shirt and black velvet suit coat. Velvet gloves covered my Gothic rings, and only my necklace was visible—all of which is my normal wardrobe—dressy and elegant or simply dark casual. The commentary I received is typical to others like me around the world, and because of such treatment we loners often keep to ourselves, or seek out the company of others with like interests in dark culture.

With that being said, not all Goths are Vampires, and vice-versa, but the two groups are greatly compatible with one another. Each person must find his or her own way through deep introspection, and with any luck they develop a healthy sense of self-esteem, which any such individual needs to shrug off the blows of the narrow-minded.

My interest in fictional vampires was not diminished, but I needed more. I acquired the film, *The Dark Prince*, starring Rudolf Martin. This film centered on the true historical account of Vlad Tepes, (Tepes meaning "the Impaler,") who became the inspiration for Bram Stoker's Gothic novel *Dracula*. The film made no references to Vampires, though to the shrewd observer much of the fiction pointed to superstitions times, poor medical knowledge and mental psychosis. I grew curious about the events and truths surrounding this man who later became such a key archetype. To further explore the life of this dark prince, I bought a copy of *Vlad the Impaler* by M.J. Trow and added much to my knowledge of vampire folklore.

Long before Bram Stoker wrote his novel, the man known as Dracula was the Voivod (prince) of Brasov of Walachia (Romania), member of the *Ordu Dracul*...

Order of the Dragon

The Order of the Dragon was an institution, similar to other chivalric orders of the time, modeled on the Order of St George (1318). The Holy Roman Emperor Sigmund king of Hungary and his queen Barbara Cilli, mainly for the purpose of gaining protection for the royal family, established the Order in 1408. According to its statute the Order also required its initiates to defend the Cross and to do battle against its enemies, principally the Turks. The original Order comprised of twenty-four members of various noble families.

In 1431, Sigmund summoned to the city of Nuremberg a number of princes and vassals useful for both political and military alliances. His primary objective was to initiate the group into the Order of the Dragon. One of these was Vlad II (father to Vlad Tepes), a claimant for the throne of the principality of Walachia who was at the time serving as commander guarding the mountain passes between Transylvania and Walachia from enemy incursion.

The Order of the Dragon adopted as its symbol the image of a circular dragon with its tail coiled around its neck. On its back, from the base of its neck to its tail, was the red cross of St George. With the expansion of the Order, other symbols were adopted, all variations on the theme of a dragon and cross. For example, one class of the Order used a dragon being strangled with a cross draped across its back; another presents a cross perpendicular to a coiled dragon with an inscription "O quam misericors est Deus" (vertical) and "Justus et paciens" (horizontal). Other emblems of the Order included a necklace and seal, each with a variant form of the dragon motif. Vlad was obviously proud of this achievement. Later he had coins minted, which show on one side a winged dragon. His personal coat-of-arms also incorporated a dragon. Even to this day, the sword of the city of York still has the Order's sigil on it. In all of these cases, the dragon was intended to convey a favorable image drawn from medieval iconography in which the dragon represented the Beast of Revelation who is slain by the forces of Christianity. Vlad took on the surname of Dracul in reference to his induction into the order. The word *dracul* is derived from the Latin *draco,* meaning "dragon."

His son, Vlad III, used the sobriquet Dracul-*a* in the context of "son of Dracul" or "son of he who is a member of the Order of the Dragon." Once again it was used as a term of honor, but soon gained the meaning of Devil, which was applied to members of the Dracula family by their enemies and possibly also by superstitious peasants. It was this second meaning that found its way into William Wilkinson's *An Account of the Principalities of Walachia and Moldavia* (1820), the book in which Bram Stoker found the name Dracula. There is no evidence to indicate that Stoker actually knew anything about the Order of the Dragon.

After the death of Sigmund in 1437, the Order of the Dragon lost much of its prominence, though its iconography was retained on the coats-of-arms of several noble families. Vlad continued to fight against the enemies of his land with cunning and viciousness, intent on continuing until it killed him. He did indeed die in battle, and his head was cut off and displayed in Istanbul by the sultan. His body is rumored to be entombed in Snagof monastery, but it cannot be confirmed or denied with complete accuracy. Both his enemies in Turkey demonized him, and the Catholic Church betrayed him.

Vlad Dracula was not a vampire, but rumors throughout history have painted him far more evil than the forsaken blood drinker of Stoker's novel. According to a 1460 writer of papal transcripts, "untold abuses, sad murders, mutilations, and sorrows were visited upon Brasov by the unfaithful, cruel tyrant Dracula, who calls himself Vlad, prince... following the teachings of the Devil."

Vlad did indeed commit acts of harsh punishment, such as impalement, which he learned by example from the Ottoman Empire. He was forced to bear witness to such horrors as a child being held captive. Torture such as he was accused of was often mirrored by the Roman Catholic Church, committed upon faithful Christian crusaders such as The Templar Knights during the next hundred years. Vlad wished for all people in his land to be free of crime, no matter their social standing. He was said to have explained his actions by saying, "If someone lies or commits any injustice, he is not likely to stay alive, whether nobleman, priest, or common man. There must be security for all in my land." Ironically, the people who he fought for eventually betrayed him. Vlad's was the first country during the Holy War to raise their banner against enemies of the cross.

It makes sense that many in the vampire culture revere this fictional and historical figure, for both have been misjudged as villains by those who are easily misled, uneducated or simply too conservative to listen to reason. Vlad Dracula is still thought of as a national hero in Romania to this day, but history created a villain out of someone who would not conform to the rest of the world's sense of order. In this way, Vlad was similar to today's youth with their dark and moody demeanor.

Fictional Vampires

Repellent and shocking tales of fictional and historical individuals circulated over centuries from the 1300s up to our current times. The fascination ingrained in peoples minds by Hollywood, brings out the surrealism and feelings harkening back to Romania, where mothers told tales to misbehaving children at night to quiet them. The changes overtime have evolved from a horrific zombie lurking in shadows, to the seductive, androgynous creature of power and beauty we see today in Anne Rice's novels.

Repression during Victorian times brought out sexual fantasies in blatant form with the Marquis writings, but vampires in books and film have lavish erotic undertones, from Stokers female seducers of Jonathan Harker to the 1970s movie *The Vampire Lover's*, and even homosexual undertones in *Interview with a Vampire,* to outright pornography such as *Les Vampires*. The dark sensuality and allure combines sadomasochism and blood with nudity to heighten excitement. This makes it appealing to any gender or sexual orientation.

One of the earliest incarnations of the romantic vampire was based off of Lord Byron by his physician in a work of fiction. The Italian, who attempted many times to become more than friends, was spurned and went back and forth in his writings from love to hate. This was no doubt part of the early ambiguous sexuality leanings that vampires have always exuded, in both males and females alike, from then till now.

Lord Byron

Born in 1788, Byron himself was considered a grandfather of Goth along with Poe. Byron is the most famous and controversial of his contemporaries. He was always a study in contrasts, a melancholy satirist, an aristocratic champion of the common man, handsome and adored but obsessed with a small personal deformity. He fled England to escape scandal and a failed marriage and died of fever in 1824. His natural gift for poetry was the only consistency in his troubled life. Yet even during his own lifetime, his personal life overshadowed his work.

The following is taken from the work titled *Loving the Dead: The Allure of the Modern Vampire*, by Michelle Belanger: "...vampire as it exists in the modern imagination is just one facet of an enduring archetype: the eternal outsider. As an archetypal figure, the vampire exists outside the bounds of normative reality. Superficially, he is a part of the human race, but he is always apart from it.

While his nature makes him an outcast, both the vampire's power and his allure arise from this outcast state. The Romantic ideal of Lucifer as the rebellious angel taps into this archetype as well. It is the Byronic dark hero, the quintessential 'bad boy' who thrills and seduces us because he breaks the rules. Consider the wild popularity of Anne Rice's vampire Lestat. People find such a liminal being sexy, mysterious, and darkly compelling."

This ideal is appealing to many, like MORBID ANGEL, who I met while researching this book.

Corvis: **"Please tell us about yourself."**
Morbid Angel: "I'm 15 and in school. Female. I know I am unusually young, but I am gifted with great intelligence and maturity and I know what I have been awakened to."

Corvis: **"What brought your attention at such a young age to this culture, and do you think the gifted are more inclined to be into things like this due to feeling alone?"**
Morbid Angel: "I was fixated with sudden interest in things of a metaphysical/vampiric nature. As perhaps ironic and stupid as it may sound a show revealing uncommon lifestyles, of people living in a house opened me up to it, and I look at it as a sign for myself. And perhaps those who are alone have the time to think about such 'New Age' topics."

Corvis: "Do you have many friends with the same interests, or is that rare?"

Morbid Angel: "Well, not many. Only one actually, my best friend is Wiccan. Don Henrie is my inspiration so to speak. I look up to him with such passion."

Corvis: "Sometimes those who are different make this world a better place, rest assured, my friend."

Morbid Angel: "Thank you, it's nice to hear that."

Corvis: "Sure, I've been there. I'm twice your age, and it does become easier...finding friends with whom you *can* relate helps. Do events like Halloween make it easier for you to be yourself, but then have to 'hide' how you are afterwards?"

Morbid Angel: "Oh yeah. I'm very proud of my nature. Though I don't flaunt it. I always dress very Gothic and have very much of my own insane style, but at Halloween. I can show it even more."

Corvis: "Do you encounter harassment being so immersed in Goth, vampire culture at your age?"

Morbid Angel: "I wouldn't say harassment so to speak, but harsh criticism, yes. Being assumed it is foolish or demonic. It's offensive and ignorant."

Corvis: "Do people in the 'Mainstream' avoid you due to the way you choose to dress?"

Morbid Angel: "Some, yes."

Corvis: "What causes this reaction and how do you respond to it?"

Morbid Angel: "Because I'm not 'like them.' I'm different to them and weird, but that's them to me. I respond to it depending on the situation. I may get angry or offended."

Corvis: "Any misconceptions you'd like to say anything about? How you wish others acted about it?"

Morbid Angel: "Some people classify it as unattractive; then again there are many that think it is. It depends on how closed minded the person is. I don't go around telling just anyone about my personal culture. But when it comes to me or the way I dress, it's more like 'if you don't like it, fuck you.' Sorry, I hope I'm not being too forward."

Corvis: "Not at all. I like honesty. In what way does accepting yourself as a Goth and Psy-vamp help you in your life?"
Morbid Angel: "Well to do that you need to have a confidence. And a sense of independence. It shows your darkness and it's less inviting to those who you're not interested in being with. It's been good for me. And I feel I can only speak for myself, really."

Corvis: "Very true. I have enjoyed our talk, and thank you for taking the time to talk."
Morbid Angel: "No problem. It was comforting."

Modern Vampires

Not only does the mystique of the vampire appeal to us romantically, but some of us rather enjoy being seen as menacing, for a lot of us are frail individuals, who belong to the same club of former victims of bullies. Think about it. Would anyone in his or her right mind pick someone who looks so menacing to mug in a dark alley? Muggers prefer spineless victims who shuffle with their heads down as opposed to any confident and aura charged individual who openly embraces the attitude that predators such as the vampire should not be trifled with.

Humanity, despite the fact we live in a modern techno-world, is still governed by primitive fears of fire and things that go bump in the night. Scare someone when the power suddenly fails, or see the panic on a survivor's face of a house fire shortly after the fact and you will see that fight or flight in animals still is under our surface. We as a society fear things that can freely exist without fear in darkness. Such courage and freedom in these nocturnal denizens conjure up thoughts like *'If they are not afraid, they must truly be more fearsome than the unknown, or deranged lunatics themselves.'* A foreboding presence is normally an inner quality that some exude naturally, giving the vampire his piercing gaze, such fame. It is hypnotizing to watch a master stage magician, whose movements captivate the outsider. These things also are second nature to the awakened. More and more people are drawn into the darker lifestyles, cast out by the mainstream because of a slew of unexplainable fears, and stereotypical knee-jerk reactions.

Common questions range from curiously mild to outright absurd. An underground film put out in 1988 by Jake West called *Razor Blade Smile* had it pegged when the main character, Lilith Silver was seated in a vamp/Goth bar among humans discussing how vampires shape shift. Her response was that shape shifting is about adapting to the situations we're in, mimicking the behaviors of animals' survival patterns, like bats that use other senses, rather than mere sight. Drifting into a room like fog as a metaphor to describe how someone can avoid being seen by simply being quiet. She was laughed at because, even now, people so wrapped up in the myths want to believe in the fantasy even moreso than those adopting the mannerisms and dress that is inherent in this subculture.

It is ironic that some of those within the vampire scene are more logical about their behaviors than are the curious hecklers. Due to a lack of respect for individuality, mainstream society sneers, ignores or outright laughs at people willing to fully embrace their Shadow.

As time passed, the subculture living with appreciation to these ideals created many groups with the structure. The Order of the Strigoii is the most organized and influential of these groups. They annually hold the largest Halloween party in New Orleans called Endless Nights. The Endless Night is an international gathering for the vampires, Gothic, fetish and dark subcultures world wide, and has even been featured on HBO, MTV, and Oxygen TV. The event brings the dark community together through a weekend of unique events, vendors, tours, seminars, celebrations and gatherings. Like the Goth subculture, the Vampire subculture allows freedom of the self, while creating a strong sense of place and identity.

Types of Vampires

It must be stressed that there are two distinctly differing types of Vampires. Vampires are either "Sang," those who drink blood from donors for energy gain (with whom a careful selection process has been done) or "Pranic," (also called Psychic Vampire), those who derive their energy from other more metaphysical means.

Pranic Vampires do not take blood, but they do remove unwanted energy to make room for fresh vital energy. It is a flow of exchange, a flushing of old with new. For those who are reminded of Reiki here, there is a connection to this Japanese healing art started by Usui. The Psychic Vampire uses energy to balance their own needs for vitality, especially when found lacking due to the excess use of psychic abilities and as a result of the drain from others around them.

Most prominent in the vampire community recently is the Sci-Fi Channel's star from *Mad Mad House*, Don Henrie, who practices both types of vampirism. "Pranic," in Don's words, "is life force. It can be found in ant living planet, insect or animal. Few of us understand how it works and how it can be manipulated. It can be given and/or taken." Don adds, "Reiki is a healing method via prana. Reiki is a method of drawing out negative energy when the body needs healing, and replacing it with positive, healing energy."

Energy Work

Energy is in and around all things, physically and metaphysically. Scientists have acknowledged that aura blueprints can be photographed by way of thermal imaging. At psychic fairs and carnivals people can have their thumbprints printed out with bluish-green glow around them. Tantra and other eastern belief systems have known about body meridians and charkas for centuries before it was widely known that electrical pluses down the spine from the brain to the end of the tail bone are the strongest flow of energy in the human body. Aboriginal shaman, magicians, Reiki masters, Martial arts instructors, and Feng Shui experts all speak of the inner and outer flow of energy by many different terms, and depending on their own particular orientation, use it for different reasons.

I have personally seen energy, read the colors of people auras, and can empathetically gain information about people in person, and as strange as it may sound, do so by looking at photographs. Regardless of expression, scenery or emotions on them, I am correct about 90% of the time. When I conversed with *Llewellyn's* author Konstantino's he assured me I was not crazy, but gifted with a form of Psychometry. Years ago, I meet a Shawnee herbalist and Reiki master, Patsy Clark of Bittersweet Cultural Center, who instructed me in the proper attunements of Reiki levels one and two. She warmly told me I had a gift of reaching into people with love and healing.

The idea of taking energy from another is a difficult concept for some to accept. There are some who abhor the taking of energy, deeming it to be a form of theft, but it is not necessarily so if the donor is aware and consenting. Then there are those who deem it their right to take from the weak, without consent. Whitelighter's believe there should not be any "magical gain" for the self, and frown upon this sort of thing. They believe that taking what one needs for survival need not be theft. This is precisely why such laws of conduct, like *The Black Veil*, were created among the vampire community.

The Black Veil

The Black Veil is the official code of conduct for New York-based communities, the Sanguinarium and the Order of the Strigoi Vii. Originally drafted by Father Sebastian Todd in the late 1990s, the first printed mention of *The Black Veil* appeared in the 1998 *Vampyre Almanac,* the publication that started Michelle Belanger's partnership with Father Sebastian. Since it's beginnings, this set of ethical guidelines has been adopted by a number of groups beyond the New York area. *The Black Veil* gained notoriety on television shows such as *CSI: Vegas,* where they referred to it as a "sacred document" of the vampire subculture. It has been mentioned on numerous documentaries and has appeared in *The Idiot's Guide to Vampires.* It is mentioned in *Sci-Fi's* bio of its resident *Mad Mad House* vampire Don Henrie, and through his work this code of conduct and the culture it represents have gained unprecedented exposure in the mainstream world.

Vampire groups have been active in New York City since the 1960s, often interwoven throughout that era's fetish underground. Occultist Aleister Crowley, who lived from 1875 to 1947, practiced a form of psi-vampirism almost identical to that taught by the *Veil*. According to material compiled by occult researcher Francis King, Crowley had added these methods to the tractates of the *Ordo Templi Orientis* prior to the First World War.

The latest version of *The Black Veil* gives seven rules of behavior, which encourage a chivalrous attitude towards one's fellow vampires:

Discretion

Respect yourself and present yourself so that others also respect you. Take care in whom you reveal yourself to. Explain what you are, not to shock, but to teach and to inform. Do not flaunt what you are, and know that whether you want them to or not, your actions will reflect upon the rest of the community. Share your nature only with those who possess the wisdom to understand and accept it, and learn to recognize these people.

Diversity

Among us, there are many different practices and many points of view. No single one of us has all the answers to who and what we are. Respect each person's individual choices and beliefs. Learn about them and share what you know. Our diversity is our strength, and we should not allow misunderstanding to weaken our community. Find the path that is right for you and uphold this freedom for others.

Control

Do not allow your darkness to consume you. You are more than just your hunger, and you can exercise conscious control. Do not be reckless. Always act with a mind toward safety. Never feed because you think this makes you powerful; feed because this is what you must do. Be true to your nature, but never use it as an excuse to endanger those around you.

Elders

Give respect to those who have earned it. Anyone can claim a title, but a true leader will prove him or herself through dedication, hard work, and great deeds. Even so, leaders should be guides and not dictators. Look to them as examples, but always decide for yourself what you must do.

Respect the person, not the position, and understand that your choices are always your own.

Behavior

Know that there are repercussions to every action, and that you alone are responsible for your decisions. Educate yourself about risky behaviors, and then always act with wisdom and common sense. Do not allow others to abuse you, but also, do not selfishly abuse.

Respect the rights of others and treat them as you would be treated.

Donors

Feeding should occur between consenting adults. Allow donors to make an informed decision before they give of themselves to you. Do not take rapaciously from others, but seek to have an exchange that is pleasant and beneficial for all.

Respect the life that you feed upon and do not abuse those who provide for you.

Community

Reach out to others in your community. Exchange ideas, information, and support. Be hospitable to others, and appreciate hospitality when it is extended to you. Do not engage in illegal activity, for this can endanger us all.

Seek to nurture our community and support all those who do the same.

In addition to *The Black Veil*, Father Sebastian publishes a variety of information for and about the vampiric lifestyle. The following synopsis from the Sanguinarium website helps to clarify what would be complex to the casual reader if browsing the net after typing "Vampire" into a search engine:

"The book 'V' is a new tome about the dark path, teachings and traditions of Strigoi Vii (living vampyrism). It contains a collection of articles, essays and explanations of dreams and expressions of modern vampyrism.

Sanguinarius for Real Vampires (www.sanguinarius.org) is not a membership organization but a support page that provides resources, articles and information for, by, and about real vampires and the vampire community.

The Sanguinarium (www.sanguinarium.net) is a network, community and resource for the vampyre subculture and scene, originally founded as Clan Sabretooth in New York's underground club scene. It has expanded to include organizations, businesses, havens and individual members who are united under *The Black Veil.*

Father Sebastian operates the Vampyre Almanac, which produces and promotes many club events, publishes and promotes various documents and books, and provides publicity for the Vampyre subculture and BDSM/fetish scene, often mingling the two to provide a unique aesthetic.

Recently emerging from the scene is the Ordo Strigoii Vii (OSV), which is a dark spiritual pathway and Vampyric religion, designed for the Vampyre subculture. The OSV is a recognized church in Amsterdam and is supported by the Church of Satan."

In an effort to explain things correctly, I spoke with FATHER SEBASTIAN about his many Vampire-related endeavors.

Corvis: "Could you tell us how Sabretooth began, and the origins of the Sanguinarium?"
Father Sebastian: "Before I get into the origins of Sabretooth and the Sanguinarium, please let me explain what they are, as there seems to be a great deal of confusion. The Sanguinarium is my word for the

movement of people who employ Strigoi Vii (living vampyres) teachings worldwide; it is like one great extended Family. Many people think of it as an organization, however it is a collective soul and community with no governing body. While Sabretooth is a fangmaking business which I started in 1994 when I was working at the NYC Renaissance Faire in NYC and had a part time job as a dental assistant in New Jersey.

Father Sebastian

"Like many individuals in the vampyre subculture in the early 1990s who were trying to discover who and what they are it was nearly impossible to find others of like mind. There were few options at the time for vampyres to congregate which included the Temple of the Vampire gatherings, New York City's fetish subculture and the Vampire: the Masquerade LARPs. At this time there was only the above resources which were geared towards vampyres. I met a fangsmith named Gregor of StrangeBlades who made me my first pair of fangs in November 1992, then I had the vision of what would eventually become the Sanguinarium."

Corvis: "Tell us about your writing career, such as "V"?"
Father Sebastian: "Thank you for asking that question, my main goal ever since I was young, was to own my own publishing company. While most kids were into looking on how the record companies worked, I paid attention to the publishing business, which are actually not that different. For me there are two types of writers, the first are those who are talented writers, second are the people who are not skilled at writing as they are authorities or so passionate about a subject they by default become writers. I am the second type, I believe

I have a unique perspective which gives me the knowledge about vampyrism is actually my fangsmithing business.

"Fangsmithing is a unique business in this day of the internet, since it must be in person and thus more tangible and real. The fangsmith and the client often have to spend upwards of 30 minutes to an hour with each other per pair, the physical contract results in an energy exchange which has resulted in more awakenings than I can imagine. Since so many people in the vampyre subculture have gotten fangs as apart of their experience, thus each client became almost like an interview and I built a personal link with each one, each of us giving each other a little bit of each other.

"The more fangs I made the more interesting conversations came about and I developed in my Xeper to be apart of each of my clients and them me, thus as I noticed many things and perspectives in common which no one else really observed. The result was the evolving Strigoi Vii traditions, For years I have been working on my project the V series, which is intended to create a series of books which compile all that I have encountered and my personal beliefs.

"To further expand upon the concept the "V" series includes three 'outer books,' which include *Vampyre: Liber Jahira, The Black Veil, Vampyre: Liber Bellah, The Strigoi Vii Codex,* and finally the adept book *Vampyre: Liber Calmae Sanguinomicon.*"

Corvis: "Future goals, plans for House of Elorath?"
Father Sebastian: "Well there is really no 'House of Elorath;' there is the Sanguinarium (our word for the Strigoi Vii community) and many families. I am working to retire now and move on to focus on my dayside and a theatrical bondage website, so my only real involvement directly with the community will be through writing. The magisters and council of my household of Sahjaza are moving forward with major plans of establishing a worldwide network of noir havens (vamp clubs) and other projects."

Corvis: "What about *Vampyre Magazine*? What does it provide, and how do we get it?"

Father Sebastian: "The original *Vampyre Magazine* and *Vampyre Almanac* were two different projects and have various incarnations over the years. When the print on demand technology began to develop I decided to put an editorial team together and re-launch the project as a combined bimonthly publication entitled *Vampyre Almanac & Magazine (VAM)*. Since it is print on demand technology this magazine is available via mail and web order as well as in a few select underground stores. Eventually I would like to get the magazine to be more frequent, however I am not sure.

"Each issue will feature interviews with real personalities in the subculture, features, news, articles, a directory to the vampyre subculture in each issue, rituals, a calendar of the months of interest and of course, to add a little spice, a bio a 'centerfold' of a real life vampyre diva. I like to think of *VAM* as a 'vampyric magickal' version of *Maxium*."

Corvis: "What are your feelings on *The Black Veil* being more commonly known about, in books, television, and in documentaries?"

Father Sebastian: "Interesting question, actually I am not sure what to think or how to react, I am waiting to see actually what happens. We are seeing something incredibly special and unique in the world develop and *The Black Veil* has been the center of this entire concept, something that has really spoken to people in all of its variations and incarnations. All The Black Veil is just common sense organized into a presentable form and is truly the center of the entire vampyre movement. I do feel it is good to be discrete and today the world is in love with vampyres since we have romanticized and made it a tragic hero.

"We support *The Black Veil* as a great basis for common sense, etiquette and respect amongst the vampire/vampyre communities. We work towards the growth and prosperity of the vampire community and vampyre subculture. Together our goal is to set an example for harmony and cooperation between the diverse aspects of our communities."

Co-author of *The Black Veil*, MICHELLE BELANGER also heads up House Kheperu, a multi religious society. According to the official site, most models of organized religion in the west are anathema to individuality. "Organized religions promote one definition of God with only one approach to God for many diverse believers...Spirituality, as opposed to religion, is conductive to individuality, since a spiritual path provides basic guidelines for progress toward self-realization while at the same time allowing a great deal of personal expression within the bonds of those guidelines." It is a spiritual group that looks upon divinity as a multi-faceted reflection of many cultures, with no one facet as having more worth than others. Everything including the self and its life force is an aspect of the spirit with a direct personal relationship to the divine.

In 1991, Michelle graduated with honors in the top ten of her class, receiving numerous awards for her academic and creative accomplishments. As a National Merit Scholar, she attended Cleveland's John Carroll University on a full ride scholarship, studying English, creative writing, psychology, and religious studies. Around that time she started a Gothic literary magazine, *Shadowdance*, which explored issues of metaphysics and vampirism through the mediums of poetry and fiction, and firmly established her within the blossoming vampire community.

By 1995, Michelle had earned a B.A. Currently she also holds a Doctorate of Metaphysics and a Doctorate of Divinity. She is trained in Shamanism and Reiki, and is a licensed and practicing minister in the State of Ohio. In April 2003, she appeared on the Women's Entertainment Network in a documentary about the archetypal appeal of the vampire.

Through these and other projects, such as the International Society of Vampires, Michelle came into contact with a number of other scholars and distinguished personalities in the vampire scene: Dr. J. Gordon Melton, who included her in the first edition of his *Vampire Book: the Encyclopedia of the Undead*; Martin V. Riccardo, who corresponded with her while researching his book *Liquid Dreams of Vampires;* Jeff Guinn, who used her as a significant resource in his book *Something in the Blood*; Katherine Ramsland, biographer of Anne Rice; and "Father" Todd Hoyt (aka Father Sebastian), founder of the Sanguinarium. While working with these people, she continued her metaphysical studies, exploring shamanism, ancient Egypt, neo-Paganism, ceremonial and chaos magick, Eastern mysticism, Reiki, and Qi Gong. During this time, she was compiling information for the book *The Vampyre Codex*. Her latest work,

Michelle Belanger

Spirits of Transformation: Vampires, Healers, and House Kheperu is the longer work combines the expanded *Codex* with a framework of chapters intended to introduce new readers to the vampire community, House Kheperu, and the metaphysics of psychic vampirism. This book is currently being considered by a publisher.

In addition to her work on the *Codex*, Michelle has also written articles on a variety of topics published in the *Cleveland Plain Dealer, Fate Magazine, Connections Pagan Journal, The Azrael Project Newsletter, Circle Magazine,* and many others, and is frequently called upon to investigate hauntings and supernatural disturbances, using her skills at energy work to perform "spiritual house cleanings"—in layman's terms, a "ghost buster." She is also a consultant and researcher for projects dealing with vampires, metaphysics, and the occult. Monolith Graphics recently published *The Gothic Tarot* (a beloved deck by Joseph Vargo coveted by myself and patrons of my occult shop!), that was in part inspired by Michelle's suggestions.

Weiser Books recently released Michelle Belanger's *Psychic Vampire Codex*, the first book ever to reveal secrets of the vampire subculture—from the inside. The term Vampire is not totally accurate, for they do not believe they are immortal undead; it is simply the closest term to fit.

Not only is she an author but also a gifted lyricist and singer. Michelle been with Chicago-based Metal/Industrial band URN from its beginnings, and still finds time to be a guest vocalist on many a tour. Michelle and I originally met online and spoke for a few months before I got the opportunity to meet her in person at URN's concert in Indianapolis.

Corvis: "How did you come to write the *Codex* and what is it about?"
Michelle: "The Psychic Vampire Codex is something I've been working on since the fall of 1991. I suppose you could say it's my magnum opus. Getting it to a state that I consider complete has certainly been a near-obsession of mine. The book has gone through many editions and revisions over the years, and it has been circulated throughout the occult and vampire communities since about 1996. The *Codex* has served as the educational text of House Kheperu, the spiritual collective I founded in the late 1990s, and it has inspired a vast number of other metaphysical groups.

"Sanguinarium Press published portions of the book in conjunction with the *Vampyre Almanac* in October of 2000. Although this abbreviated version of the *Codex* was extremely well received, the audience was very specialized, and so it had a limited print run. I felt that the *Codex*, if given a chance, could reach a much larger audience, and so I set about doing what was needed to make that happen.

"In the summer of 2002, I undertook a complete expansion and revision of the book, based in part upon work I had been doing with the members of House Kheperu. Book proposal in hand, I started shopping the *Codex* around to respected and established occult publishers. To my utmost delight, the work was accepted by Weiser Books earlier this year, a publishing company whose well-written tomes make up a good portion of my personal library.

"The new edition not only includes a significantly expanded version of the *Kheprian Codex* with sections on advanced energy work, past life recall, and interaction with spirits, but it also opens with five weighty chapters that explain the concept of psychic vampirism, the development of a world-wide community of vampires, the growth of House Kheperu, and the influence that Kheprian teachings have had on many peoples' understanding of psychic vampirism."

Corvis: "What is psychic vampirism and its history?"

Michelle: "Psychic vampirism can be best approached as a metaphysical condition. A psychic vampire is someone who regularly and actively needs to take in life force in order to maintain their physical, mental, and spiritual well being. Psychic vampires are unable to process anything but the vital energy of others. It is a well-known phenomenon in the metaphysical community, yet it is widely misunderstood.

"The many authors that have tackled this subject have been experts in their fields, but where vampirism is concerned, they have remained outsiders looking in. Information on what psychic vampires are and what they do remains incomplete without the perspective of the vampires themselves.

"There is a definite Gothic element to the most visible portion of the subculture, but don't let this retro aesthetic fool you. The eighties and nineties saw the vampire subculture make huge strides in becoming a community as independent groups started reaching out and communicating with one another. However, real vampires were alive and well long before that. Vampire groups were active in New York City as early as the sixties, often interwoven throughout that era's thriving fetish underground. Further, occultist Aleister Crowley, who lived from 1875 to 1947, practiced a form of psi and sang vampirism almost identical to that taught in the vampires' most-read instructional tome, *The Vampire Codex.* According to material compiled by occult researcher Francis King, Crowley had added these methods to the tractates of the *Ordo Templi Orientis* prior to the First World War. A case could be made that conscious psychic vampirism was practiced even before this. For example, there is evidence in the private letters and papers of poet Lord Byron (1788-1824) that suggest he may have been a psychic vampire."

Corvis: "Isn't the reality of the mythic vampire one of tragedy? To be dead but live while watching friends and family die? Why use that as an archetype to model a subculture from?"

Michelle: "I have often been asked why anyone in his or her right mind would want to be called a vampire. The truth is, it is not something most people start off wanting to be. The majority of self-defined psychic vampires did not wake up one day and decide that they were going to identify themselves with a folkloric entity believed by most people to be damned. Typically, these individuals were vampirizing energy long before they had a term for what they were. Their abilities frightened and confused them, and they searched wherever they could for answers, and especially for a name."

Corvis: "Why call yourselves vampires and identify with this label?"
Michelle: "The 'v-word' is a communication tool. It's not the best word for what I and others like me are, but it's the closest word we have in the English language. I know it was the v-word that I was finally drawn to when I first started understanding and coming to terms with my nature. It follows that many others who are just trying to understand themselves will also be drawn to that word. If I'm going to fulfill my mission of reaching out to others like myself and educating them so they can control their vampirism and choose to feed consciously from aware and willing donors, then I have to speak in the language that the majority of people will understand. That includes using words like vampire, psychic vampire, and psi-vamp.

"Of course, using the word "vampire" only helps me communicate with people who already understand that it doesn't mean blood-sucking Undead. With all the folkloric and cinematic trappings the image of the vampire has obtained over the years, there are a lot of connotations that come along with the word "vampire" in the popular imagination. It's pretty hard explaining to people outside of the community that we're not laying claim to all of these silly trappings when we define ourselves as vampires. It's kind of like the difficulty the Wiccans had for a long while of convincing the general populace that they didn't ride on broomsticks or wear black, pointy hats."

Corvis: "What of the Vampire is an archetype, an identity?"
Michelle: "Vampirism as I have defined it is really just a condition of the soul or energy body. It's not exactly an identity so much as it is just a characteristic. However, people can choose to define themselves as

vampires just as people can choose to define themselves as left-handed. Being left-handed is just one characteristic a person may have. They could be male or female, black or white, but for whatever reason, they choose the label "Southpaw" when defining themselves. They think of themselves as "lefties." They buy little books like *The Left-Hander's Guide to Everything*. They wear T-shirts that proclaim them to be left-handed. They use special pencils or other tools that cater to their inherent left-handedness.

"Some people take it a bit far. When your entire house is redone with left-handedness in mind, it's probably gone *way* too far. But people do just the same thing with vampirism. Sometimes it's a matter of accepting it in themselves—I've met some left-handed people who are pretty bitter that they live in a right-handed world. So they make it a point of pride and rebellion to proudly proclaim themselves "lefties." I've met vampires like that. They've really got something to prove, maybe to themselves, maybe to others, so their vampirism affects the way they dress, the jewelry they wear, and virtually every other aspect of their life.

"Then there are people who just happen to write with their left hands — they don't make a big fuss over it, they don't proclaim it to the world, but they'll admit that they're left-handed if you ask. And I've met plenty of vampires like that as well. For them, it's just another aspect of who they are—nothing to be proud or ashamed about, just a fact of life. Is either approach good or bad? I think it's a matter of personal choice. People are people, whether they're Southpaws or vampires, and everyone has to find their identity on their own."

Corvis: "What about energy, psychically speaking?"
Michelle: "Because the West has a very materialist world-view, peoples' relations to energy are poorly understood. It is telling that all of our words for vital energy are imported from other cultures. Chi is Chinese. Prana is Sanskrit. Ki is Japanese. For Westerners who have a fundamental and undeniable experience of vital energy, there is neither a language nor a context for them to put this in. This places awakening psychic vampires in a very difficult position. Here they are having these profound and extraordinary experiences that have a significant impact

on their physical, mental, and spiritual well being. And yet they have no word for this, no guideposts to know where to even begin to formulate a definition. With parallels in Reiki, Qi Gong, Yoga, magick, and shamanism, the techniques detailed in the *Codex* have a wide reaching appeal that is not limited to psychic vampires alone."

Corvis: **"How does the vampire fit into this?"**
Michelle: "As an undead being romanticized in fiction and film, the vampire really has very little in common with psychic vampires. Yet for those who encountered the archetype through books or movies, there was an obvious connection. The vampire feeds upon life. The need to take vital energy is typically the first and most undeniable quality awakening psychic vampires notice in themselves. Thus, even though they realized the term did not quite fit, there was enough of a resonance for these people to begin tentatively identifying themselves as vampires. Within the community, it was tacitly understood that someone who claimed to be a vampire was neither undead nor physically immortal, but had this underlying hunger for life energy."

Corvis: **"What about the other organization you're in, Kheperu House?"**
Michelle: "Kheperu means 'transformation'. We've tried originally to keep the House and my musical career separate, but depending on where we are playing, sometimes the vampire subculture will know me and show up. We have as many of those as URN fans. It crosses over a little bit. I mean, the idea, I do this because this is what I am, what empowers the self. I consider following my dream with the band as an example to those that follow the House. Do whatever you want to do."

Corvis: **"You don't have a problem with Catholic, Pagan or even Satanist?"**
Michelle: "I am open to anybody's belief system. I have a catch phrase. 'Seek your own truth'. Which is pretty much "Find what works for you". The thing I object to is people denying who they are. If they are living like that, hiding from their inner truth, then they're living a lie. I see many, too many, like that. Anybody who can live the life they

want to live, I deeply respect that. Dominic, who grew up with the 12 step program is someone who lives his beliefs. He's a little Christo-Pagan. He's got his own shrine. Jesus is his deity."

Corvis: "It's safe to say then that it matters not what you believe, as long as you're sincere."
Michelle: "True. I don't care as long as you follow something."

Corvis: "I started as Native Spirituality and a little Asian philosophy. My ancestry is Irish-Cherokee. Then I stepped into Satanism because life is harsh and I needed a realistic grounding in how to deal with people I don't like. I merge the LHP and Goth because of its comfort in realism and philosophy, and being sensitive to the light. I think it can be very well blended together. It's like viewing puzzle pieces. If you step back the lines blur and you see a whole image that makes sense."
Michelle: "I'm a Universalist. I blend Taoist with Buddhist ideas, Egyptian. One of the first things I started to study outside of Catholicism was Hinduism. I was reading the *Bhagavad Gita*, studying Yoga, the principals and use of breath. Obviously, working with eternal energy appealed to me. I found myself leaning a little towards the Tao. Whatever works, I go with it. I lean toward Dark Paganism. I would say I am LHP. Thy will be done. My will be done. I am empowered in my own deity. As Don would say, my own godhead."

Corvis: "I studied Reiki, Jeet Kun Do, did a lot of introspection. I was a quiet kid. Similar experience?"
Michelle: "All of us were the squeaky wheels. We're way too intelligent for our years. Nose in a book and no clue how to socialize. A pariah as a result. One thing I've noticed with the Goths is that there is a lot of pain growing up. The punks/industrial like to throw it out to the rest of the world…"

Corvis: "The anarchy, with anger and violence."

Michelle: "Yeah. With Goths it's all internal. It makes them turn inward. Becoming even more introspective."

Corvis: "The part in 'Forsaken' [*Queen of The Damned* Soundtrack] about walking alone. I feel that way walking around at night in my hometown. So many stare at me as if I'm a lunatic. I get it constantly, everywhere. People don't understand I'm trying to be me. I can't exist not being true to myself."

Michelle: "In moving into a new house in Suburbia, a couple of my neighbors were a bit horrified to see groups of people dressed in black. I know they thought cats would start disappearing in the neighborhood. Have to watch the kids. One neighbor finally started speaking, to clear up misunderstandings (like calling the police variety). Someone filed a police report. Just my presence in the neighborhood alone apparently warranted it. When I had my housewarming he came over and said, 'You know, you guys are really quiet.'

'I told you we were quiet,' I said.

'I expected you'd be...um...'

'Like loud, drinking and doing drugs? Doing a Satanic Mass?' And he was like 'Well, I saw your website and saw all that vampire stuff...'

I told him, 'I'm just like you. I live out here. My business is in Los Angeles, New York City, New Orleans. Yes, I run with some people that would make your hair turn white but when it comes to living, I like my house quiet too.' At least he learned not to judge a book by its cover. I actually got an apology out of him. He wanted to sit down and talk."

Corvis: "That's great!"

Michelle: "One of the things I try to do with House Kheperu is show faiths are just a language with the same meaning. I mean, new agers and Pagans...they act like 'A witch! Oh my god!' and freak out about it. Well, you guys believe the same thing. 'But they sacrifice cats!' and I say 'No, actually they're more like hippy dippy tree huggers. Get over it!' Not all, but they're freaking out about things they don't understand. I say sit down and talk together. It's the labels that are hurting us, misleading us. It's all language. I'll admit, I used to have a negative view on Satanists because I'd only meet the 'I'm pissing off Mom and Dad' types and I assumed the LHP was that but someone explained it and I said 'Oh, so I'm LHP! No wonder all the LaVeyans really dig my work.' I make a point in not bringing deity into the *Codex*. The principles there work, no matter if you believe in God, a Goddess. I teach principle. If people want to turn it into a faith, ok, but I left God out on purpose."

Corvis: "What about Stragoii, any connection?"
Michelle: "I've pretty much helped influence them from the get go. Strigoii vs. the Kheperian tradition is they are more showy. High ritual. We are low key as a path; they are…flamboyant. They take it to the level of energy being a religion."

Corvis: "What would you like to say about how the darkness has a positive aspect, for those who don't understand it?"
Michelle: "Well, first of all, I can't have one without the other. A world without it, in an existence of blinding white light, you see nothing as much as one that is completely dark. With shadow, everything is thrown in relief. You see two things. Those that feel they follow a light path, exclusive of anything else; I want them to think about if they cut out that darkness no one would be able to appreciate light anymore. It's the dynamic balance of things. It's Tao, of yin and yang. To assume that darkness is evil is wrong. Being a Goth growing up I knew pain, but it wasn't evil. I grew up with people who believe anything is evil that inconveniences them. I think a lot of people that are drawn to the darkness come to appreciate it. They come from painful experiences, these things made them who they are. The bad things that other people might shy away from, these are the things that test and build them. Once you realize all the pain and suffering you've gone through in your life is not a bad thing, you begin to appreciate it. It built you up. You can't deny the darkness. There is goodness in both things. Anything taken to an extreme is wrong. A balance between them is needed. Another thing is people who have perfect lives. We don't grow unless we're challenged."

Corvis: "The psychos are dressed in normal clothes. It's the ones dressed like Wednesday Addams that are balanced inside."

Michelle: "They're comfortable with their darkness. I've a Sadistic streak, a side of me. I could go the route of a nice, white lighter and in the back of my head, deny it. Then it would come out when I couldn't control it. I looked in and saw, wow, there's some dark stuff in there. I choose when and where to act on it. Once it's in my hands it's in my power. I choose if I'm going to do it in a constructive way."

I later had the chance to speak to **DON HENRIE**. I called him from late one evening, and I enjoyed our conversation immensely. Don clarified some of his views and expressed his feelings about dealing with people, coming out publicly, and misconceptions.

Don has always been interested in the genre, stating, "I have decided long ago, to collect as many vampire related books, movies and memorabilia that I could find. Just as I have a fascination with learning new things. I also especially love to learn about the history and culture of vampirism. My personal favorite movies are: *Queen of the Damned, Interview with the Vampire, Underworld, The League of Extraordinary Gentlemen, Shadow of the Vampire,* and Bela Lugosi's classic, *Dracula.* As a big fan of Bela's, I also like Ed Wood's behind the scenes portrayal of him."

As far as stereotyping and misconceptions go, he feels that it comes from Hollywood, saying, "Negative portrayals give a negative stereotype. I don't want to make it sound as though vampires are completely happy all the time. I would like to represent a balance— balance is something we are all trying to find in life. Many of the so-called myths about vampires have an explanation or story behind them. for example: Long ago, in the old days, corpses of suspected vampires were dug up, decapitated, and the heads were stuffed with garlic. Garlic is a symbol of crucifixion to vampires. Most of us still eat it though, I think it tastes great in Italian foods and salsa."

"Regarding the myth that vampires cannot see their reflection in a mirror, that vampires are immortal and that they can fly, here is my theory: If you think of yourself in terms of body and soul, the soul is the immortal part of our being. It is invisible and cannot be seen in the reflection of a mirror, only the mortal shell of our body reflects itself. I choose to associate myself with my soul because the body serves simply as a vehicle for the soul, while the essence of our spirit will remain long after the death of our body. Those of us who can astral project could say that vampires can fly, but this also does not relate to the body. Aside from those who have had astral projections or out of body experiences, anyone 'undead' or anyone who has had a near-death experience, who has actually left their body behind for a moment, and then returned to it and lived to tell about it would clearly understand this kind of association in relation to the soul and the body."

Don Henrie

Other aspects he has mentioned in various forums and interviews on himself on what is factual was wide ranging. "Holy water never burned me. Now sunlight, on the other hand—I am very sensitive to energy in all forms. Sunlight is an intense blast of energy. To my senses it is harder to handle than the night. I could go out in the day but always wear shades and try to avoid it whenever I can. I find sunlight annoying and irritating, but bursting into flames in the sunlight hasn't happened to me yet. I do try to protect my moon-tan from the sun, and if I must go out in the day you'll always see me wearing 'sun-armor,' full clothing to keep the sun off my skin as much as possible. Some people I know burn very easily from the sun. I would rather just sleep through the day and wait until nighttime to go out. A stake through the heart or a silver bullet could probably kill anyone, alive or undead."

As for sleeping in a coffin, Don explains, "I like the sensory deprivation it gives me. I have a condition called fibromyalgia. We all have protective sheaths over our nerve endings; I have less than other people which makes me hypersensitive. It's hard for me to get a good night's sleep so the coffin helps. It cuts out noise."

He has explained that as far as blood work goes, "We have our sanctioned feeding circles. It's a self-contained society with our own doctors. There are worries in normal society about HIV and such and we worry about the same things. Also, for some, it can be bad. Blood can give people a really bad stomach ache. You have to be taught how to take the energy it gives. I only do it when I feel undernourished spiritually. You can eat as much as you want and take all the vitamins you need and still feel down. It's at times like that I will drink blood. When you look at other disciplines you have things like chi or life force energy. You have chakras that can be out of line. We believe similarly in that blood-drinking restores them. The blood is just a tangible and crude means of transferring energy. The only type of blood I am interested in is someone who has been tested and someone from my circle."

Don has mentioned in an interview online about his appearance that is was not always the way that you see him now. "No, it was a gradual progression. It is a constant metamorphosis or evolution that has taken place over the last decade. Moving out from my parents' gave me some self-realization. Moving through life, you gravitate towards certain people and they gravitate to you. Vampirism is another type of faith, really. One of your secretaries could be a vampire. We have houses—which are like covens for Witches."

Don acknowledges and respects the code of caution and discretion in revealing one's nature. Yet for Don, he is not one to hide in the shadows, and would like to see a day where other vampires like him could feel comfortable letting the world know they exist. In regards to secrecy he may have broken in the minds of some in the vampire community, Don often explains passionately that he disagrees, stating, "*The Black Veil* code of discretion by going public about the vampire lifestyle. On my showcase, one part that was edited out was when I mentioned *The Black Veil* as a code of ethics for many vampires. It is not a list of rules or laws, but a guideline of common sense to serve a vampire at their own discretion. In no way am I going against this. In fact I am very good friends with Michelle Belanger who is the author of *The Black Veil*. She had also auditioned for the part of *Mad Mad House*, so I know that being on the show was not something the she goes against."

Following is an interview with Don Henrie contributed by Michelle Belanger:

"It's 4 am in San Diego. I've finally caught up with Don Henrie. He's had a long day, shopping and traveling out and back to Hollywood. He keeps telling me that he's tired, but he's as well-poised as always, perfectly coiffed, perfectly dressed. He's at home, so he settles down in the Zen room, decorated throughout with an Asian theme. The dragon candle-holders are especially striking. He eases back onto the couch and lights up a clove, closes his eyes, and sighs a plume of smoke to the ceiling. After composing himself a moment more, he turns his attention back to me. He's very relaxed this morning, so his eyes are kind of far away and dreamy, but his aura of charisma spreads its usual intensity throughout the room..."

Michelle: "What was it like, being the vampire on *Mad Mad House*?"
Don: "Oh, where to start? It was an experience. First of all, it was wonderful being able to live in that kind of decadence. The house was gorgeous—huge and haunted—a bit drafty, though. They had space heaters running constantly, and they didn't really help. But otherwise, it was like living in my future home—without the moat of course. (laughs).

"Now, a lot of viewers know that I had to get used to living in that house with the contestants and the other alts, but there were other, shall we say, residents, that we all had to get used to living with as well. The mansion was haunted—that's one reason they chose it for the show, and I can affirm that it really does have ghosts. I spent the first few days getting acquainted with these. I would lie asleep in my coffin and have these extended conversations with several different female spirits—there were quite a few of them in that house. Now, some people might want to say this was my imagination, but here's the thing. I would sleep with the lid of the coffin closed. So it was closed when I went to sleep. But each night, I would wake up, and the lid was completely open. Now, the coffin was solid wood—very heavy, very expensive. The lid itself weighed about 60 pounds, so it's not like it could really open on its own. And for various reasons, if a living person walked up and opened it—let's just say I would notice that for sure."

Michelle: "So you were living with a witch, a modern primitive, a naturalist, a voodoo priestess, and ghosts. Did the presence of the spirits bother you?"
Don: "I never had a problem with the spirits. They played around with the coffin lid, but they never did anything threatening or even annoying, really. In fact, they helped me feel more at home, I think. I felt completely comfortable, knowing they were there with me. Of course, I'm not the sort to freak out at the presence of a few spirits and run around smudging rooms, if you know what I mean.

"Now, I don't know if they're going to release it on the website or on DVD or anything like that, but they did actually catch one of the ghosts on camera during our stay. You figure, they had to at some point, having cameras all over the house. It's an image of a woman walking through one of the rooms. Somebody on the staff asked who it was. I guess it looked a little like Fiona, the resident Witch, but Fiona was somewhere else entirely at the time, on camera, as well. After asking around among everybody, they realized there was no one who was supposed to be in the house anywhere near that room. So the ghosts made their presence both felt and seen."

Michelle: "Since you sleep during the day, you pretty much were up when everyone else was asleep. What did you do to amuse yourself?"
Don: "One of the things I would do at the mansion was walk the grounds at night. I really wasn't supposed to be doing this—at least, not as extensively as I explored things. But I'm a very curious person, and I have ways of sneaking about without being seen. So I got to see some things on the mansion grounds that were technically off-limits. Things they were setting up for the coming weeks, things off-set, so to speak. Because of my Nocturnal hours, I got to see many different aspects of the show that were otherwise invisible to everyone else.

"Another thing about that was seeing everyone else asleep. It's a different kind of feeling being in a house that big, filled with people, and you're the only one who's awake. I was on camera, of course—you were always on camera in that place—so it's not like I was doing anything sneaky, if you know what I mean. The producers knew I would wander at night. But sometimes I would creep up to the bedrooms just to see the other people in that state. It was like seeing a whole different side of them. There they lay, totally asleep, totally at peace. There was none of the drama, none of the posing that you would see during the day. It was like getting a different perspective on all of them. I would use that to help me keep a balanced view during waking hours."

Michelle: "Overall, do you think your experience with *Mad Mad House* was a good one?"
Don: "Yes, I believe the experience on the show was a good one for me. I made some lasting friends there. I've spent time with Noel and with Avocado since the show ended. That seems to be pretty well known. But there's a friendship I made that isn't so well publicized, and that's with Ia Ta'shia. How this came about was very interesting to me. In addition to my Nocturnal ramblings, I did a lot of exploring the house during the day—while I was asleep. As you may know, I practice astral projection, and I actually sleep very little. I spent most of the time out of my body, observing everything that was going on. This is one way I always knew what was going on behind the scenes—I was almost always there, watching, invisibly.

"Iya Tashia, as it turns out, saw me. Pretty early on in things, she saw me projecting in the corner of her room. She took me aside afterward and spoke to me about it, kind of called me out, if you will. But that was how she knew I was real, and not just someone playing at being a vampire. Some respect was earned at that point, I think. Later, I made me this special necklace consecrated to the spirit of Eshu. In Voodun, Eshu is a spirit of the crossroads—very appropriate for a being like me, who walks the places between. I still wear the necklace—I treasure it, in fact. Eshu is so appropriate for me, because I'm all about the crossroads of things, the balance—not Heaven or Hell but the path between, you could say. That's part of the power of the vampire, really."

Michelle: "While we're on the topic of vampires, what does vampirism mean to you? You practice magick and astral projection, and you hold some definite spiritual beliefs, but it's clear that the fashion and the aesthetics appeal to you as well. How do these things relate if they relate at all?"

Don: "I've ranted on this one before, so here goes. Basically, you've got people who just live the lifestyle. They wear the clothes, they like the aesthetic, but that's about it. Then you've got people who only follow the spiritual side of things. They'll admit they're vampiric, but they wouldn't be caught dead in a Goth club if you paid them to show up there. And then there are people who embody the archetype. That's me. I embrace the vampire as a whole. For me, it's not about one thing or the other. It's everything—the aesthetics, the fashion, the magick, the lifestyle, the spirituality—I take all of these things and weave them together until I have something very unique, very special to me. I guess you could say it's a kind of alchemy—I take all the different parts of this archetypal image and distill their energies into something that's very powerful for me.

"Now, I've heard some people criticize me for how much I like the fashion side of things. But I'm a very social creature. To me, image is a part of empowerment. How I dress influences how I feel, so I always make an effort to wear something that's going to help reinforce what I want to project, how I want to be. There's such a thing as over-doing it, of course. I don't want to come off like a Liberace, if you know what I mean. But in Mad Mad House, for example, I chose my clothes each day knowing that people were going to see me, knowing that I had certain emotions, certain energies I wanted to project. That's why when we were doing judging, I would wear my red jacket. That's my powersuit, so to speak. I get a very grand feeling when I'm wearing that jacket. I manifest a lot, projecting my charisma to an audience—it's my craft, if you know what I mean. And wearing clothes like that, they help put me in a better place for that. I guess you could look at the clothes as ritual tools, in a way. They help give me a focus, and let me tap more into the energy of the archetype, and channel it through me."

Michelle: "I think it's safe to say that you were one of the sexiest people on Mad, Mad House. With 5000 fans professing their attraction for you on your website, has that changed you at all?"

Don: "Aw, thank you. (giggles). You know, people keep asking if this has changed me, and this is what I see. I see them making all these assumptions about what I'm doing now, how I live my life. I didn't have an agent until just recently, and in a lot of ways, my life is still pretty normal. I still have to shop at the grocery store and clean up after the cats, after all. So I don't think stardom had changed me. But people's perceptions of me have changed, and what they keep seeing are all these things they're projecting onto me.

"Now, I have to admit—I love the attention. I've got fansites and a couple of my fans have done artwork of me. My favorite right now is one that shows me with these beautiful black wings. A nickname I have for myself is Mourning Star, so of course I like the whole angel theme. But I like all of the fan art—it's all very flattering. Still, I make sure I don't get conceited about all of this. The attention—sure, it sends a lot of energy to me, but I want to do something with that energy, harness it, give it back to people. There are ways I could get over-zealous and let this all go to my head. So it's a balancing act, doing things for the fans like making posters and T-shirts, but also making sure I'm doing these things for them, not just taking their money. There are ways to harvest that kind of attention that make it more of a fair exchange. That's what I'm going for, really. I don't want to be out of the spotlight, but I want to do something with my time here, make a difference for people, for the community."

Michelle: "There's so much left we can talk about, but it's getting late and I don't want to keep you up past sunrise. So let's close this interview for now. Are there any parting words you'd like to say?"

Don: "Yes, actually. I have something very important I need to say. I know that I've become a kind of role model for some people, something a lot of people want to grow up to be, if you know what I mean. I know because I've had the courage to come out about who I am and wear that for the world to see, it's given a lot of people in the community the courage to come out as well. I'm very thankful about that. I'm glad I could do something that's empowered so many people. But I just want to tell people not to be stupid about things.

"This is kind of a 'don't try this at home, kids' message, and I don't want to sound preachy, but I think it's very important to say that I'm not trying to get people to follow me. I don't want a whole community of Don clones out there, because that's not the message I'm trying to get across by being me. What I'm trying to show people is that you can harness your inner soul—the you that you really are and not the you that society or family wants you to be—and you can wear that on the outside. You can draw power from that and use it to really live in your Godhead. That's what all of this is for me, but I don't want people thinking that they have to be exactly like me to be empowered like that. All of us are different. I like a lot of groups, a lot of people, but I follow no one but me. So I don't want to inspire followers. A great leader is not one who commands many followers, but one who creates leaders. I want people to find the strength and the courage within themselves to be who they need to be."

Michelle: "Wow. I think that's a good message, and something a lot of people need to hear. And I'm going to let you go for now. Everyone say good night—or good morning— to the vampire Don Henrie." —*Michelle Belanger, Author of* The Psychic Vampire Codex

Over time fame has brought it share of troubles to Don Henrie. Like any other celebrity he accepts it as coming with the territory, but none the less it perturbs him. "I had to put our phone on a timer so that we wouldn't be disturbed by calls all day, while we sleep. It's a strange feeling meeting complete strangers who know who you are and you are clueless about who they are because you've never met. We caught a vampire digging through our trash one night and that was somewhat disturbing. Things nobody would care about suddenly become a big deal and as I had mentioned earlier, people sometimes talk up to me as if I am superior or try to butter me up when I just want to have a normal conversation. My girlfriend and I have had to secure our private life because anything anyone knows about us will spread like wildfire. We have to be picky about our friends, even some people we thought we could trust have done things like spread the word for the invite of a private party we once had."

Don has likewise experienced avoidance and rudeness in social situations. "I have had people who are very ignorant. People lack common courtesy. If I nod at someone as I walk down the street, I often do not get people replying, even though I mean no harm. It leaves a bad taste in the mouth. It's all down to prejudice. I keep to my own circle and keep to Nocturnal hours to avoid it."

We both encounter the same reaction publicly but also agree that this weeds out the people we don't want to speak to. He explains, "I cannot spend all my time trying to educate people. It's a double-edged sword, of course." Despite all that, he still finds time to "smell the roses," play with his two cats, and relax enough to just enjoy the moment.

Another member to the Vampyre culture is DRAGAN DRACUL, Father of Clutch Arcane, and an online acquaintance of mine. We both are members of a few online groups, Don Henrie's official site most notably. I asked him a few questions on how it felt to become aware of his talents at an early age and what he has done with his life from those experiences.

Corvis: "Please tell us a bit about you and how you became involved in vampirism?"
Dragan: "Well first, a little bit about me. I am an Eclectic Vampyre but primarily feed sanguinely, I started my awakening around 16 and I was really pushed off the deep end for that. Prior to my awakening I wasn't aware of vampires. I was just like the other millions of people when I thought of vampires, I thought of movies. How ironic to find out I am just that...It was hard. If it wasn't for the Net I would have been completely lost. There are no other people of my kind around here. Looking back now it is amazing I made it through. I think it is that way for all of us that are just awakening and embracing it;

accepting it was hard. But like most others. I grew out of my old life and was reborn into my new."

Corvis: **"What about your early experiences?"**
Dragan: "Finding a Donor; that was quite an experience because I am Eclectic and I can adapt to many ways of feeding. But it's harder to feed many ways than it is to have one and stick with it. I tried a few but the sanguine path seems the best. Pure energy condensed into a liquid form. But with today's threats or diseases I can't just feed from anyone, so I went on to look for a donor, which is not a very fun thing to do, it took a lot of talking and probing minds to find someone I could connect with on a level so deep. After many attempts to gain trust with someone, I finally found a willing friend that I could open up to without being made fun of, or called a liar. We drove to the local doctors office and we both got check ups and had our blood screened. Everything was ok and I gained a donor and a good friend. But without a doubt I would have to say the best part of awakening, was becoming aware of what I am. The worst aspect was the not knowing. I was running blind and I was so hungry for knowledge...Just the learning and growing was a great experience. I have met many friends on my path, all who have helped me in a great way."

Corvis: **"What do you feel is misconstrued about the culture versus what positive aspects we actually have to offer?"**
Dragan: "The biggest misconception, in my opinion, is the idea that vampyres are all about darkness, but that is the farthest thing from the truth. Most vampyres try to stay equal with a balance of Darkness with Light. We are open with our darkness, and we show that, so when the mainstream sees us they will only see dark individuals. But the light is easier to see when you are in the Dark. Another Misconception is the idea that Vampyrism is a religion, which again, is false. Vampyrism is the way one is born and lives, not a religion. Vampyres are free to worship and believe in what they want. There are Christian vampyres, Pagan vampyres, Satanic Vampyres, even Buddhist vampyres. So the idea that vampyrism is a religion is wrong."

Temple of the Vampire

The Temple of the Vampire see power not as energy in psychic physicality, or in blood, but in power gained through any means necessary. Blood drawing to them is too dangerous to tamper with and they feel the power of prey and predator is simply a metaphor to demonstrate acquiring gain by taking from the weak.

Magister Nemo is elusive and difficult to find, but has been interviewed in the Satanic magazine *Not Like Most,* published by Purging Talon's Matt Paradise. In it, he details the differences between his church and the Church of Satan.

Temple of the Vampire, a vampiric organization with heavy Satanic ideals—such as pragmatic occultism, is one of the few in existence that has obtained the legal status of a church under U.S. Federal government requirements in 1989. Its leader, Magister Nemo, is a registered member of the Church of Satan. They view vampirism to be one of true energy exchange, differing from the public persona of traditional vampires, having nothing to do with coffins and the like. Vampirism as a romantic figure in popular view is a metaphor useful to disguise their true methods and agendas. It is the skill of being on the receiving end of things desired more than not. Predatorily acquiring goals, whether it is of words, money, time by cunning and skill. A winner wins and losers lose, with no emotional compunction regarding the seeking of victory. Life force, according to the Temple Vampires would be an exercise of raw power flowing from the stronger, more skilled in any exchange. A truly Machiavellian attitude of 'might makes right,' where members attain rank by self-proclamation. The motivation to be honest in this is by knowing others will know the truth eventually, and expose them. The Church of Satan grants rank by judgment on the members efforts outside the organization, opposed to a need to give to them and 'work up within it'. Each group requires its members to prove themselves for their own benefit. Ability, regardless of title is needed. Belief in the self, drive and determination are healthy aspects in the left hand path. They contend that the stupidity of the masses is something to exploit for their own benefit, and like Satanists, feel enlightenment is for the elite.

According to the Temple of the Vampire creed:
"I am a vampire, I worship my ego and my life, for I am the only God that is. I am proud that I am a predatory animal and honor my animal instincts. I exalt my rational mind and hold no belief that is in defiance of reason. I recognize the difference between the worlds of truth and fantasy. I acknowledge the Powers of Darkness to be hidden natural laws through which I work my magic. I realize there is no heaven as there is no hell, and I view death as the destroyer of life. Therefore I will make the most of life here and now. I am a Vampire, bow down before me.

"The Temple does not care what members do in private, provided such actions do not risk drastic public consequences. We simply require that our members be sensible. To be explicit about the most important details, we have four very straightforward rules for our members. These are:

Abide by the law. The Temple will not tolerate any member who commits any jailable crime. Traffic tickets and other minor law infractions (those which cannot result in jail time) are not considered to be criminal acts and are not violations of this Temple Law.

No drinking physical blood. We wish to avoid exposure to criminal liability and what many consider cannibalism. Our path does not require drinking blood. Hence, to simplify much for the Temple and its members, we do not permit this.

Do not represent the Temple without our explicit written permission. While members may reveal the public website URL or postal address of the Temple to non-members, we wish to keep control of what is said in our name. Members may not discuss the Temple with anyone without special permission.

Do not betray the Temple Mission. Temple members are welcome to join virtually any organization or support nearly any cause they wish. However, we will not retain any member supporting an organization or cause which attacks the Temple's image or supports criminal activity or blood-drinking. For example membership in racist, neo nazi or similarly anti-social fringe groups is not only unacceptable, but is contradictory to the Teachings of the Temple.

"One additional clarification. True members of the Temple are Vampires. They have performed Communion and obtained verified Contact with the Undead Rulers Who Guide this Temple. Those who have thus found the Temple willingly try to honor the intentions of their found Family. If a member were to resist these four simple requirements this would be clear evidence that they were human after all and be removed from membership. The Temple is for Vampires alone and would only be a source of frustration to any human. You are what you are. The Temple is not for everyone. The Temple's disclaimer regarding truth vs. metaphor does not apply here. Temple Law is as written. Within lies fact and fancy, truth and metaphor. Discriminate with care." © *2004 Temple of the Vampire.*

MAGISTER NEMO, founder of Temple of the Vampire was quite cooperative when I approached him to clarify the differences between his Church and those belonging to Father Sebastian's Order, and the Temple's Satanic views.

Corvis: "I understand Temple of the Vampire is an actual church, legally speaking. How and why was this decided?"
Magister Nemo: "In 1989 it was decided to permit a public testing of an effort to offer the Vampiric Teachings by means of conscious instruction through the written word. The intent was to reach more of those with the Vampiric Potential. The desire to do this has had a long history and many false starts."

Corvis: "What is the definition of 'Psychic Vampire' to you and the multiple other versions? (i.e., Sang, Psy, and Psychic Vampire, a la Anton LaVey?"
Magister Nemo: "The term 'psychic vampire' used by Doctor LaVey in

The Satanic Bible refers to the human being who attempts to control others by means of guilt. These social leeches have nothing to do with real Vampirism. The Temple deals only with real Vampires, those persons who are members of the Vampire Religion and who are able to successfully rise above the mortal human condition. The full definition and meaning of this condition is outlined both at the Temple website as well as in our primary text The Vampire Bible."

Corvis: "What separates you from others about blood in your organization? Isn't The Temple a group of Satanists who identify with the vampiric archetype?"
Magister Nemo: "The Temple forbids the drinking of physical human blood primarily because the reality of Vampirism has nothing to do with neither silly Hollywood stereotypes nor sexual blood fetishes. The Temple is not a subset of Satanism and while we enjoy the presence of many members of the Church of Satan, and also have great respect for the Church of Satan, the vast majority of our members never were Satanists. Additionally the Temple does not recognize any validity to the claims of those who try to identify with the Vampire as a lifestyle. We do not recognize any others who lay claim to Our Heritage. We are the only Vampires. And We can prove this."

Corvis: "What good comes from being a 'vampire' in your group, and how is it a positive thing for people instead of the 'freak' stereotype affixed to the label by society?"
Magister Nemo: "Actually you are born with the Potential of recognizing that you are a Vampire such that it is not an issue of joining to 'become' one. At the same time if the Potential is not exercised the Vampire is, so to speak, 'stillborn.' The Temple also leverages and relies upon the misunderstanding of the human masses with regard to what the Vampire is. The Temple Teachings refer to this as 'The Truth of the Lie.' It serves Us well. The advantages are many. The Temple offers proven tools for wealth acquisition and personal mastery. Additionally we advocate the achievement and maintenance of physical immortality for the member."

Corvis: "**Anything you'd like to say to clear up any misunderstandings or words of advice for interested future vampires?**"

Magister Nemo: "The Temple's motto is 'Test Everything. Believe Nothing.' Absolutely everything with regard to the Temple requires that the member obtain personal proof. We do not debate nor proselytize. The Temple is a test at every step. Those willing to take the test need only read details at www.vampiretemple.com."

The opinions here do not necessarily reflect those of anyone else in this same chapter, and while the relationships of these people range from best of friends to bitter parties who contest each other's set of ideals, the core thought is similar in behavior to the outside world. No matter how varied, each and every group has a code of ethics that promote respect, knowledge and betterment of the self.

Power, either by energy transference or physical gain, along with presence conveyed through one's own sense of style is what ties Goths, Vampires of any of the three types described here, Satanists, and Dark Paganism together—all of whom are dark individuals alienated by a differing mindset from that of mainstream society, all misanthropic without becoming deranged sociopaths.

DESCENT
by Corvis Nocturnum

⊰THE 𝒟EVIL'S DUE ⊱

"Don't worry, you who have been fooled into believing the paper tiger displayed by today's media; we Satanists aren't after your children, for they are probably as hopelessly mediocre as their parents. But we are moving the world towards a state wherein the freeloaders will either work or starve, and the parasites will be removed to wither and die. So, you need only fear real Satanism if you are a criminal, a parasite, or a wastrel. Are you afraid?"
— Peter Gilmore, High Priest of The Church of Satan

"As LaVey has stressed over and over again, Satanism is not about heavy metal or the sacrifice of children or animals to a horned Deity. These are antics for the weak and confused."
—Adam Parfrey, The Devil's Notebook

Satanist. The one word that is bound to generate fear from the general populace. Satanists are certainly the most misunderstood of all the dark groups on the face of the earth. It has been called out on television, from the mouths of preachers and so-called experts for three decades. The media has made a sensation out of Satan's hold over the youth, and lies about the Church that uses Satan in its name and about its founder, Anton LaVey.

Long before the Church of Satan was even founded, people who fought against hypocrisy and societies flaws were called Humanists, Atheists, or worse. In typical mass hysteria for ratings, literally hundreds of unsubstantiated horror stories have been told to the public without a single member of the organization being given the chance to speak up in its defense.

Myself, along with thousands and thousands of other people, from King Diamond and Sammy Davis Jr. to leaders in corporate business, have turned to Satanism. Not for spirituality, but for a logical belief system based on common sense and realism. This path does not force its practitioners to abhor a peaceful mindset, like those discussed in the chapter "Dark Spirituality."

EGO DIABOLUS, a member of an online discussion group called "The Hellfire Network" based in my hometown, spoke to me about our city's tolerance and reception, as well as to why he chose Satanism for himself. Though he is not affiliated with any Satanic organization he still considers himself a Satanist.

Corvis: "As a Satanist in average America, what is your reaction to the stereotypical thoughts most have on your path?"
Ego Diabolus: "I wonder at the image most people create when they hear the word Satanist. Immediately, it seems, they assume that we are black-garbed sorcerers who light our homes with black candles, maintain a collection of obscure odds and ends related to death and destruction, speaking in strange languages and practicing foul rituals. They are often surprised if they discover that we also can be very, well, normal. There may be hints of our beliefs and interests around our home and in our demeanor, but more often than not an outsider would find such things interesting or even desirable.

"Other misconceptions have to do with our attitudes toward other religions, especially Christianity. It is assumed that we must, as Satanists, oppose all things Christian. This is not the case, as our religion is not dependent on the scriptures of another for its form. Satanism stands on its own. It is when our values and beliefs are challenged by others that we must stand opposed. Some of the basic ideals of Satanism and Christianity are the same; the values of truth, property, against murder are shared by both religions. However, we Satanists take our values more seriously than the majority of Christians, and our faith does not have the history of ignoring those ideals that Christianity and its institutions have.

"Another idea I find strange about how people view Satanism comes from some Satanists themselves. There are those that seem to think that Satanism should be the religion of all, and want to see the world converted to our ideals. This would, in my opinion, be harmful to Satanism if it were true. Not everyone is cut out to be a Satanist, and we Satanists not only accept that, we are glad of it. Satanism is a religion of elitism and internal strength and many are simply not equipped for it. In our world, however, such people have a place and purpose; even if it is merely carrying out the ideas and building the society of our design. 'The world needs ditch-diggers,' even if they cannot grasp the structure of the world around them."

Corvis: "What lead you to Satanism, and how were you introduced to it?"

Ego Diabolus: "Satanism, I feel, was always there, in the back of my mind, without any real formal structure. As I studied religion, I turned away from my traditional training. There was no horrible or scarring event that made me hate the faith of my fathers, it simply did not ring through as truth to me, and I sought out my own answers. I learned as much as I could about a variety of faiths, and agreed with some ideas there, but still finding the same feelings about the religion in question as a whole. Many of the authors I was reading had been contrasting their religion from Satanism, so I decided to pick up the *Satanic Bible* and find out why.

"In reading the *Satanic Bible,* I found all my random thoughts and ideas about reality and society given voice and form. I felt like I had discovered a kindred spirit in LaVey; the more I read, the more I thought, 'yes, exactly!' I read everything I could find about LaVey, the Church of Satan, and Satanism, and continued to find my own ideas re-enforced. It was like trying to find out what you are, and then finding a mirror and really seeing yourself undistorted for the first time. It felt like 'oh, there I am. I am a Satanist.'"

Corvis: "Has any change in the last few years taken place in peoples views on it locally?"

Ego Diabolus: "Locally we have a very conservative segment of society. The changes I am seeing are really happening in the younger generation, those folks in their 20s and 30s, the future leaders and policy makers. Those people have become more tolerant and interested in other religions, including Satanism. They are more likely to ask what Satanism is about than they are to dismiss it outright. Sadly, it has remained something to keep to one's self in many situations, but more often than not religious discussion is not welcome at all. Religion as a whole has become less a means of acceptance in our society, and zealots of any stripe are considered undesirable, which has made being a Satanist much easier than it would have been in the past. Whereas years ago Satanists would be expelled from the social scene, now Satanists and Satanism are generally agreed with in their views, but people still have issues with the name 'Satanist.' I think, in a short few years, even that will dissipate."

Corvis: "What of 'Devil Worship?"
Ego Diabolus: "The question of Satanism and devil-worship can be a bit confusing; due mainly to it being a matter of perspective. The Christian mind will never accept a division between the worship of a Deity other than their God (and often their means of worshipping their God) and worship of the entity who is their God's nemesis. In fact, the acknowledgement of an entity of evil and subsequent empowerment through blaming it for their misdeeds and negative occurrences is in itself a form of devil-worship. Most of us would disagree with this view, but it does provide an illustration of why this issue is debated.

"In my opinion, there are as many variations of Satanism as there are Satanists. Some feel that they truly worship and entity above and beyond themselves, and call this entity by a number of names. Some see these entities as abstract energies which require those of us with a physical presence in the universe to guide and define them; an acknowledgement of existence without worship. Others deny their existence entirely, suggesting that they represent abstract ideas and not actual entities. Few in any of these schools of thought consider what they do devil-worshipping, though they often suggest that what another does is precisely that.

"For my part, when attempting to sort these answers out for myself, I find it helpful to look at the etymology of the words; their history and meaning. If we can properly decipher the words themselves, we can be better equipped to discuss them.

"Devil-worshipper' seems fairly straightforward; one who worships and is subservient to the Devil or a devil. We all are in certain agreement of what it is to worship. This issue often hinges on what a 'devil' is Devil travels through old English after a couple permutations to the Latin 'diabolous,' which is literally 'one who throws against' or one who is opposed. This comes from the Greek 'diabolos,' which is even more literally 'to throw against,' and was the direct translation of the Hebrew 'satan,' 'one who opposes' (Ego Diabolus, by the way, is broken Latin for 'I oppose'). In none of these translations are those who are opposed necessarily 'evil.' Devil-worship is not necessarily an evil act, at least by direct translation. 'Demon,' by the way, is Greek and refers to any spirit, good or bad. Furthermore, 'angel' is the Hebrew 'Ma Laahk.' or 'messenger,' and again referred to good or bad sorts. How does this help us? Inherent in the term 'devil' is the idea that there is something to be opposed to, that a force or ideal is being resisted or stood against.

"Satanists, in general, are not opposed to any particular idea as the main thrust of their philosophy; rather they stand for something, which as a result finds them opposed to other things, not the reverse. A 'devil-worshipper' would therefore need to be opposed to an idea before they could act. Satanists are Satanists with or without opposition; a devil worshipper requires opposition to be. This would simply be an inversion of the Christian who inadvertently 'worships' their Devil through maintaining that this entity has power in their lives. A Devil-worshipper would inadvertently worship God by acknowledging such an entity through their need to oppose it. Satanists, for the most part, deny the existence of the Christian God or that entity's impact on their lives; typically it is that God's worshippers and institutions which we find need to stand against. Of course, this is an etymological viewpoint. No doubt, others will proudly call themselves 'devil-worshippers' and act much as many Satanists do, while some 'Satanists' will be driven by their 'calling' to base their beliefs on the inversion of the beliefs they suggest they oppose. Deeds may continue to confuse the issue, but perhaps the words will help sort it out."

Corvis: "What positive factors does this contribute into your life not found elsewhere?"

Ego Diabolus: "As with any religious conviction, I find myself no longer searching for some means to structure my world view, and now can work on building from that foundation. Knowing where you come from is one of the first steps in determining where you are going. Through Satanism, I have discovered a community in which I feel welcome. Through my interactions in that community, I have discovered new ideas and directions for my research and growth. Satanism has provided a clearer definition of self, which has added to my over-all confidence and sense of well being."

The Black Pope

Anton LaVey was a student of the occult for most of his life. Who exactly was this mysterious man with such negative stigma associated around his name and life's writings? I felt an introduction to him would be best described by the current High Priest of the Church of Satan, and longtime fiend of his, Peter H. Gilmore. He wrote the following in the official website, and with his permission, I have copied portions of the writing to give some background about one of the world's most wrongly hated individuals.

ANTON SZANDOR LAVEY (1930–1997) was the founder of the Church of Satan, the first organized church in modern times promulgating a religious philosophy championing Satan as the symbol of personal freedom and individualism. Unlike the founders of other religions, who claimed exalted 'inspiration' delivered through some supernatural entity, LaVey readily acknowledged that he used his own faculties to synthesize Satanism, based on his understanding of the human animal and insights gained from earlier philosophers who advocated materialism and individualism. Concerning his role as founder, he said that, "If he didn't do it himself, someone else, perhaps less qualified, would have."

Born in Chicago in 1930, his parents soon relocated to California, that westernmost gathering place for the brightest and darkest manifestations of the 'American Dream.' It was a fertile environment for the sensitive child who would eventually mature into a role that the press would dub "The Black Pope." From his eastern European grandmother, young LaVey learned of the superstitions that are still extant in that part of the world. These tales whetted his appetite for the outré, leading him to become absorbed in classic dark literature such as Dracula and Frankenstein. He also became an avid reader of the pulp magazines, which first published tales now deemed classics of the horror and science fiction genres. He later befriended seminal *Weird Tales* authors such as Clark Ashton

Anton LaVey
Photo courtesy of the Church of Satan

Smith, Robert Barbour Johnson, and George Hass. His fancy was captured by fictional characters found in the works of Jack London, in comic strip characters—like Ming the Merciless, as well as historical figures of a diabolical cast such as Cagliostro, Rasputin and Basil Zaharoff. More interesting to him than the available occult literature, which he dismissed as being little more than sanctimonious white magic, were books of applied obscure knowledge such as Dr. William Wesley Cook's *Practical Lessons in Hypnotism*, Jane's *Fighting Ships,* and manuals for handwriting analysis.

His musical abilities were noticed early, and he was given free reign by his parents to try his hand at various instruments. LaVey was mainly attracted to the keyboards because of their scope and versatility. He found time to practice and could easily reproduce songs heard by ear without recourse to fake books or sheet music. This talent would prove to be one of his main sources of income for many years, particularly his calliope playing during his carnival days, and later his many stints as an organist in bars, lounges, and nightclubs. These venues gave him the chance to study how various melodic lines and chord progressions swayed the emotions of his audiences, from the spectators at the carnival and spook shows, to the individuals seeking solace for the disappointments in their lives in distilled spirits and the smoke-filled taverns for which LaVey's playing provided a soundtrack.

His odd interests marked him as an outsider, and he did not alleviate this by feeling any compulsion to be 'one of the boys.' He despised gym class and team sports and often cut classes to follow his own interests. He was an avid reader, and watched films such as those which would later be labeled film noir as well as German expressionist cinema such as *M, The Cabinet of Dr. Caligari,* and the Dr. Mabuse movies. His flashy mode of dress also served to amplify his alienation from the mainstream. He dropped out of high school to hang around with hoodlum types and gravitated towards working in the circus and carnivals, first as a roustabout and cage boy and later as a musician. His curiosity was rewarded through "learning the ropes" and working an act with the big cats, and later assisting with the machinations of the spook shows. He became well-versed in the many rackets used to separate the rubes from their money, along with the psychology that lead people to such pursuits. He played music for the bawdy shows on Saturday nights, as well as for tent revivalists on Sunday mornings, seeing many of the same people attending both. All of this provided a firm, earthy background for his evolving cynical world view.

When the carnival season ended, LaVey would earn money by playing organ in Los Angeles area burlesque houses, and he relates that it was during this time period that he had a brief affair with a then-unknown Marilyn Monroe. Moving back to San Francisco, LaVey worked for awhile as a photographer for the Police Department, and, during the Korean War, enrolled in San Francisco City College as criminology major to avoid the draft. Both his studies and occupation revealed grim insights into human nature. At this time he met and married Carole Lansing, who bore him his first daughter, Karla Maritza, in 1952. A few years earlier LaVey had explored the writings of Aleister Crowley, and in 1951 he met some of the Berkeley Thelemites. He was unimpressed, as they were more spiritual and less 'wicked' than he supposed they should be for disciples of Crowley's libertine creed.

During the 1950s, LaVey supplemented his income as a "psychic investigator," helping to investigate "nut calls" referred to him by friends in the police department. These experiences proved to him that many people were inclined to seek a supernatural explanation for phenomena that had more prosaic causes. His rational explanations often disappointed the complainants, so LaVey invented more exotic causes to make them feel better, giving him insight as to how religion often functions in people's lives.

In 1956 he purchased a Victorian house on California Street in San Francisco's Richmond district. It was reputed to have been a speakeasy. He painted it black; it would later become home to the Church of Satan. After his death, the house remained unoccupied until it was demolished by the real estate company which owned the property on October 17 of 2001.

LaVey's final companion was Blanche Barton, who bore him his only son, Satan Xerxes Carnacki LaVey on November 1, 1993. According to LaVey's wishes, she succeeded him as the head of the Church after his death on October 29, 1997. In 2001, she passed-on this position to Peter H. Gilmore, a long-time member of the Council of Nine.

Through his 'ghost busting,' and his frequent public gigs as an organist, including playing the Wurlitzer at the Lost Weekend cocktail lounge, LaVey became a local celebrity and his holiday parties attracted many San Francisco notables. Guests included Carin de Plessin, called "the Baroness" as she had grown-up in the royal palace of Denmark, anthropologist Michael Harner, Chester A. Arthur III (Grandson to the U.S. President), Forrest J. Ackerman (later, the publisher of Famous Monsters of Filmland and acknowledged expert on science fiction), author Fritz Leiber, local eccentric Dr. Cecil E. Nixon (creator of the musical automaton Isis) and underground filmmaker Kenneth Anger. From this crowd LaVey distilled what he called a 'Magic Circle' of associates who shared his interest in the bizarre, the hidden side of what moves the world. As his expertise grew, LaVey began presenting Friday night lectures summarizing the fruits of his research.

In 1965, LaVey was featured on the *The Brother Buzz Show*, a humorous children's program hosted by marionettes. The focus was on LaVey's 'Addams Family' life style—making a living as a hypnotist, psychic investigator, and organist as well as on his highly unusual pet Togare, a Nubian lion.

In the process of creating his lectures, LaVey was led to distill a unique philosophy based on his life experiences and research. When a member of his Magic Circle suggested that he had the basis for a new religion, LaVey agreed and decided to found the Church of Satan as the best means for communicating his ideas. And so, in 1966 on the night of May Eve—the traditional Witches' Sabbath—LaVey declared the founding of the Church of Satan as well as renumbering 1966 as the year One, Anno Satanas—the first year of the Age of Satan.

By the end of 1969, LaVey had taken monographs he had written to explain the philosophy and ritual practices of the Church of Satan and melded them with all of his philosophical influences from Ayn Rand, Nietzsche, Mencken, and London along with the base wisdom of the carnival folk. He prefaced these essays and rites with reworked excerpts from Ragnar Redbeard's *Might is Right* and concluded it with 'Satanized' versions of John Dee's Enochian Keys to create *The Satanic Bible*. It has never gone out of print and remains the main source for the contemporary Satanic movement.

The Satanic Bible was followed in 1971 by *The Complete Witch* (re-released in 1989 as *The Satanic Witch*), a manual which teaches "Lesser Magic"—the ways and means of reading and manipulating people and their actions toward the fulfillment of one's desired goals. *The Satanic Rituals* (1972) was printed as a companion volume to The Satanic Bible and contains rituals culled from a Satanic tradition identified by LaVey in various world cultures. Two collections of essays, which range from the humorous and insightful to the sordid, *The Devil's Notebook* (1992) and Satan *Speaks* (1998), complete his written canon.

Since its founding, LaVey's Church of Satan attracted many varied people who shared an alienation from conventional religions, including such celebrities as Jayne Mansfield and Sammy Davis Jr., as well as rock stars King Diamond and Marilyn Manson, who all became, at least for a time, card-carrying members. He numbered among his associates Robert Fuest, director of the Vincent Price 'Dr. Phibes' films as well as *The Devil's Rain;* Jacques Vallee, ufologist and computer scientist, who was used as the basis for the character Lacombe, played by Francois Truffaut in Spielberg's *Close Encounters of the Third Kind;* and Aime Michel known as a spelunker and publisher of *Morning of the Magicians.*

LaVey was a skilled showman, a talent he never denied. However, the number of incidents detailed in both biographies that can be authenticated via photographic and documentary evidence far outweigh the few items in dispute. The fact remains that LaVey pursued a course that exposed him to the heights and depths of humanity, full of encounters with fascinating people; it climaxed with his founding of the Church of Satan and led to notorious celebrity on a worldwide scale. The Church has survived his death, and continues, through the medium of his writings, to continually attract new members who see themselves reflected in the philosophy he called Satanism.

Why the name 'Satan' then if he is nothing more than an archetype to emulate philosophically? To answer the question that skeptics keep asking me, I often refer them to various writings of LaVey and leaders who came after him. From the beginning, the Church of Satan has made it explicitly clear that Satan is not an entity, conscious or preconscious. Many examples are available to the studious: "In LaVey's view, the Devil was not [an anthropomorphic Deity], but rather a dark, hidden force in nature responsible for the workings of earthly affairs, a force for which neither science nor religion had any explanation." —*Burton Wolfe, Introduction to* The Satanic Bible.

I was honored to have the chance to relay my work to HIGH PRIEST GILMORE, who agreed to answer some questions here in order to clear up some misconceptions.

Corvis: "Many people, especially teenagers, flock to 'dark' imagery for a sense of rebellion, and so may be attracted to surface elements of Satanism. Once they find out Satanism requires the practitioner to be independent and responsible for themselves,

High Priest Gilmore
Photo courtesy of the Church of Satan

they might flee to make up some form of pseudo-Satanism based on what they had hoped to find. Would you agree that they are the reason that true Satanism gets bad press?"

Gilmore: "I don't see that there is a large contingent of these misguided, desperate young people, nor are the few that exist getting noticed by the general public. There are definitely some pathetic web sites and hilariously goofy 'organizations,' which are usually some disturbed fellow with a web site and his equally naive online pals pretending to be 'evil.' That sort of rebellion, using pre-packaged 'dark' imagery, usually is short-lived. The only folks who regularly see these antics are people who take a good deal of time to search them out, as the sites and chat rooms that these few wannabes frequent receive little traffic. The danger of having them being presented as if they were real Satanists happens when lazy journalists, television producers, and 'hackademics' doing shoddy research use these losers as exemplars, as if they represented some major faction amongst Satanists. We know that are not, and these 'researchers' would too if they got off their backsides and separated fact from the fictions spewed on various web sites. Some of these folks actually want to make it seem as if these pseudo-Satanists really are some kind of mass movement, and so facts mean little in the face of a desire to create proPaganda. Otherwise, evangelical Christians and those who support their agendas persist in spreading disinformation and outright lies about there being some sort of conspiracy lead by Satan himself. Certainly this demonstrates the validity of the Ninth Satanic Statement, and of course rational people know that such claims have been debunked by secular investigators. But that is often the real source of 'bad press,' the falsehoods and fantasies promulgated by this bunch, not the clowns wearing black nail-polish and calling themselves by names out of Dungeons and Dragons."

Corvis: "Warped views from would-be Satanists try to excuse excess in drinking and drug use by claiming it to be their 'indulgence' which is part of a 'given right.' Why is it so difficult for people to separate indulgence from addiction, and who draws the distinction?"

Gilmore: "It is simply part of their natures that it is difficult for many people to see their limits. They are incapable of being responsible for their own actions. That is why laws are needed, and police forces, as most humans are irresponsible and therefore dangerous. In Satanism we are epicureans, who indulge in balanced pleasure from all avenues, not hedonists who binge on just fleshy pursuits and thus find themselves slaves to their compulsions. Satanism isn't for the masses, as very few people have the strength to be their own masters. From my experience, it is natural for Satanists to see when their indulgence could be bordering on compulsion - and they take immediate steps to balance themselves, but it is generally rare in most others. Many people seem to lack enough self-awareness to make that decision, and find themselves in hospitals and clinics when their loss of control leads them to behavior which intrudes on others. They put the decision on family or society. Finally, the Satanist also understands that rights of any sort are a myth. The only rights you have are privileges given out by governments. That is why we want to live under a government that guarantees as much personal freedom as is possible."

Corvis: "The projection of one's own fears and hates onto one's enemy—from a person or an entire country— seems frighteningly common in history and now. Does the need for an 'enemy' so weigh on society that it will always create scapegoats?"

Gilmore: "Humans have always done it and always will. As a species we are xenophobic and quick to externalize our shortcomings and project them on some adversary, whether it is deserved or not. With that always in mind, we Satanists walk carefully, seeing our life journey as if we are in a zoo filled with rabid primates. We never take respect, awareness, and justice to be the norm. Ignorance, maliciousness, pettiness, and bigotry are the main behaviors we can see—watch the news from around the globe for proof. Being pragmatic, Satanists never forget the true nature of mankind and thus take great care in any exchanges with other people. We never expect them to behave with the integrity and honesty that we bring to the table, but we are delighted when we do find such unique experiences. This is also why we have adopted Satan, the ultimate adversary and scapegoat, as our symbol for we have found it to be a means for moving beyond our species' paranoid self-righteousness."

Corvis: "'The Devil' exists in us all; some chose to embrace that part of them honestly. Do you find it ironic that some of the most outwardly extreme lifestyles are the most inwardly balanced?"

Gilmore: "If you mean that 'The Devil' is that driving 'black flame' of self-determination and embracing of carnality, then no I don't think that everyone shares that. I think that many people actively reject this 'Luciferian' responsibility because they at heart have no sense of self. They look outwards to find something that will define them, whether it be a God, a dictator, or an ideology. So there is no 'Devil' within them to be embraced. We Satanists are almost like a different animal when compared to that kind of person. And amongst Satanists, those who have what the herd might see as 'extreme lifestyles,' of course they are inwardly balanced as only a person with a surety about their own individuality can make such a lifestyle function on a long term basis. The Satanist being certain of his self, being his own God, lives life with passion, and can balance a broad range of experience."

Corvis: "How would you respond to the question I get asked, "If Satanism already existed in a secular humanistic way, via Thomas Paine, Nietzsche, Jung and Machiavelli, then what makes LaVey and his Church so special?"

Gilmore: "Satanism only existed as a literary fiction before Anton Szandor LaVey founded the Church of Satan. People like Paine, Nietzsche, Blake, Machiavelli, and Rand are precursors and inspirations, but they didn't see themselves as Satanists. So, the unique achievement of LaVey was that he saw something in common between certain ideas espoused by these and other supporters of individual sovereignty, and he saw that the best metaphor to unite these threads was that of Satan as the avatar of personal liberty. He created the Church of Satan to be the first organized body in history to promote this philosophy, and brazenly called it a church. That is certainly of historical significance."

Corvis: "The quest for power, especially for the individual, is considered by some to be an antiquated and barbaric relic of civilization. It is considered evil for someone or especially a group to advocate its pursuit-not to mention when it uses the trappings we enjoy. How would you explain our position to the skeptic in a positive, healthy way?"

Gilmore: "I think it can be practically impossible to explain to certain human types that there really are individuals who can handle personal power, as many people can barely control themselves and must be treated by our societies and laws as if they were horses in bridles. Since they don't feel that they'd 'behave' were it not for drastic societal consequences to keep them in line, they may never be able to grasp that for Satanists it is natural to command oneself. We don't require an external authority to force us to act in a civilized manner. It really comes down once again to the fact that there are different human types.

"We Satanists belong to the subset of our species that can regulate our personal behavior as we see it being beneficial for getting the most out of the one life we have. Other folks who require an authority to force them to 'play nice' will never grasp this concept—it is alien to their nature. They cannot see that people like us could exist. Likewise, we must not project upon them the ability to be productive and responsible on their own. That is a mistake some humanists make, thinking that there is some basic shared 'good' in all people who would act decently if given the chance. Satanists know that this is idealistic nonsense, and that most people tend to behave despicably when not being monitored, as they hope that they will not have to suffer any consequences for their actions. Satanists bravely take the position that we are fully responsible for all of our actions, for our successes and failures, and we accept that there will be consequences for every action that we take. That is not a widespread stance.

"For the average person I might encounter, I liken Satanists to the Addams family. Our aesthetics might be seen by them as 'creepy, kooky, mysterious, and spooky,' but they have nothing to fear from us as we just want to be left on our own, to pursue our creative goals and spend time with people whom we cherish. We aren't out to convert anyone, and we know that one has to be born into our 'family' to truly be one of us."

Blanche Barton, author of the book *The Church Of Satan,* writes: "People, even those who call themselves 'practitioners of the Old Religion,' can't conceive of a philosophy beyond Christianity, beyond good against evil. It's like 'worshipping the Devil.' We don't worship Satan; we worship ourselves using the metaphorical representation of the qualities of Satan. Satan *is* the name used in the Judeo-Christian tradition for that force of individuality and pride within us. But the force itself has been called by many names. We embrace Christian myths of Satan and Lucifer, along with Satanic renderings in Greek, Roman, Islamic, Sumerian, Syrian, Phrygian, Egyptian, Chinese, or Hindu mythologies, to name but a few. We are not limited to one deity, but encompass all the expressions of the accuser or the one who advocates free thought and rational alternatives by whatever name he is called in a particular time and land. It so happens that we are living in a culture that is predominantly Judeo-Christian, so we emphasize Satan.

If we were living in ancient Roman times, the central figure and the title of our religion would perhaps be different. But the name would be expressing and communicating the same thing. It's all context."

Satan is an archetype, which personifies in our minds the aspects we identify with—the rebel that we ourselves are. We each are the Godhead 'Satan' ourselves. It is frustrating to hear of other so-called Satanists who follow ninety-percent of LaVey's work, then add the contrary opinion that Satan is their controlling deity. To do so would be totally against the non-theistic principals of this path.

Yes, there are forces of magic and energy in our midst, but we direct our wills with it, not by its choosing or direction but by our own. The aspects taken from works of LaVey in his writings and from the Church of Satan are geared towards the truths behind the doctrine established during the advent of The Holy Roman Empire, when the masses were expected to either follow one school of belief or be killed.

The following Statements are referenced from the Church of Satan official website:

The Nine Satanic Statements

1. Satan represents indulgence instead of abstinence!
2. Satan represents vital existence instead of spiritual pipe dreams!
3. Satan represents undefiled wisdom instead of hypocritical self-deceit!
4. Satan represents kindness to those who deserve it instead of love wasted on ingrates!
5. Satan represents vengeance instead of turning the other cheek!
6. Satan represents responsibility to the responsible, instead of concern for psychic vampires!
7. Satan represents man as just another animal, sometimes better, more often worse than those that walk on all-fours, who, because of his "divine spiritual and intellectual development," has become the most vicious animal of all!
8. Satan represents all of the so-called sins, as they all lead to physical, mental, or emotional gratification!
9. Satan has been the best friend the Church has ever had, as He has kept it in business all these years!

Next we see the decree by Satanists on how to behave properly without the fears of eternal punishment, but rather through a humanistic and quite logical system of common sense and respect.

The Eleven Satanic Rules of the Earth

1. Do not give opinions or advice unless you are asked.
2. Do not tell your troubles to others unless you are sure they want to hear them.
3. When in another's lair, show him respect or else do not go there.
4. If a guest in your lair annoys you, treat him cruelly and without mercy.
5. Do not make sexual advances unless you are given the mating signal.
6. Do not take that which does not belong to you unless it is a burden to the other person and he cries out to be relieved.
7. Acknowledge the power of magic if you have employed it successfully to obtain your desires. If you deny the power of magic after having called upon it with success, you will lose all you have obtained.
8. Do not complain about anything to which you need not subject yourself.
9. Do not harm little children.
10. Do not kill non-human animals unless you are attacked or for your food.
11. When walking in open territory, bother no one. If someone bothers you, ask him to stop. If he does not stop, destroy him.

Satan's Child

The above is quite unlike Shaun Sellers, nicknamed 'Satan's Child.' His story was the focus of episode one of *Inside the Criminal Mind*, a series which airs on Discovery Health channel which was originally created for CBS. This documentary spoke about a killer who, in 1985, performed Satanic Rituals, and claimed to have invoked demons to inhabit his body. He liked the power and fear it gave him to be the occult student in high school and the reactions from people while he carried a *Satanic Bible*. I wonder if he ever read it. If he had, he may not have killed his parents or any animals. Unfortunately, neither the show nor the judges bothered to get the facts from the author/founder of Satanism, who was very vocal about what Satanism is and isn't. Seeing as how this show aired on September thirteenth of 2004, it is proof that the mainstream media wishes to continue to propagate myths and lies in reference to LaVey's works.

Sellers was diagnosed with Multiple Personality Disorder (MPD), whereby one of his personalities was a killer, and the other side of him was a Born Again Christian, (this revelation came about while in prison). By pretending to be saved (as argued by some psychologists during the trial), he attempted to reduce his death sentence to life in prison. Severe trauma as a child, and sexual abuse was alleged. This might be true, but either way, he was disturbed. It is obvious at this point that he forwent the clause in Satanism about "Responsibility for the responsible." Most around him say he was a psychotic, posing as if he suffered from MPD. Lack of empathy is a common trait in Devil worshippers who block their horrific actions, whereas true Satanists are elitist, who attempt to find their faults critically, realistically and systematically, eliminating mental problems to become their own stylized 'perfect' God.

Ironically, I was reading *The Church of Satan* by Blanche Barton during the airing of the show with Sellers, and was reminded of LaVey's opinion on why people equate Satanism to the crazy antics of deranged killers. He was quite understandably upset when people talked about killings committed by someone owning a *Satanic Bible*. If one were to look on page 89, LaVey wrote in plain and direct English, "Under NO circumstances would a Satanist sacrifice any animal or baby!... The purest form of carnal existence reposes in the bodies of animals and human children who have not grown old enough to deny themselves their natural desires... A Satanist holds these things in high regard..." LaVey was the father of three children and owned a great deal of pets, himself being one of this country's foremost animal rights activists. As to why the media and the brainwashed believe such charges his retort was, "Can't people read? Of course, I know the answer. There are just too many people making money off purposefully not understanding."

The Perfection of The Self

From time to time people make mistakes. However, the elitist that a Satanist is by their very nature often needs reminded on what not to do and why, to ensure perfection of the self to the best of our abilities. Thus the "Sins" were created by The Church of Satan, as follows:

The Nine Satanic Sins

1. **Stupidity**—The top of the list for Satanic Sins. The Cardinal Sin of Satanism. It's too bad that stupidity isn't painful. Ignorance is one thing, but our society thrives increasingly on stupidity. It depends on people going along with whatever they are told. The media promotes a cultivated stupidity as a posture that is not only acceptable but laudable. Satanists must learn to see through the tricks and cannot afford to be stupid.

2. **Pretentiousness**—Empty posturing can be most irritating and isn't applying the cardinal rules of Lesser Magic. On equal footing with stupidity for what keeps the money in circulation these days. Everyone's made to feel like a big shot, whether they can come up with the goods or not.

3. **Solipsism**—Can be very dangerous for Satanists. Projecting your reactions, responses and sensibilities onto someone who is probably far less attuned than you are. It is the mistake of expecting people to give you the same consideration, courtesy and respect that you naturally give them. They won't. Instead, Satanists must strive to apply the dictum of "Do unto others as they do unto you." It's work for most of us and requires constant vigilance lest you slip into a comfortable illusion of everyone being like you. As has been said, certain utopias would be ideal in a nation of philosophers, but unfortunately (or perhaps fortunately, from a Machiavellian standpoint) we are far from that point.

4. **Self-deceit**—It's in the "Nine Satanic Statements" but deserves to be repeated here. Another cardinal sin. We must not pay homage to

any of the sacred cows presented to us, including the roles we are expected to play ourselves. The only time self-deceit should be entered into is when it's fun, and with awareness. But then, it's not self-deceit!

5. **Herd Conformity**—That's obvious from a Satanic stance. It's all right to conform to a person's wishes, if it ultimately benefits you. But only fools follow along with the herd, letting an impersonal entity dictate to fall to you. The key is to choose a master wisely instead of being enslaved by the whims of the many.

6. **Lack of Perspective**—Again, this one can lead to a lot of pain for a Satanist. You must never lose sight of who and what you are, and what a threat you can be, by your very existence. We are making history right now, every day. Always keep the wider historical and social picture in mind. That is an important key to both Lesser and Greater Magic. See the patterns and fit things together as you want the pieces into place. Do not be swayed by herd constraints—know that you are working on another level entirely from the rest of the world.

7. **Forgetfulness of Past Orthodoxies**—Be aware that this is one of the keys to brainwashing people into accepting something new and different, when in reality it's something that was once widely accepted but is now presented in a new package. We are expected to rave about the genius of the creator and forget the original. This makes for a disposable society.

8. **Counterproductive Pride**—That first word is important. Pride is great up to the point you begin to throw out the baby with the bathwater. The rule of Satanism is: if it works for you, great. When it stops working for you, when you've painted yourself into a corner and the only way out is to say, I'm sorry, I made a mistake, I wish we could compromise somehow, then do it.

9. **Lack of Aesthetics**—This is the physical application of the Balance Factor. Aesthetics is important in Lesser Magic and should be

cultivated. It is obvious that no one can collect any money off classical standards of beauty and form most of the time so they are discouraged in a consumer society, but an eye for beauty, for balance, is an essential Satanic tool and must be applied for greatest magical effectiveness. It's not what's supposed to be pleasing—it's what is. Aesthetics is a personal thing, reflective of one's own nature, but there are universally pleasing and harmonious configurations that should not be denied.

The sins are not doing this lest you be punished, unless of course the punishment is your own losses through your own choices in life. Every action has a reaction, including lack of action.

Responsibility and the Malignment of Character

In the architecture and landscape of the world of how people are perceived, we are placed upon gleaming pedestals or cast out among the rubble and ruin not by the thoughts of others, but by our own actions. Mere words of others are of no consequence and have no true worth by those who accept us for who we really are. Persons who are swayed to and fro in their ideas of who are good and bad or right and wrong just by others stories and opinions in conversation are dimwitted and scant attention should be paid to them. For those who know you despite all whispered things, will judge you by words they themselves hear. To those who misjudge you unfairly, let them say what they will. A poor reputation by another's word alone dies quickly if there are no actions or evidence to support it. Lies and truths speak for themselves. The memory of most is thankfully short, and in most cases damage is minimal. Gossip is usually just that, consider the source and weigh it for the truth it contains.

That having been said, take responsibility if you are deserving of slander. People, who commit felonious activities, cheat on their spouses or excessively lie; panic and backpedal when they are exposed to the public eye. Those most fearful of their 'ruined reputation' are deservedly anxious and paranoid. Had they concerned themselves with what lies or truths to the audience would lead to, they might have conducted themselves better in the first place. For all things there are ramifications, and do not ever expect those you have wronged to lie still. Retribution is either swift or lengthy in coming. To avoid this, consider the fact that when dealing with other people it always requires some level of diplomacy. Karma, in this case, is simply cause and effect, a mere chain reaction leading to poetic justice. If you find it necessary to subvert and lie, do so with meticulous detail. If you cannot accomplish this then live by the following advice:

> *"Do not complain about that which*
> *you need not subject yourself to."*
> —Anton LaVey

The core of Satanism is not in responsibility, but deeper. It is pride and allowing success or failure to be attributed to oneself. We of the left hand path never expect anyone to shoulder our burdens or fuss when another is unable to assist us in a given task. Accept the problem as your own and be courteous to those who have helped you. A true friendship—with no strings attached—is a rarity. Any sense of pity or care taking, let alone whining about the lack thereof is totally disgusting, humiliating, and proves the complainer is not worthy of a shred of respect. Anton LaVey wrote, "Nobody gives a shit about anyone else's grievances. When one caterwauls his troubles to another, it simply weakens the complainer in the listener's eyes."

When someone's life has taken a severe plunge into a downward spiral, it is not your job to give advice, give financial help or anything that does not benefit you. Family loyalty often blurs into feelings of guilt leaving the real victim feeling as if they have been used beyond necessity simply due to the fact you 'had to.' Assist others because it makes you look good, if the time is unimportant to you, if you feel it may be appreciated and someday returned. Only you know who will and will not fall into what category. Those who fail to live thier lives without taking care of themselves fully, those who would use you out of laziness if you let them, are "psychic vampires." LaVey coined this term in the late 60s, not to be confused with the second use of psychic vampirism in the chapter "Vampires Among Us."

Why We Need To Be Elitists

Mediocrity and regrets are our only Hell, and accepting our awful fate is our own stupidity. Heaven is always within our grasp one needs just to reach higher for the next prize. Being around other like-minded people who seek better in life will encourages all to strive for more, whether it be of riches, companionship (quality, looks and or intellect), each acquisitions knocked off the list will only encourage the individual to strive for more. However, I do not mean to say, 'Keep up with the Jones.' Attempting to be what everyone else is shows ignorance of an enormous magnitude, for no two persons have the same income, wants, or outgoing expenses. Do live a life balanced. Common sense, apposed to blind greed that leads to stupid errors, often will cost everything gained. Blind ego is equal to blind stupidity.

Proud and rightly so are the few who struggle as elitist, especially those who do so for their legacy, children. How pathetic is it that poor people from elsewhere gaining so much when we who dwell here do nothing more than sit around daydreaming about being 'somebody?' Pride is not a sin, nor envy. Elitists know that it is the lack of wants that is the root of laziness, stagnation, and failure. One must take pride in themselves, or be guilty or another sin—Sloth. Not having pride in ones appearance prevents friends and employers from wanting you around! The consequences of that should be obvious! Pride makes us want better than the Jones's, if we are clever enough to amass wealth or at least appear well off enough to look worthy of having others around us.

Envy of others spurs us to acquire that which we desire; else we never get better quality cars, furnishings or the ability to properly entertain our friends or ourselves. How is that evil? Living in a hovel as a monk is fine and dandy if your friends are rodents and cockroaches! If all our natural instincts lead to 'sins' then at least you can enjoy your life as it is in the here and now. The desire to be intellectual promotes education, which includes home schooling. We know what's best for us and we should make that clear in teaching our own young. Taking the time to educate open minds to the truths around us is a Left Hand Path ideal as well. Who wants to be surrounded by idiots? Intelligent people think for themselves and so they soon seek answers outside the box and question the rule makers. This is the common denominator between Satanists and Goths, the mindset mixture of cynicism and intellect.

The path of a true follower of Anton LaVey's Satanism is a lonely place at times. It is a place of detached aloofness, with few in our ranks of fellow human beings that maintain the opinion and constant mentality of being superior in so many aspects. Not many realize the effort it takes to remain vigilant on the faults of ourselves. One must perpetually remind oneself of the belief system they have pledged to, a quality lacking in weak-minded people. The cruelest taskmaster is always the self, ask any dedicated students of the arts.

It is out of our unique natures, the self awareness and of being 'born' into it by one day waking up into the harsh world and seeing everything as it really is without illusions. To see the faults and frailties of our fellow man and ourselves, humanity's delusions and emotional weakness of mass mind control through politics, the pious and melodramatics of people in our daily life and noticing that the masses are quite comfortable wallowing in self pity. If not, they would rectify the situation. Too many people are too fearful to break away from the mental security of routine.

The normalcy of daily life is a comfort zone, and facing the actions required to push themselves is difficult if not impossible. This is the psychology factor in societies conditioning that Nietzsche hated about mediocrity. "A human being who strives for something great considers everyone he meets on his way either a means or a delay and an obstacle. Or a temporary resting place." —*Fredrich Nietzsche,* Beyond Good and Evil

Jung talked about the Shadow and Archetypes as figures to hold up as a mirror in order to shed light hidden parts of us to face without fear. Thinkers holding truths in such Humanist philosophies made up of harsh logic consisted of a lot of Anton LaVey's approach to his religion. Exactly how to use logic above "morality," which is a belief based concept, for governing large amounts of people properly and how exist in society filled with real Satanic practitioners is raised often.

Due to the fact that Satanism is more of a solitary path, how can it be made useful as a large-scale concept?

The following is an article written by High Priest Gilmore on LaVey's *Lex Talionis*, from the Official Church of Satan, well covering this thought.

Lex Talionis

"The Church of Satan pursues a five point plan to move society in directions that are considered to be beneficial to Satanists. The first point is the avocation of general recognition and acceptance of stratification, which is no less than the elimination of egalitarianism wherever it has taken root. Mediocrity shall be identified and despised. The stupid should suffer for their behavior. The truly beautiful and magnificent are to be cherished. Each individual must choose for himself his own aesthetic standards, but we think that there are certain elements of achievement that are undeniable, even if they are not satisfying to everyone. For example, one cannot deny the undeniable, even if they are not satisfying to everyone. For example, one cannot deny the superior accomplishment inherent in a Beethoven symphony, a Michelangelo sculpture, a DaVinci painting, or a Shakespeare play. Many Satanists are working to create their own citadels of excellence outside of the cultural mainstream and have preserved the worthy from the past and continue to create new works of power to be unleashed to those who will be appreciative.

"The second point is the enforcement of strict taxation of all churches. This would remove the government sanction of religion and force these parasites to live off of their own members alone, and if they can't, then they will perish as they should. The Church of Satan has never pursued tax-exempt status and challenges all the rest of the world's churches to stand on their own feet. Let us expose the vampiric nature of the organized religions and see if they can withstand the light of day.

"Third, we call for the re-establishment of *Lex Talionis* throughout human society. The Judeo-Christian tradition which exists secularly under the guise of liberal humanism has exalted the criminal over the victim, taking responsibility away from the wrong-doer with their doctrine of forgiveness. Such thinking is a disgrace towards the ideal of justice. This must stop! Individuals must be held accountable for the consequences of their actions, and not be allowed to scapegoat society, history, or other supposed "outside" influences. It should come as no surprise that many Satanists are part of law enforcement agencies, and a large number of people throughout this and other criminal justice systems who fully agree with Satanic philosophy on this point. If the law is not being enforced, Satanists advocate the practice of seeking personal justice, but you are warned to be fully aware of the consequences of such actions in today's corrupt society. With the present state of affairs, the outcry may yet come to welcome justice back to stay.

"Fourth, Satanists advocate a new industry, the development and promotion of artificial human companions. These humanoids will be constructed to be as realistic as possible, and available to anyone who can afford one. Recognizing that the human animal often raises himself up through the degeneration of another, this would provide a safe outlet for such behavior. Have the lover of your dreams, regardless of your own prowess; every man a king who can purchase his own subject; or contrariwise, buy the master you wish to serve. Freedom of choice to satisfy your most secret desires with no-one to be bothered is now at hand. What could be better for blowing-off the tension that exists throughout our society, and promoting healthier interaction among true humans?

"Finally we advocate the construction of total environments, technologically up-to-date but theatrically convincing, to be literal pleasure domes and places of amusement and delight. We have seen the beginnings in some of the major theme parks, but let us take them on to the heights depicted in films like *Westworld*. Here you will be able to indulge in whatever environment you can imagine. Re-creation of past history would not only be ripe for these constructions, but science fiction and fantasy will provide fertile sources for many of these playgrounds. Even now such projects are gearing up.

"The first theory is put into place by people more often than they might realize, from private schools or home schooling to promote children above the mediocre standards of public education."

Interestingly enough 'The Real Doll' (an anatomically correct sex toy mannequin made of latex and real human hair), 'Data' from *Star Trek: The Next Generation*, and films from *Terminator* to *Bicentennial Man* have clearly proven man's desire for companionship created by his own hand, much like Mary Shelly's *Frankenstein* during the Gothic period. What was once considered macabre and blasphemous is now commonly viewed as fiction or progressive science for the convenience of modern man. The controlled environment has been in development for some time, albeit available to the wealthy alone.

I discussed *Lex Talionis*, modern Satanism, and the beginnings of a popular Satanism magazine called *Not Like Most* with MAGISTER MATT PARADISE, publisher. He also heads Purging Talon, a video/DVD production company.

Corvis: "How in 30 years is it that we are still termed "devil worshipers who sacrifice children" when proof exists to the contrary?"
Magister Paradise: "If you are referring to the Church of Satan, the organization has been around for almost 40 years (since 1966).

"Truth be known, I really don't hear much of this accusation in modern day, and particularly when compared to the 1980s 'Satanic Panic' era. If a minority of folks are still dredging up tabloid news and outdated fundamentalist Christian propaganda, then perhaps their adherence to belief denies even the fact that the FBI debunked all of the 'Satanic Ritual Abuse' nonsense in the early 1990s. Belief is powerful in that weak-minded people find a false sense of empowerment through avoiding the facts and putting their unquestioned trust in something outside of themselves. And this extends beyond conventional religion, reaching into other areas of culture such as politics, pop culture, sex, ethics, etc.

"Some of these same weak-minded individuals, by having no real personal power in their lives, find it necessary to invent an enemy to battle against, fulfilling a sense of purpose that they cannot (or will not) achieve in their real lives. Perhaps, their idea of 'Satan' serves that purpose — certainly not a new observation as Dr. LaVey covered some of this in The Satanic Bible. And if they have convinced themselves so thoroughly that we, as agents of the Devil, simply must fit the image of what they need us to be, then the illusion might feel a bit more grounded by having a less figurative representation to rail against. Belief is the negation of fact. Moreover, the believer must shut out all reason and evidence to keep the illusion of belief alive. Otherwise, it's back to having to face the real world and the reality of carnal existence—a scary proposition for the inept, the lazy, or the stupid. All advancement in cultural evolution throughout world history has occurred in opposition to spiritual belief systems. Conversely, all obstacles in the way of this advancement have, at their core, the influence of these same belief systems behind them."

Corvis: "Do you feel the principles of Satanism are timeless and flexible enough to withstand evolution of societies change?"
Magister Paradise: "Satanists (and, hence, Satanism) will always exist. In fact, by other names or no name at all, Satanism has been an operative force throughout human history—because it is an eternal reminder that existence is purely carnal. It is a fact that the laws of Nature do not require approval; they operate regardless of how they are perceived. Satanists recognize this fact, unfettered by pipe-dreams of how things 'should be.' Therefore, the caprice and timeliness of a society's views are inconsequential. Nature is not listening, nor is any sort of 'God.' Satanic forces already rule the world. Only time and intelligence will see whether or not people become tired of their distractions and fantasies, and acknowledge what remains once belief is abandoned. If not, then we as Satanists will proceed as we always have—ever forward, and to live our lives to their fullest."

Corvis: "Can *Lex Talionis* be slowly worked into the mainstream despite people's fear and misconceptions of Satanism?"

Matt Paradise
Photo courtesy of Purging Talon

Magister Paradise: "*Lex Talionis* isn't exactly a foreign concept for people. When the attacks on 9/11 occurred in the United States, the majority of American were not crying out for forgiveness — they were wanting justice. Whether or not people get over their misconceptions of Satanism isn't reliant upon formally accepting Lex Talionis because the latter is already built into our carnal natures. For the herd, they are allowed to be perceived as separate issues. However, those who are able to look beyond belief and investigate this concept will find that it is nothing new, that it has been with us for millennia, and that Satanism is its primary champion in modern times. But, since the 'mainstream' is comprised of folks on various levels of learning and ability to learn, the outcomes will vary."

Corvis: "Please tell my readers about your publication, *Not Like Most,* its background, and your reason for publishing it."
Magister Paradise: "*Not Like Most* was first published in 1995 and was, initially, a vehicle for my official media representation for the Church of Satan. As an Agent and a writer, I put my strengths where they belonged. Since, *NLM* is now on its 15th issue and is considered by many to be one of the most respected and well-received publications on Satanism."

Baphomet

Baphomet, described as a monstrous head, a demon in the form of a goat, a figure with the head of a goat and the body of a man, was thought to symbolize the burden of matter from which arose the repentance for sin. The human hands formed a sign of esotericism to impress mystery upon the initiates and represented the sanctity of labor; two lunar crescents, the upper being white and the lower black, represented good and evil, mercy and justice. The lower part of the goat's body was veiled but expressed the mysteries, the universal generation is symbolized by the phallus. The goat's female breasts were the symbols of maternity, toil, and redemption.

Baphomet was affiliated with many great occultists and organizations over the centuries; The Knights' Templar, Levi, Crowley, and LaVey to name a few. Each person has his or her own personal opinion of what Baphomet represented. The Knights of the Templar looked upon the skull of Baphomet as being symbolic of personal wealth, and fertility, and many were charged with heresy for worshipping this idol.

Other than the goat's skull within the inverted pentagram, the other most common depiction of Baphomet is the illustration of the goat-headed man perching on a platform. This illustration was given to the world by the classical occultist, Eliphas Levi, and it first appeared in his work *Rituel Et Dogme De La Haute Magie*. Levi believed that Baphomet was symbolic of the Astral Light, which has roots in primordial matter. Levi was also insistent that there was a correlation between Baphomet and Pan. According to Anton LaVey, Baphomet was one of the infernal names used in conjunction with the Enochian calls. LaVey believed that Baphomet was symbolic of indulgence.

Baphomet is a force which can be summoned by mages, but it cannot be easily controlled. Some groups of Witches invoke this being during Sabbats to strengthen the link between themselves and the weave of life.

Baphomet is pan genitor and pan phage, All-begetter and All-devourer. It is man, animal and plant. It is ever-changing, ever-growing and dying. It is mindless, only filled with a Dionysian will to grow, feed, mate, survive and die, again and again. It is filled with the ecstatic joy of life and death, and it exists inside every living being. The purpose for the invocations that the Witches & magicians do is to awaken this force and set it free.

The worship of Baphomet has survived since time immemorial. Baphomet was worshipped by the cult of Mendes in Egypt and the Bacchants of ancient Greece. The worship survived in some mystery cults during the Classic Period, and well into the Middle Ages. Some of the myths about Witches Sabbaths may well be distorted legends about the cult of Baphomet. The Knights Templar were accused of worshipping it (of course, it is hard not to name any perversion or heresy the Templars have not been accused for). Today magicians are actively interacting with Baphomet.

By invoking and worshipping Baphomet, one may gain insight into the secrets of life, and feel its power. Baphomet is the sum of all life, and knows all its secrets and desires. In the current Church of Satan, Baphomet is a symbol, but in other organizations, such as the Temple of Set and The First Church of Satan, both Satan and Baphomet take on the form of a dark god as well as a symbol of "self."

JOHN ALLEE, founder of The First Church of Satan relates his thoughts and ideals:

Corvis: "How did the First Church of Satan come about?"
John: "I started thinking about it back in the 80s. I founded the FCoS in 1994 to bring Satanism back to its roots when Anton LaVey started his church. This was in my mind and this was why I called it what I did, where I wanted it to be—where the magazine I had published, *Brimstone*, had been going. Lillee and I changed the scope of the *FCoS* in 2003—we opened it up as an educational and religious tolerance organization for Satanists of all beliefs, Pagans and others who wanted to talk and learn about the left hand path and the philosophy and beliefs of Satanism. I can tell you we have more members than ever. We are doing more offline events and more community oriented work. We are now on the path that I want to follow. I now can say I am proud of how far we have come. Often people will ask us—can Satanists and Pagans get along?

"Yes, there is often a problem, but it does not have to be that way. Satanists are as much to blame as the others. Wiccans often demonize Satanists so that they are seen as devil worshippers and can market themselves as the good guys. That is sad. Pagans often are misinformed that most Satanists do not even believe in the devil and go with the same pre-Christian roots that they do

"Witchcraft, remember, is the art of practicing magic and there are Christian Witches, Celtic Witches, Satanic Witches, Eclectic Witches. etc Paganism is earth-based spirituality. Witches have this as well no matter what path they follow, and Theistic Satanists definitely are earth based. Some Satanists will never fit in and be able to involve themselves with Pagan events. Devil worshippers or traditionalist and modern Satanists are perfect examples. Inverse Christianity has nothing to do with Paganism. Also, modern Satanists are mostly atheist or agnostic so again would not have a spirituality that similar to Pagans. The bottom line is that we need to find common ground. After 9/11, we should all be looking at our faiths and our communities and say that this can not happen. No religious group should feel so righteous that they feel justified in killing innocents because they have the only direct line to God. I think anyone with a brain understands just how dangerous this type of agenda can be."

Corvis: "Can you explain the combination of Satanism, Hermetic and the 'middle pillar approach' for my readers?"

John: "First off I want to explain what I am—Oh if I had a dollar for everyone who asks me if I am Pagan or Christian or if I have changed

John and Lilee Allee
Photo courtesy of First Church of Satan

my beliefs. I have been a Theistic Satanist as long as I can remember and remain one. I consider Theistic Satanists to be different from Traditional Satanists and similar to Dark Pagans. I am comfortable with the term Pagan as Satanism is often just seen as a philosophy, especially by the Modern Satanists. Moderns and Traditionalist are not Pagan. Theistic can be Pagan if we must use labels at all. I do not wish to use the term devil worshipper—as that is not what my faith or philosophy is about and it gives out the wrong message, Hermetic Philosophy is a philosophy of natural law that can be used in conjunction with any religion or no religion, and is a basis to understand magical workings as well as the way life works.

"Satanism, whether you believe in a Satan or not, is basically about learning about the self. It is about going inward and seeing the darkness in yourself. This is different than the right hand path which is about others, and community, the middle path is, in my opinion, taking the best from both sides, using the strength of yourself and applying it so you can function more effectively in the world I like Lillee's explanation of Satanism: She says, 'If you do not define Satanism by the Judeo-Christian construct but see it in the Vedic SAT (being) plus TAN (becoming), it is an interesting combination of the left and right hand path and a philosophy where you are your own devil's advocate in terms of when to use which—call it a study in self-control and self-exploration. We do not try to use fantasy or escapism to avoid talking about death or other serious and unpleasant things that happen. We embrace our shadow side as much as we do our light side. Light and dark are as natural and masculine and feminine. To deny either is to deny an important part of your life experience. We look at things from a Hermetic perspective and see science as working with religion... It really is a true acceptance of self.'

"I would have to say that the Allee Tradition is Witchcraft but it is also Satanism and Paganism combined. So this is a new form of Satanism. Other groups incorporate Satanism and the left hand path beliefs with a balanced approach. I think the reason is that this is the new generation of Satanism and we are getting away from the shock value and looking at the pure value of the philosophy and incorporating it into an earth-based religion."

Corvis: " Any connection currently with members of COS?"
John: "There is no connection. We certainly have friends who are *COS* members, and have members who are in the *COS* as well. The *COS* is all about philosophical Satanism and for modern Satanists. It is an exclusive organization. The *FCoS* is inclusive, and involves Satanists, Pagans, Witches and others."

Corvis: "Tell me about acceptance at PPD events and the Tolerance organizations you are a part of?"
John: "Lillee, as a Witch, has always been proud of what she is. She had always supported Pagan Pride. We felt that those Satanists who wish to identify as Pagans should be able to be a part of the Pagan community, and be accepted. The first step to acceptance is education. The fact that Lillee and I can find a middle path where we can work together is the

first way... to demonstrate that Satanists and Pagans can get along. Further, we then explain the differences between the left hand path and the right hand path without a bias for either side. In fact, we advocate for an understanding of both paths and philosophies.

"What we are doing has never been done before possibly, but we have found that people are listening and do understand it. We started what we call the SWitch project, a project designed to build bridges between Satanists and Pagans to find common ground."

Corvis: "Future plans for the Church?"
John: "To continue to grow, teach, holding workshops and talks and to continue the work with Lillee on religious tolerance. I hope to speak at more conferences and Pagan events. I hope to continue with the CD series and possibly move to video. I am still working on my books and I am still committed to taking Satanism out of being a fringe and unacceptable religion. I would like to be remembered for that. I now know better than anyone that you visualize the end result and not the means. I wanted to see the Church change and grow, but honestly would never have foreseen how this has been done in the last year and a half. However, there is still so much work to be done. I am enjoying where the Church is at right now, and we are taking our time as we continue to find another project or area to explore, we work to help others find that connection to themselves and within themselves."

When he was asked about the morbid trappings of Satanic ritual, LaVey explained that creating such an atmosphere depicts the sobering reality of our own finality. Coffins, dark clothes and black candles often unnerve people from outside of Satanism, Goth or Vampire subcultures. They don't love death anymore than do Christians who wear an agony stricken Jesus on a crucifix. Surprising to the mainstream, these groups all love their existence, with only a few random exceptions. Whereas some faiths worry about how to live now for a better afterlife, Satanists feel that deprives us of fully enjoying the time here on Earth. "We keep our death close to us... keep constant reminders of our own mortality around, *momentos mori,* to spur us to enjoy each moment as if it were our last. Truly like Satan, we find ourselves dismayed at the complexity and pain people purposely call into their lives." If we did not do so, we could not pursue our dreams and be remembered by our works for generations. Few have to ask, "Who is Mozart," or any other icon from any time period.

The use of magic and ritual is more concisely described in the chapter "Dark Spirituality," but logic is the balance sought by Satanists to counter satisfying our primal urges. That is where responsibility comes into play. The prideful misfit who creates his own world, rather than abide by foolish rules in order to fit in, echoes the logic of the members of the Church of Satan. They see beyond exact labels and stereotypes by being honest with themselves, and so do not fit in with most of society who think conformity is not only what has to be done, but is a safe mental haven.

Equally disturbing to me are people who wear a pentacle, ankh, or sigil of Baphomet and act as if they are a serious practicing Witch, Goth or Satanist when their only knowledge of these beliefs may be from *Charmed, Harry Potter, Edward Scissorhands,* or a seldom-opened copy of LaVey's Bible. Many of them have not even read the *Satanic Bible* let alone any of LaVey's other works. You can't say "I know the rule of three" or "I read the Satanic laws and statements," and expect me to believe you are more than a poser that lives for the new anti-social conformity that Wicca or Witchcraft, devil worshipping and Goth-punk seem to represent. It needs to be more than this is 'cool' and if you want to be 'in' with dark freaky people and accepted by them you have to do this, wear that. Herdism is for the weak willed and weak minded, disgusting to those of us who truly *are* more than the outer trappings we wear.

It is as if people are secure in talking about vampires, engrossed in the latest Rice novel, wanting to be dark and mysterious, playing with the thought of being one of the undead complete with fangs at the theater. Few live the role in their heads without making it obvious that they are nothing more than nut jobs. To immerse yourself in the dark culture because it is deep in your nature, to express the shadow self openly is quite unsettling to the rest of the world. Talk is cheap; action without substance is no better.

Show me that you celebrate the Sabbats, that you can write a thesis on why *Edward Scissorhands* or *The Crow* (any version) is Goth, other than their wardrobes, makeup, etc. and show by example how you live your daily life in either thought or actions as Satanic. Show me how you fight the status quo, stupid rules, how you fight conformity and herdism while improving your life for yourself by striving for the best in life for yourself and your loved ones. Then I will be proud to say, yes I believe you are a Goth, a Witch, or a Satanist.

Satanism is labeled a 'brutal' as well as a selfish philosophy. The philosophies of Satanism are beneficial in self-improvement and self-awareness without the denial of our needs and the useless burdens of guilt that not only harms the practitioner but those around us. The universe is not 'benevolent.' Take a hard look at the realities of natural disasters obliterating millions of lives, works of art, science and monuments of our peoples over the eons, and ask yourself if it's the premeditated act of nature against humanity. It is not. We simply live in a cause-and-effect world which Satanists view as neutral, beyond the concepts of vindictive acts of 'Mother Nature' or the 'Wrath of Gods.'

We are different; we are elite.
Welcome to the enlightenment.

THE MESSENGER
by Corvis Nocturnum

BONDAGE
KNOT FOR EVERYONE

"I wanted only to try to live in accord with the promptings which came from my true self. Why was that so very difficult?" —The Marquis De Sade

The Marquis de Sade

About the Marquis de Sade, everyone knows too much, and too little. Even during his own lifetime, the myth of Sade was growing, taking on a shape of its own, larger than his own life, so that he came to live not just behind the stone walls of the Bastille, but behind an equally impenetrable mask of false notions perpetuated by other people. In the end, he became a being not entirely of himself, but rather a kind of collaborative construction, a being of myth, a force in the consciousness of humanity, known by only one name: 'Sade."

Even stripped of exaggerations, Sade's real life was as dramatic and as tragic as a cautionary tale. There's much to the saying about truth being stranger than fiction, but the Marquis de Sade wrote, "Truth titillates the imagination far less than fiction." Certainly, Sade was in a position to speak knowledgeably about both imagination and titillation, although his ability to distinguish between truth and fiction is a little less apparent.

Donatien Alphonse François Comte de Sade was born into privileged French nobility in 1740. A spoiled child, he grew up on various country estates, including an ancient castle with a dank, miserable dungeon, which no doubt played a factor in his developing psyche. He was also the subject of a Catholic school education. Unlike the current Catholic school setup, in which youngsters are subjected to mostly mental abuse and molestation, the Jesuits of the day included public whippings as part of the daily routine. He often speculated that everyone indulged as he did, just more quietly. Writing later in life, he said, "So long as the laws remain such as they are today, employ some discretion: loud opinion forces us to do so; but in privacy and silence let us compensate ourselves for that cruel chastity we are obliged to display in public."

He was married (against his wishes) to a middle-class heiress for money, and caused scandals with prostitutes. He enjoyed orgies, blasphemy and subversion in equal measure.

Within months of his marriage, he was arrested for mixing those pleasures. Sade invited a prostitute over for what at first appeared to be the usual procedure, but quickly diverted from foreplay into... well, something else. According to the woman, Sade masturbated into a chalice, called God a "motherfucker" and inserted communion hosts into her "naughty bits," all the while screaming for God to strike him down if God was so tough.

Sade was sentenced to the first of what would be many stints in prison. After a few months, he was released to exile outside Paris, the equivalent of house arrest. Under close surveillance from the authorities, he returned to debauchery—albeit apparently without the aid of religious artifacts—and with his sister-in-law. This enraged his mother-in-law, who had him imprisoned under a *lettre de cachet* for 14 years until the Revolution freed him. To pass the time in prison, he secretly began scratching out writings, which he wisely concealed from his jailers.

The ex-marquis became a Revolutionary, miraculously escaping the guillotine during the Terror, only to be arrested later for publishing his erotic novels. He spent his final 12 years in the insane asylum at Charenton, where he caused yet another scandal by directing plays using inmates and professional actors. Ironically, his jailers practiced his ideas, and the asylum sold his writings in attempt to avoid bankruptcy. Sade died at the asylum in 1814, virtually in the arms of his teenage mistress.

De Sade didn't think he had done anything wrong. In a letter written from prison, he said, "Man's natural character is to imitate; that of the sensitive man is to resemble as closely as possible the person whom he loves. It is only by imitating the vices of others that I have earned my misfortunes." It's hard to imagine which "others" Sade could have been imitating.

Between his squalid surroundings and his even more squalid brain, the Marquis produced exactly the kind of writing you would expect. Horrific. His writing features the sum total of bad things that people can do to other people, including rape, necrophilia, oral sex, sodomy, incest, and gang bangs. Suffice to say, the Marquis, no matter how depraved, had hit upon a few gems of wisdom during his disturbed life. "Wolves which batten upon lambs, lambs consumed by wolves, the strong who immolate the weak, the weak victims of the strong: there you have Nature, there you have her intentions, there you have her scheme: a perpetual action and reaction, a host of vices, a host of virtues, in one word, a perfect equilibrium resulting from the equality of good and evil on earth."

Current Ties

Many of the activities that Sade preacticed are a part of the BDSM scene today, in one form or another, although some are avoided due to legal issues or personal conscience. Modern critics have rightly pointed out that Sade foreshadowed the age of psychoanalysis, identifying the power and the nature of the sexual obsessions that would later be more clinically obsessed over by Sigmund Freud. Ironically, it takes one mad man to understand another. Sade himself wrote, "lust is to the other passions what the nervous fluid is to life; it supports them all, lends strength to them all... ambition, cruelty, avarice, revenge, are all founded on lust."

Based on a decade of research, *The Marquis de Sade: A Life* by Neil Schaeffer reveals an astonishingly non-sadistic Sade, his capacity for deep romantic love, his inexhaustible charm, his delusional paranoia. And through a dazzling reading of Sade's novels, including the notorious masterpiece *120 Days of Sodom*, Schaeffer argues powerfully for Sade as one of the great literary imaginations of the eighteenth century. —*www.neilschaeffer.com/sade*

Other factors in the meantime have been part of the BDSM and Fetish lifestyle, such as psychologist John Norman from the 1960s, who wrote a fictional series starting the Gorean Society, which started the Master-Slave situation common today.

Media, such as the film *Eyes Wide Shut, The Story of O*, and *Nine and a Half Weeks*, portray elements of the BDSM lifestyle. Two films have been made about the life of DeSade: *Marquis,* which portrayed how society influenced his development, and *Quills,* which showed how a determined (or deranged) man can accomplish anything, despite the restraints put upon him by society. The theme of BDSM even made its way into the pilot of the comic-book-turned-television-show *Witchblade,* which had a character that was a BDSM clubber. The film *Exit to Eden* was a comedy about a Dom-Sub island getaway, which at least succeeded in exposing the subculture in a more positive way. In it, the creator of the resort explains that society's harsh views surrounding sex has, over the generations, created a situation where people can't release their feelings. When they do come out, it is without restraint.

Screw the Roses, Send Me the Thorns is possibly the most famous book on the subject, but *Different Loving* is the first and only mainstream book to explore and demystify the worlds of BDSM, sexual power relationships, and fetishism. Drawing on extensive scholarly research and interviews with hundreds of consenting adults, *Different Loving* has been called "the Bible of D&S" and has been critically acclaimed as a ground-breaking study into who the adherents are, what and why. To quote the book, "We start from the premise that sex for pleasure is a normal human drive and is acceptable when it brings pleasure to both partners. From this perspective, D&S is simply a 'different' kind of loving." —Brame, Brame, and Jacobs.

The book was selected by the *American Association of Sex Educators, Counselors and Therapists* (AASECT) as a top pick for their 1993 Christmas book list. *Playboy* has called it "A detailed, eye-opening account of the real sexual underground in America... a thorough and serious study." Over 300 D&Sers participated in this study, and roughly 90 interviews appear in it, with hundreds of quotations from books and articles by and about sadomasochists. Chapters present a wide range of opinions and practices from interviewees who self-identify as straight, gay, lesbian, bisexual, pansexual, top, bottom, sadist, masochist, dominant, submissive, master, mistress, slave, fetishist, leatherman or leatherwoman.

BDSM Terminology & Definitions

It is a very difficult task to find facts on the history of BDSM. Although one can find erotica from circa 1930s France, much of the discussion and interest centers around the "Old Guard," which most say is the basis of the scene today, along with the gay lifestyle. It appears the term BDSM did not appear until somewhere in the early 1990s, but the traditional terms for this acronym are as follows:

—Boston Dungeon Society: www.bdsbbs.com/define.html

Bondage & Discipline—Bondage is restricting someone's freedom of movement through either physical or mental restraint,whereas Discipline is the use of punishment or correction in response to certain behaviors. **Dominance & Submission**—The consensual exchange of personal power in which one person (the submissive) turns some level of control over to another (the dominant). **Sadomasochism**—The consensual and intentional infliction of pain, discomfort, or suffering by one person (the top) upon another (the bottom) for the mutual satisfaction of both parties.

The following is an introduction to the world of Dominance & Submission. It is a short explanation and a gathering of basics and safety tips for those who have only dreamed and fantasized, but never dared to take that first step.

BDSM—Umbrella term for activities of B&D, D&S, S&M (also an acronym for Boston Dungeon Society Member).

B&D—Bondage and Discipline. A subgroup within D&S which is largely involved in making the submissive physically helpless and applying stimuli which outside of a scene would be painful.

Blood Sports—A group of techniques in which the submissive's skin is broken and blood is allowed to escape. Since the advent of AIDS and the spread of hepatitis, interest in blood sports has declined and those who practice it have developed techniques to protect themselves. The most common blood sport is cutting. See Cutting.

Bondage—A group of techniques for rendering a submissive physically helpless. These include rope ties, handcuffs and manacles, wrapping and mummification. See B&D. See Mummification. See Decorative binding. See Immobilization.

Bottom—A submissive.

CBT—Cock and ball torture.

Cutting—A technique in which cuts are carefully made in the submissive's skin to produce an aesthetically pleasing pattern and stimulation to the submissive. The cuts are sometimes made into permanent markings by placing sterile foreign substances in them before they heal. See Blood sports.

Decorative Binding—Using rope or cord to compress or tie a portion of the body where struggle will not cause it to tighten or cut into the submissive. See Immobilization.

Discipline—The application of stimuli which, outside of a scene, would be considered painful. Common discipline techniques are whipping, spanking and strapping. See B&D.

Dominant—An individual who accepts the submissive's power and uses it for their mutual pleasure. See Sadist.

Edgeplay—These are particularly dangerous D&S that are looked upon with some trepidation. Because there is no formal 'ruling body' in D&S, what is called edgeplay is up to the individual. Therefore, something that to one person might be considered edgeplay might not be edgeplay to another.

Edgeplayer—A person takes part in edgeplay. Example: "The guy is a real edgeplayer; he's into heavy bloodsports and asphyxia."

Go Word—A signal by the submissive that everything is all right and you can continue with or increase the present level of stimulation. See Stop word See Slow word.

Golden Showers—A humiliation technique where the dominant urinates on the submissive. Consumption of the urine may be part of this scene.

Immobilization—Using rope or other bondage tools to render a submissive relatively helpless despite his or her struggles.

Masochism—The ability to derive pleasure from pain. Derives from the writings of Leopold von SacherMasoch. See S&M.

Panic Snap—A linking device used with cable and chain that allows two lengths to be disconnected even when there is tension in the system. A safety device.

S&M—Sadism and Masochism; A term often used to describe the D&S scene; however, it is falling into disrepute because it is both inaccurate (Dominants are not sadists.) and overly limited (All submissives are not masochists.). See Sadism. See Masochism.
Sadist—An individual who enjoys causing pain in a nonconsensual manner or regardless of the presence of absence of consent. Derives from the writings of the Marquis de Sade. See S&M.

Safe Word—A word or phrase which permits the submissive to withdraw consent and terminate the scene at any point without endangering the illusion that the dominant is in complete control.

Scat—A slang term for scatophilia, taking pleasure in playing with and sometimes eating feces. While this is occasionally used as a means of humiliation, it presents a relatively severe health risk, not limited to AIDS and hepatitis.

Slow Word—A signal by the submissive that things are getting too intense and you should change or decrease the stimulation. See Safe word. See Go word.

SAM—Smart Arsed Masochist. A pseudo submissive who attempts to control everything the dominant does. A term of contempt. Example: "She's cute and willing, but she's a real SAM; you will spend most of your time trying to keep her from telling you which whip to use and how to swing it." See 'Topping From the Bottom.'

Scene (The)—The gamut of D&S activities and people considered as a whole. Example: "The scene contains some of the nicest people I have ever met."

Scene (A)—An individual session of whatever duration where the participants are in their D&S roles. Example: "It was a tremendously hot scene last night when Master Jim waxed Lisa at The Vault."

Slave—Often used interchangeably with submissive. However, generally reflecting a more intense level of submission or non-sexual or sexual-plus submission. For example, a slave might be someone who remains in a 24-hour-per-day submission and cooks, cleans and, otherwise, takes care of a dominant's house. See 'Submissive.'

Strapple—An elongated paddle with a bit more flex so that is something intermediate between a strap and a paddle.

Submissive—An individual who gives up power in a D&S relationship for the mutual pleasure of those involved.

Suspension—A set of techniques for suspending a submissive using ropes, webbing or chain so that no part of the body touches the floor. This is a highly specialized technique and great care must be used to prevent damage.

SWitch (SWitchable)—A person who enjoys both the dominant and submissive roles. A sWitch may be dominant to one person and submissive with another or may be dominant or submissive with the same person at different times.

Top—A dominant.

Topping from the bottom—For a submissive to dictate the precise action in a scene. A term of contempt. Example: "She's cute and willing, but she's always topping from the bottom; you will spend most of your time trying to keep her from telling you which whip to use and how to swing it." See 'SAM'

TT—Tit torture. The term applies to both males and females.

Vanilla—Not in the scene. A term used to describe ordinary, conventional life both sexual and otherwise. While it can be used in a pejorative sense, it is more often used to distinguish between scene and non-scene activities and people.

Crossing Culture Boundaries

Not surprisingly, BDSM, Goth and Vampirism have common ties, partly for the sexual freedom and escapism associated with BDSM, and also due to the outcast stigma shared by each group. Following is an interview with a close friend of mine, CRYINGGYPSY about the overlap of Vampires and BDSM.

Corvis: "Here's something for everyone to think about... What do you consider vampyrism?"
CryingGypsie: "What does this girl consider Vampyrism... like any question you ask a hundred people and will get a hundred different answers but I guess I can give a shot. Most know me well and my passion for vampyrism and the occult. On a personal view, I see

vampyrism as a form of evolution or state of transcendence to everyday humanity. I mean if you see that mankind sees them as top of the food chain then why cannot there be those that human kind does not realize are predators for them. If you notice in the wild, most animals are aware of the dangers of life but go on with a daily living as if their predators did not exist. So is it possible for a predator of man to exist but they are not aware of.

"Most certainly, I agree that we have come a long way from simple superstitions, folklore and progressed greatly in science as well, but we cannot explain all truths in life. If we did why would we need religion or faith ? All follow their own truth in their own strange way.

"Many who know me would say I take on a lot of the traits and that I have a passion for vampires; but am I one of them? If you consider a bloodlust, and affinity with the darkness to define what a vampire is, then yes I am, but if one delves deep into the legends and lore's and occult books about vampires there is more to that restless spirit than a mere taste for blood or psychic energy... as for the fact that some have bad heartburn from garlic, those that I have met and known who either are or live as vampires actually love garlic. And they don't have heartburn. I just wouldn't stand downwind of them if I where you..."

Corvis: "Do you feel that it belongs as part of BDSM?"
CryingGypsie: "Yes and No, because all creatures in this world are so varied and different even within their own species that for some it seems like the 'horse and carriage' scenario in that they go together, but you will also have those vampires that love the taste of blood, but fall whimpering to the floor over a simple swat on the butt. While you have a masochist that loves being black and blue, but will faint at the mere sight of a paper cut."

Corvis: "With the ever-growing fascination with Pagan culture and religion, is it possible that vampyrism in the BDSM lifestyle may actually have a historical or factual basis?"
CryingGypsie: "If we where to go by the romantics of the modern day vampire that we see in movies and books then no...but if one were to

go by the occult myth and lore, then most definitely. Many look at Vlad Dracula as being the first vampire because of his grisly way of executions, which most people look upon with disgust, but if one were to talk to the people of his empire they would tell you he was a savior, for he delivered his people from the Turks. Then there are some interesting theories of where did the myths rise? For many

attribute them to things we didn't understand because mankind was not as advance in the sciences as they are today. But what of the theories of Lilith the first wife of Adam that is rumored to be the mother of demons and all such wicked creatures? What about the fall of Cain and the mark that God placed upon him so that all who look upon him know who he is? Could it be that mark was a thirst for blood? Could Lilith have given birth to a race of man that are the ultimate predators of their own species? Who knows, but many try to answer these questions and come up with many different answers. Each one different from the last, when we all must seek the truths that work for us."

Corvis: "What are your feelings about this lifestyle?"
CryingGypsie: "Hmmm ask my dark companions and they will tell you I am very much into the vampire lifestyle as well as BDSM. For me they go hand in hand because they both give me something that most religions don't give to me (at least) but may give to others. And that is the heightening of personal and spiritual awareness. Most have sub space but this girl experiences not sub space but raw and pure emotion that does not stem from what is happening without but the stretching of this spirits wings that are reaching into new realms for enlightenment."

Corvis: "It was enlightening to speak with you; thank you."
CryingGypsie: "Your welcome, Corvis. May all have a safe and joyous journey in the crazy thing we call life."

Dungeon Masters

BDSM has a concept whereby the submissive is truly in control through safe words, and in group situations there is a Dungeon Master who safeguards the area. Pain is a vehicle to mental euphoria, similar to the phenomenon called 'runner's high.' The release of endorphin's in the brain causes a euphoric feeling. Some have been known to cry during flogging, not in pain, but because conditioning does not give them the ability to do so normally. It can be a therapeutic experience, but should only be done with trusted people.

GRIFF is the head of a Munch group in my hometown who was very happy to explain his position at parties, and to dispel some of my own misconceptions.

Corvis: "What is the role of Dungeon Master?"
Griff: "The role of Dungeon Master is basically that to protect the people coming to the play parties, or to be a stand in for any activity that's going onto insure that the rules of the club are adhered to. It's basically to keep everybody safe. We're the security, walking around keep an eye on things to make sure things don't go to far and make sure nobody's breaking the rules. It's their job that no matter if it's an open door or locked door to enter and deal with the problem. If someone has a problem they don't take care of it themselves, they come see one of us. We stop unwanted guests, if someone is too drunk."

Corvis: "It's one of the common misconceptions that there is no safety in BDSM, that it's all abusive."
Griff: "Usually the DM knows everything that's going on in every situation, they know the people in charge and where everyone is at all times. If they hear a safe word, which is 'Red,' or something. If they hear that more than once from the same person, they know that means the scene has not stopped, or we go in to investigate the scene and put an end to it immediately."

Corvis: "Most popular misconception of all that bother people that

I encounter is the history of the Marquis De Sade, being so over the top, having done illegal and cruel things, how do you counter that as this being a healthy expression of the self?"

Griff: "The Marquis? Yeah, were talking ancient times back when they let the Spanish Inquisition go by, and then there are us...the misconception is that we beat people that don't want it. Were all adults over the age of 21, and we know what we want. We have a saying: sane, safe, and consensual. None of us are like Jeffery Dhamer, or Manson. Anything we do is asked for. We are a conscientious group some consider us kinky, fine. Some people think if you do anything other than missionary that is kinky."

Corvis: "What about safe sex? That is a big concern these days."
Griff: "It depends on the individuals, sex is sometimes not even involved in the scene, our lifestyle with some people is what builds up to sex. I mean, in Sub and Dom, they just get turned on by the power exchange in the fantasy of it. They get put into a situation where their wide open for anything and say, lets go have sex."

Corvis: "Out of all the subcultures I have interviewed, or read about, the people in them are more outwardly different, but you guys are the opposite seem normal in appearances. But the activities themselves are more extreme."
Griff: "You're talking more about the Marquis here though, if I'm with a woman who likes being beat, they assume the worst. It's something most people can't grasp. We have our own little things about us. You could walk up to any of us and ask, you wouldn't know if they were into BDSM. You have Executives, high power people they like to be dominated in a situation were they are actually still in control, but have a release not found in their daily life. There are groups, not like Whorehouses, put them in an aspect were you put several women that are in a big building or apartment complex, whose job it is to basically to beat, tie up, cliental who are in big business. They get so stressed out they have to run every little aspect of a company that they want to give up control. I our lifestyle the Submissive actually has all the

power, control when the scene continues, when its stops, what happens, period.

"Now in the clothing styles one concept is Doms wear black. Not true, some look like a rainbow. But we have two types of collars; we have a c collar that is shown outwardly an actual collar, and impressed collar. That can be a simple necklace that looks like a fashion statement. But it shows the Subs submission to their Dominate."

Corvis: "What's the difference between a Sub and a Slave?"
Griff: "That's kind of like asking what love is. It all depends on who you ask. There are cases in where a Slave has no say so; they want to make no decision making what so ever. They give it all up."

Corvis: "Do they have no safe words at all?"
Griff: "That would be up to the Master. In most cases the two have an actual contract, that states this is what they want to accomplish, the responsibility of both. Now, a Sub does have free will, in what happens to them"

Corvis: "The Sub is not in play 24-7."
Griff: "Right. A Slave is."

Corvis: "Why would someone give up their human urge for freedom?"
Griff: "Well, that depends on the type person. Some people were raised in a strict military environment where it was 'Yes Sir,' 'No Sir,' and their job was to be slave like as a child. They got used to it and want it in their adult life. Some people have it in their nature just to please another person, which they can give themselves to, no matter what."

Corvis: "It's a psychological security blanket, to be needed?"
Griff: "Yeah, being needed, being wanted. It's more the aspect of being somebody has taken them. They are put into humiliating situations they thrive on it, the being wanted."

Corvis: "What is the benefit in a positive way as opposed to the negative stereotype were used to thinking about?"

Griff: "The healthy aspect of this is that every body has a dark side. And some people are afraid of it. Our lifestyle is that if you ask somebody to do something like simulate rape fantasy, it is done safely in controlled environments. We have limits."

Corvis: "What psychological benefits are there they the participants get out of it?"

Griff: "It power exchange that they don't get normally, the feeling of control in their lives. They can feel safe; people get tested for disease and live out fantasies with somebody they trust."

Dominant & Submissive

To better understand exactly what is involved in a DS relationship, I spoke with HAWK AND DOVE, a couple who live the DS lifestyle. They graciously agreed to explain about their roles and how it works in their daily life.

Corvis: "Can you explain what the role is relationship-wise between master and slave to the people who may not understand the difference between that, and a normal dom/sub relationship that's a little more typical?"

Hawk: "All that… I was informed Saturday that the DS relationship most of us in the lifestyle seem to have apparently mimics the Amish and the way they are. The man holds the domination, the one that everybody goes to, he makes all the decisions, and pretty much determines what they're going to take care of. The woman would never raise her voice to him at all and their very submissive in there own right. So if you want to look at the DS relationship as far as submissive and dominant or master and slave, you can look into some other religions as well."

Corvis: "So instead of being something more...."
Hawk: "Dark and alluring?"

Corvis: "It's more traditional than what people would think. Its not so kinky that people would freak out."
Hawk: "Correct. If people would actually just sit back and look at it, and forget about what it's called, as far as the day to day DS aspects of it. In our respects, I make all the decisions; she makes none, in a perfect situation.

"There are times when she has to make decisions, and she finds it quite difficult in some respects, because that's not what she wants, she wants me to make them all. She doesn't want to make any decision, including what she wears. I could be at work and a crisis could flare up here and she has to make a decision."

Corvis: "Something else I was curious about when it comes to raising kids in a normal family life. How is it for the child?"
Hawk: "They learned the same thing you learned from your mom and dad, from your grandma and your grandpa. They learn manners, and how to be good, right from wrong."

Dove: "Especially morals and ethics. My daughter being 15 and having been sexually active, I'm more up front with her with what goes on. She asked me point blank 'why do you still call him sir?' I told her, 'Out of respect. Same as I've always taught you.' And she says, 'Yeah, but why?' And I did tell her, 'One, he is older than me and two, we do live an alternative lifestyle.' And she says, 'Oh, you're kinky.' And she knew more than I thought she knew and so we since have gone from there. There is still a lot she doesn't know and she won't know until she's 18, and she knows that."

Hawk: "There's a common code that you don't bring children. Minors into this alternative lifestyle. You can discuss things with them, but they do not actually see or actually know until the age of 18."

Dove: "DS is one thing, but kink is separate. And I'll explain the DS with her, but the kink is what we do in our bedroom and is none of her business."

Corvis: "That's understandable."

Dove: "Like with my boys. For all appearance, what they see in the house is what they saw when I was married to their dad. Except Promise made one observation. You're doing the same things you did with Dad. You're cooking the meals, you're taking care of the laundry, and you're taking care of us. Except instead of being called worthless, fat, lazy, lacking ambition, you're getting praised and rewarded for those things."

Corvis: "So instead of it being a servant, a downtrodden servant type role, its actually more respectful then what typical America's couple can degenerate into."

Hawk: "How long would you do something if you weren't getting respect or praise?"

Corvis: "Probably not at all, or you would be miserable and commit suicide."

Dove: "I once had a 'trainer,' and I kept doing the best I could to take care of him. And all I would hear about are the things I didn't do right or where I lacked and he was very into humiliation. So one day I asked him, 'Don't I do anything that pleases you? Isn't the laundry okay? Isn't my cooking okay?' And he looked at me and said, 'If you want praise, go to a fucking puppy show.' And I said, 'Okay, see ya.' Because that wasn't the type of relationship I wanted. That was the kind he wanted. He was coming from a military background and he thought you had to tear the spirit of the submissive first and build her the way you wanted. I wasn't going to survive that."

Corvis: "So clearly different types of people, personality wise, within this lifestyle that go from one extreme to the next?"

Dove: "You have Victorian, your Military, your Gorean, your Edwardian, your Old Guard, your different cultures within the subculture."

Hawk: "And we border on about four different types. We've been considered Edwardian, we've been considered Gorean; our beliefs and ethics are the same. Edwardian is an era piece or period, is it sixteenth or seventeenth century."

Dove: "There's a link at www.shadowfind.com. Look into that because he does run a BDSM bed and breakfast and it is Edwardian style and there's a lot of detail on that site about what goes on there. I don't have a lot of info on that."

Hawk: "Also, it makes Elizabethan."

Corvis: "So this mirrors the old Gothic, Renaissance period, mentality wise, the people involved in it Is there any sort of broad coverage between the people into the Renaissance reenactment?"

Hawk: "You will find that a lot of those people are into the BDSM lifestyle. They walk both paths because not only are only walking the actual lifestyle of the period, the eighteenth century, and the nineteenth century. Where the man walked forward, he was proud of his household, his household upheld him, his household was slightly behind him in the shadows, and that's pretty much the way the lifestyle is. It's more based on that type of arrangement."

Corvis: "So it wouldn't come as a surprise to people that get more immersed in the lifestyle that it's more akin to that period, alternative religions as well? A normal religion like Christianity or Judaism wouldn't be so open to this wide range?"

Hawk: "I wouldn't say that, because there are Christians who are into the BDSM lifestyle. And that goes off onto another tangent all onto itself.

They live a Christian life, their religion is Christian, so they worship that way, but they still have a BDSM kink, and it's all tied together."

Dove: "There's a group called CADS (Christianity and Domination Submission).

Hawk: "When you were saying BDSM and Renaissance, they get to live the lifestyle, they get to dress the period that went along with the lifestyle that their trying to live. They really thrive and get a thrill on it. For example, I was talking with a man on Saturday who gets a thrill out of seeing Amish women because they don't show a lot of skin. So when he sees an ankle come protruding out of one of their dresses, it gives him a thrill, he gets really excited, then he wants to see if they'll do anything else. Of course, it never happens, but he's always on the move to see. Everybody has their little idiosyncrasies about themselves, that turns them on, that doesn't necessary doesn't turn on somebody else. It could be as something as simple as seeing a ladies ankle."

Corvis: "And in some ways, psychologically speaking, we've become desensitized. The owner of a BDSM club told me, 'I don't care about seeing naked people anymore. People come in and out of here in all shapes and sizes, so nothing is that much of a thrill anymore.' He doesn't get into porn or anything, he just plays it for the guests. It takes actual emotional connection to his wife to get him excited. That shows a little bit of a link they're, whereas what you were talking about is somewhat of a mystery, unwrapping the package so to speak. It's the thrill of what might be there instead of just right away..."
Hawk: "But his submissive is totally different than that. She's kind of brassy; sometimes she's a little bit alluring on her dress. She's not quite what I would imagine if he's got the kink to unwrap the package. Why is he?"

Corvis: "Back to what you were saying about raising kids and society. Would society pretty much be shocked overall at this?"

Hawk: "I think if society knew what happened within a DS lifestyle with children, they might look back on his or her own and wonder why their kids don't have the manners or be as they could hold up to what these kids are who live in this lifestyle. They are held to a higher standard than what the average kid on the street is. I heard they took a poll and found out that the manners of the children today have degraded another 40% of what they were 10 years ago."

Dove: "I think more to the question would be, would society be shocked by it? If you put the label on their DS, if you said you were raising the kids DS, that's a scary concept for vanilla society, that itself would probably shock them. If you took that label or that title off and just said we're teaching our kids in a strict, moral environment, you get a lot further. Its all about how you choose to label and word things."

Corvis: "Labels are one of the things that do the opposite of what people in it are actually like. One of the major points of this whole book is to show people what this is what it is, instead of stereotyping a mental image that just clicks in your head. When I think of BDSM fetish, you know, conjure up dungeon beatings."

Dove: "Whips and chains and leather. A true scene starts that morning. If we know we're going to a play party, if he tells me we're going to a play party next week, I'm already planning my headspace. Okay, I need to make sure he has XYZ in his toy bag, I need to make sure we have our first aid kit with us, make sure I'm properly bathed and shaved in case he's going to do fire play or anything like that. I don't want body hair catching on fire. I have to make sure to have his glucose and his diabetes stuff so he can check his diabetes. There are a lot of things to consider. I have to make sure my hair is up, because the last thing you want when you're doing a heavy flogging scene is to have your hair get caught in the flogger, because it will stop the scene and the flow of the energy."

Hawk: "Make sure we have munchies for afterwards."

Dove: "Make sure we have snacks for afterwards."

Hawk: "She gets ravenous because she's spent all that energy, and she's on an endorphin and adrenaline rush. So she's flying nine feet high and your sitting here wondering why she's crashing; because she's hungry."

Dove: "Making sure that there's the necessary equipment for aftercare. It's different for everybody. For me, I want my blanket and I want some water to get some fluids back into me."

Corvis: "It's like a good workout in a way?"
Dove: "Exactly. It's like running a racehorse. When you're done with that racehorse, you want to clean and feed and brush down that horse. You know, make sure it's taken care of for the next race."

Corvis: "What is the biggest positive aspect for your relationship as a couple?"
Hawk: "Well, we haven't been able to play in quite awhile. It's been a real downer on our relationship. But when we do play, it brings us closer together."

Dove: "I think just the DS aspect of the relationship. When some couples get married, they just go, 'Okay, we're getting married.' There are really no defining thoughts, no real roles of who's going to do what in the marriage. In a DS relationship, your role is already defined as what he expects of me, what I expect of him and what are responsibilities are towards each other. Whereas, I know for myself, from my first marriage, I expected my husband to be the breadwinner and head of the household, to do certain things, and that I would caregiver and the nurturer and the wife and all that stuff. And he had different expectations from me. So sometimes you walk into marriage with false hopes and false expectations. As a DS, I know what he expects of me, it's been prenegotiated before he ever walked through that door. He knows what's expected of him. When I got into the relationship, I knew that he was going to take care of my health, medical needs, my food, my clothing and my shelter. I'm going to take care of his health by making sure he takes his meds, his diet is appropriate to his diabetes, his house is cared for and whatever errands he needs to be run or anything else."

Corvis: "It sounds a whole lot mentally more adjusted then the way a lot of other people live their lives."
Dove: "It really is. That's why after my marriage, I purposely sought a DS relationship. I wanted the structure, I wanted to know what was expected of me, what the rules were before I jump in and start playing the game. Unlike my first marriage, where I jumped in and for 13 years the rules changed all the time."

Corvis: "What draws someone in, like the term vanilla, who doesn't know anything their than the misconception?"
Hawk: "What I see in a restaurant or you go into a grocery store and these people are in a DS relationship and don't even though their in one. And if you watch people, you can find out whose dominant and who's submissive without them realizing it. They just take it up without thinking about it."

Dove: "You saw an example of it at work."

Hawk: "Yes, my boss' boss at work came in and pointed and said, 'You! In my office, right now.' And away she went, she put her head down and away she went. She just put her head down and that was it."

Corvis: "Is there any freedom for the submissive in this? Or do they have no freedom?"
Hawk: "Oh, the submissive has more freedom than the dominant does and don't you ever think that that's not the case. In actuality, the slave is the Dom and the Dom is the slave because the Dom constantly has to take care of their needs. Because the Dom has to have control of everything."

Corvis: "How do you handle being so decisive?"
Hawk: "I'm not sure that I always have it under control. I know that for a fact. Like when the finances get tight, I get hard to deal with, because I know its going out faster than I can replace it."

Dove: "But a good or well trained submissive will, instead of feeding into that, of getting pissed off and angry, always try to meet and or anticipate the master's need. Instead of ranting and raving about finical situations, I'll gently say something like, 'Well, what can we do to fix this? Or maybe we should put this on the backburner for awhile.' I just try to be more peaceful instead of feeding into it."
Hawk: "The dominate has dominated his own feelings, he takes in his own feelings before he takes in some else. That's something you strive for, that's perfection."

Dove: "We strive for spiritual perfection. Forget it, it's an unobtainable goal, it's the Holy Grail. However, we still strive to attain this goal."

Fetish

The difference between BDSM and fetish is that bondage, like flogging, is a form of fetish, whereas fetish is an attraction to something specific, such as feet, breast play/tying. It is more specific, one example of which would be latex. Both fetish and BD/SM offer an expression of our inner desires. Whether we openly admit to it or not, each of has a streak of both fetish and BD/SM deep inside. It is simply a matter of entering with an open mind and being willing to communicate our wants with a responsible, loving partner.

BIANCA BEAUCHAMP is from Montreal, Canada, and has graced the many fetish magazine covers of *Marquis, SkinTwo #48,* and *Whiplash #10.* She also has appeared in *Playboy Lingerie* (Oct-Dec 2004), on both its cover and inside pages. Most recently she is up for model of the year and appears on the front of *2005 SE Calendar* by *Playboy* as well. This stunning model began her career rather reluctantly at first, but as her eyes were opened to the sensuality of it, she embraced that aspect of herself with a passion.

I became online friends with Bianca after finding her image on the net and requesting to paint her portrait ("The Messenger" page 166). I am happy to say I continue to work with her longtime boyfriend, agent and photographer Martin Perreault on various upcoming projects using her likeness. She not only agreed to an interview, but explained to me what her lifestyle was about, and the aspects of her career, early experiences, and some background basics of fetishwear.

Corvis: "What is the most common misconception on fetish you encounter, and how do you react to people who don't understand?"
Bianca: "Fetish is very often mixed up with (S&M). You can have the fetish of something like latex, leather, high heels…without being into pain and games related to S&M. It is true that lots of S&M players will often even always wears fetish clothing while they play, but you can find also people that will be dressed with kinky outfits without being into the S&M world. Unfortunately, when you speak with someone who doesn't know a thing about fetish, as soon as you say that word: fetish, they tend to think about S&M. It makes me sad sometimes to see that concept is often mixed up together and with my web site, I try to express my love for the fetish of latex."

Corvis: "When you first walked into the shop with your boyfriend, how did you feel, and what caused the initial emotion? And how did taking the step into this fetish feel afterwards?"
Bianca: "I was very afraid when I first saw the latex clothing in the sex shop. I was a very open girl when I was a teenager, and I used to be the one to surprise my boyfriend with kinky lingerie and PVC clothes. But I had no idea that latex existed and when I saw that dress, I got scared because it was the unknown. I was afraid too because my boyfriend was really turned on about something I didn't know. I felt lost a little bit and not in control of the situation. Of course, I felt all those feelings in a second or two. It happens so quickly in your mind and you heart. We left the store without buying the dress because I wasn't ready. I was 17 years old then. I came back a month later to buy

it because I didn't want to stay trapped in my fears and the best way to deal with that material was to wear it myself. So I surprised my boyfriend with the dress, but I surprised myself even more because I fell in love with the material as soon as I wore it. I looked at myself in the mirror and I thought I was looking like a super hero comic strip. Since that day, I keep buying latex clothes and I still love that material very much."

Corvis; "Can you describe the difference in being a model of 'normal' for more known or mainstream type of shoots compared to the Gothic/fetish look?"
Bianca: "Can't speak for the Gothic because I am not into that world really. A glamour shoot will be with sexy regular clothes without necessary heavy make-up. The style will be a little bit more natural and romantic. The expressions of the face must be soft, romantic and sensual. You can have those looks for a fetish shoot, but you may also have more power strong eyes looking, with smokey eyes or kinky weird make-up and hairstyle. You can laugh out loud at the camera, scream, and cry… I think it can be more theatrical. It is for me. That's why I really enjoy shooting for fetish. It helps me to express many feelings and side of myself."

Corvis: "The Playboy shoot. You are known by both looks. Did it bother you that they seemed to want you to look like everyone else (make up, etc.) than what you do for your own indulgence?"
Bianca: "Playboy is soft. I don't think they wanted me to look like everyone else. They just wanted to show the more natural, soft Bianca, which is ok by me. They have their own style, and shooting for Playboy help me grow a lot in my ability to model. I worked on my body and myself for 2 years before I did the casting and I worked a lot of my modeling face expression. When I started to model, I was maybe 18-19 years old. I was still a teenager. It was though for me to show sensuality without a smile or cute eyes. Working to be part of the Playboy team made me realized that I would need to discover my soft sensuality inside me and let it show. That's was not that easy at the beginning."

Corvis: "If you get *Playmate of the Year,* will you use that prominence to expand people's awareness in fetish, or will you keep it more 'underground'? If so, why?"

Bianca: "I don't want to become a playmate because they then have to sign a contract of exclusivity for 2 years I think. So, I don't wish to stop working with fetish magazines because of that kind of contracts."

Guidelines For The Novice

There are a lot of people who enjoy bondage. There is nothing to be ashamed of and nothing to fear as long as you know the basics. First I will attempt to clear up a few misconceptions about both the practitioners and the practices of bondage: Bondage is not just about getting someone into an inescapable situation and hurting them. People that practice bondage are not rapists, psychos, or other nasty, monstrous types. Bondage is all about the fulfillment of deep and primal needs. It is an act of love, not violence. There is the idea of surrendering or being in control and enacting a fantasy that is "forbidden."

Choosing a Partner

Bondage is not a solo practice. You need at least one other partner to safely satisfy that urge, whether you are dominant or submissive. Selecting the correct partner is crucial. Make sure that this person is someone you know well and that you trust implicitly. This person should be made well aware of your intentions and desires and should be 100% consenting. No ifs ands or buts.

Communication

Proper communication is an absolute must. It does not just start and end before the act. It is imperative that you and your partner/s establish effective means of communication throughout all of it. Make sure that everyone involved is aware at all times of how you feel about what you are doing or having done to you. This is not necessarily going to kill spontaneity or ruin a 'scene' for anyone. Before anything happens, be sure that you have a set of SAFE WORDS and/or signals ready and committed to memory. For those who are unfamiliar with the term SAFE WORD, it is simply put, a word, signal, or phrase that has a definite meaning to the person/s that hear/s it, usually when the submissive has been pushed beyond the limit of what s/he finds pleasurable and needs the dominant to stop or lighten up a bit. If you do not use safe words, you will find that bondage is suddenly a very dangerous game, and at the very least, people will not want to play it with you.

Mutual Support

Bondage, by its very nature is a highly emotional activity. It pushes both the dominant and submissive parties to their respective emotional and sometimes physical limits. There will be times that both sides need the support, approval and love of the other. Never ridicule your partner for not being capable of performing an act that is beyond their personal limits. Spend time after your session being affectionate and receptive. Just because your submissive can't physically handle having his or her elbows tied together doesn't make them defective. Just because your dominant squeaks at the mere idea of making you roll around in diapers acting like an infant doesn't make him or her a wimp. This is just personal taste. Some of us just can't do these things. It's nothing to criticize. Move on to something you BOTH enjoy. Trust me, you'll come upon a situation you personally can't handle, and you'll be glad of having someone tell you that you aren't defective.

Establishing Limits

Everyone has things they just do not enjoy. Bondage doesn't change that. Make sure you establish a set of limits before you even think about embarking on a session. Be honest with yourself and your partner or the experience will not be all it could. If you dislike being struck a certain way or with certain objects, let your dominant know this. If you don't, there are very good odds that you will regret it. Discuss these things honestly and openly with your partner so that s/he knows what you do and do not want. As a dominant, I am frustrated by not knowing how far I can go, or what I am expected to do. I am not afraid or ashamed to admit this. If you or your partner cannot honestly set down your limits and respect them, then maybe bondage isn't for you or them.

When securing your submissive, pay close attention to how tightly you tie them. Make sure that you do not cut off circulation or stretch muscles too much. Ignoring this can lead to embarrassing hospital trips, not to mention possible permanent damage to nerves.

When using handcuffs, the standard police issue handcuffs can sometimes cut the nerve of sensation from the wrist to the thumb. Also, handcuffs that do not have a small chain between them (these are usually attached to each other by a hinge that can fold the cuffs together) can be dangerous. If somebody falls while wearing them, they can break a wrist. If using hoods or gags, be very sure that the person who wears these objects can breathe freely. If they can not, adjust the hood or gag until they can. If you're using a rubber ball gag, it's a good idea to use one with snaps on the strap instead of buckles, in case there's an accident, and you need to get the sub out of the gag quickly.

Always use a safe word or signal to halt play in bad situations. It can save your relationship or even save your life. Never leave a bound submissive alone in a room. Not only is this emotionally dangerous, but physically as well. This goes double for someone who is gagged and bound. When using toys like vibrators, vampire gloves, butt plugs, or anything else that has the possibility of getting bodily fluids on it, make sure you WASH IT after every use. Whether or not you continue to use it on the same partner, you still need to make sure everything is clean. Infection in those areas can be at least annoying, and at most debilitating until they go away.

Always make sure that you are with a consenting partner, and that all of your activities are mutually consensual.

THE RAVEN
by Corvis Nocturnum

ᵈ DARK RESONATIONS ᵉ

*"I don't want to change the world,
and I don't want the world to change me."*

—John 'Ozzy' Osbourne

The influence of "evil" in song has been a tug of war for centuries. Music might be the "voices of angels," or a "battle cry" depending on one's persepctive. Every musical era throughout history has fallen prey to religious condemnation and censorship. Early pre-christian folksongs that told tales of magic, mythical creatures and talking to the dead were deemed heretical in their time. Classical composers like Beethoven, Mozart and Bach were at once condemned for writing the "Devil's music." Rock-n-Roll of the 50s, 60s and 70s, Heavy Metal in the 80s, Death Metal in the early 90s; all have met with with harsh resistance. Society in and of itself is an ever-changing organism, and that change breeds fear, resentment and anger.

The problem with music's secular and religious critics over the last two thousand years is that in their effort to silence this form of expression, which rages against such censorship, they only lend fuel to the very fires of the rebellion they are trying to smother—and that which is held out of reach becomes all the more desired, and becomes an aspect of the Shadow.

Other than religious expression, whether it be for or against a particular faith, music reflects classic philosophies as well. It allows us to voice our thoughts and opinions, and often provides mind-provoking stimulation, fulfilling the same role that Plato, Socrates and Nietzsche did in centuries past. The music we choose to listen to gives us our sense of individuality, while at the same time offering us a sense of belonging, knowing that others feel as we do. Music allows us to express how we feel when we cannot find the means to do so otherwise.

While mainstream society accepts that all forms of creativity can be cathartic, the self-imposed morality police of our current society harshly criticize powerful forms of music without really taking the time to *listen* to its intended message. It is easy to hear a singer scream in rage, using visual imagery to make a point, and yet it is often misconstrued by critics that seek little or no understanding to the true meaning and depth of the lyrics—they fail to hear the context of the message and rather judge by how it is delivered.

To quote Marilyn Manson, "You spoon-fed us Saturday morning mouthfuls of maggots and lies disguised in your sugary breakfast cereals. The plates you made us clean were filled with your fears. These things have hardened in our soft pink bellies. We are what you have made us. We have grown up watching your television. We are a symptom of your Christian America, the biggest Satan of all. This is your world in which we grow. And we will grow to hate you." —*Portrait of an American Family*

The manner in which music is performed, its tone and volume strike as much fear, if not moreso, into the general populace than the actual content and message, or even the appearance of the individuals who create it. Music giants of the dark cultures, like Marilyn Manson, Type O Negative, and similarly styled groups, are often misperceived as instigators, ralling the heathens to war with their battle cries, rather than a source of inspiration and comfort.

Marilyn Manson's response to the Columbine situation on violent images being televised and how visually horrifying and how wrong it was, said; "Does not having a body of Jesus hanging from a cross with blood dripping from his side seem to you a violent image?" The pot often calls the kettle black without realizing they are both similar instruments.

As disturbing as some bands may look visually, they bring out shared feelings of both the creator and the listener, playing a role, psychologically expressing pain, loss or anger. These bands reach out to the audience for connection, empathizing with the listener's own feelings and giving them voice through lyric and song. It enables the listener and the musician to release feelings which might be normally repressed.

The inability to express oneself emotionally is the cause of anger problems and often leads to self-destruction. Being able to identify with another person or group via any creative outlet is a basic requirement for stable mental health. Viewing oneself as part of something larger instead of feeling alone; reflecting on problems and focusing on what needs fixed; understanding society's flaws and reacting to them; sharing a bond against the false mask of what is deemed "normal;" coming together en mass yet in peace; all of this contributes to the subculture overlap.

Music fills the role of muse for artists, writers, and healers of the heart and soul. In *Thus Spoke Zarathustra*, Nietzsche states: "Companions, the creator needs, not corpses, not herds and believer's. Fellow creators the creators seeks—those who write new values on new tablets." Without inspiration we would not have a base for continuing. Without change and challenges to the rules of conformity, we would stagnate.

For those who inspire us musically, I wanted to give several bands the chance to speak for themselves, on topics ranging from society's perceptions of them, religious fanatic persecution, and reasons for doing what they do.

The Magic of Music

Much has been discussed throughout this book on the subjects of aesthetics, attitude, and expression through the arts within dark subcultures. How does music heal and what have been the results in the people within these groups is a compelling thought to ponder. One of the best examples of artistic diversity is exemplified by Michael and Mark (a.k.a. the Riddick brothers). Both are artists and members of the bands THE SOIL BLEEDS BLACK and HEXANTENZ, operated under their own record label, THE FOSSIL DUNGEON.

The Soil Bleeds Black

Corvis: "First, please tell me a bit about yourself, your brother and the formation of your company."

Michael: "The Fossil Dungeon is a record label which is owned and operated by my twin brother Mark and I. We use the label as a medium to publish our own original music as well as the music of artists whom we appreciate and admire. Likewise, the label also serves as an outlet for our creative design interests. The Fossil Dungeon was born out of our interest in music. We observe music as a powerful and unique medium of communication. The artists on our label vary, yet they all serve to create an atmosphere that can move consciousness to deeper levels while also remaining suitable as entertainment. Jointly, my brother and I have been involved in 'underground' music for more than a decade. Our interests first began in the underground death and black metal movement of the early nineties, later blending into an interest with other forms of 'dark' music. We have always actively participated in these different movements through artistic and musical contributions and still do so to this day."

Corvis: "Has the acceptance of Goth in music, film, etc. become more palatable to the mainstream do you think? I see a huge increase in films like *Van Helsing, Blade, Gothika, White Noise, Underworld, Constantine,* and *The Grudge,* not to mention music groups like Evanescence in the last two years. If so, what motivates it?"

Michael: "Indeed, it appears 'gothic' themes have become more prominent in mainstream American culture over the past few years. I would attribute much of its popularity to Marilyn Manson. His accessibility brought this aesthetic to a mass market. Now we have chain stores in malls dedicated to this aesthetic (e.g., Hot Topic). In respect to the recent resurgence of horror films in Hollywood, I find this refreshing. The nineties seemed rather devoid of horror films, whereas the eighties provided many classics."

Corvis: "Your personal involvement in so many aspects of the culture must have made you more aware than others of the heavy overlap in every subculture... Goth, Vampire/Vampyre, and neo Dark Paganism. What is the bond that ties them together?"
Michael: "I trust one of the bonds between various 'dark' cultures is their related attitude against complacency. Particularly among youth, the notion of embracing themes of death and darkness go against the standard of popularly esteemed values. Youth are often seeking out ways to establish an identity for themselves, and this results in these themes remaining attractive to them. Similarly, these themes attract those who have experienced particular setbacks and hardships in life. Often, these cultural communities will act as a place to share the discomforts of existence. Finally, there are those who understand these themes to hold much more profound significance, hence why they choose to engage them."

Corvis: "Art, music and spirituality in the broad spectrum of darkness. In what healthy way does this bring out the positive aspect of people? Is there justification in the mainstream's paranoia of us?"
Michael: "The layperson is generally afraid of any circumstance or individual that does not meet their expected criteria. Criteria are defined by what is familiar. Those with little discipline above their reactions will intrinsically react with intimidation when engaging something they are unfamiliar with. If the layperson is not interested in understanding something they are unfamiliar with then their 'paranoia' will continue. This is not to say that their 'paranoia' is justified, it is simply a matter of their choice to not be concerned with understanding. In general, it is ignorance. Embracing themes of death in a sincere manner can challenge one to consider the value, meaning, and purpose of life. It shakes the foundation of complacency and prompts one into living life with fulfillment and reward. This is one great benefit that can emerge from a concentration on those subjects

that most laypeople select to ignore. One could say, it is only when one has died, that true living begins. Of course, this is largely a metaphorical statement.

"Though it is true that an old 'personality' can perish after facing death with deep sincerity. Darkness concerns itself with the mysteries of life. Those who would explore its depths may find many unique surprises and perhaps develop an understanding that is not commonplace for the layperson. Hence, we have the term and subject of 'occultism,' or that which is hidden. In contrast, there are hazards involved in exploring themes of death and darkness. Those who are incapable of accepting the pains of experience might not have the strength required to survive or to realize pleasure. Additionally, those who 'identify' with death and darkness have only opted to add another label to their growing list of personal descriptions about who they are. In honesty, who they are may not be a description to be 'had,' inasmuch as a nature to be 'realized.' Further, there is the trap of developing a culture of complaints.

"The gothic movement is notorious for its plethora of gossip and daily protests about problems. This leads to a nihilistic attitude where the possibility for potential and action are ignored. This sense of hopelessness is a quality of weakness, as opposed to the strength I referenced previously. These are my own observations, however. In sum, for those who desire something greater from their experience, death and darkness are rich areas of exploration that can yield much wisdom and a deeper experience of life."

Corvis: "I understand you are a member of the ToV. How does this influence/affect your perspective?"
Michael: "The Temple promotes three different perspectives with regard to understanding what is true about reality (i.e., metaphysics). These perspectives assist in my categorization of experience. However, I cannot say that the Temple is simply a series of perspectives, as it has more to do with a condition of being through applied action. My involvement with the Temple of the Vampire has challenged and rewarded me throughout the course of my

experience. Realizing the Vampiric condition, through application of the Temple's instruction, has unfolded a deep understanding and psychophysical condition unlike anything I could have imagined in my early youth. It is a misfortune when I observe other 'vampires' who imitate Hollywood stereotypes, when there is indeed the true presence of Vampires among us.

Corvis: "What does the future hold for us all? Acceptance, or dwelling in a different world than other people? And should we really mind if 'they' don't understand?"
Michael: "We should not mind that laypeople fail to understand those who have chosen to explore death and darkness. When I attempt to discuss these deeper issues with a person, I often find that they become uncomfortable. Quite simply, there are those whose nature it is to explore life and there are those who are comfortable in their complacency. It's not necessary to require that people understand the depths of life. If we sought acceptance about this problem it would point to some need on our own part to find wholeness in some exterior condition, when in truth wholeness rests with acceptance of our own interior natures. Mind you, we ought to be concerned when we witness the ignorant layperson reaching for the nearest steak and hammer with which to crucify us!"

Corvis: "What of your future projects can we keep an eye out for?"
Michael: "With respect to my own musical projects, we are presently recording a new Equimanthorn album. This project involves members from metal groups such as Absu, Melechesh, and Zemial. The music focuses on mythology from the ancient Near East while incorporating a musical influence from this region. Overall, the musical format might be considered 'ritual music.' Likewise, we will continue recording with our Hexentanz project that is another 'ritual music' collaborative effort. Hexentanz is focused on themes of medieval witchcraft and incorporates members from the industrial band Psychonaut 75 and the black metal group, Black Funeral. Our main band, The Soil Bleeds Black, will continue recording medieval

music. I have an occult metal project known as Yamatu. This effort shall continue. Finally, there is our band Moonroot that performs a unique cross between epic metal, Celtic folk music, and progressive rock. This project includes Dawn Desiree as the lead vocalist. With respect to our record label, we will continue publishing albums from artists like Dark Muse, Butterfly Messiah, Mephisto Walz, Chirleison, Funerary Call, Violet Tears, Arkane, Dawn Desiree, The Soil Bleeds Black, Hexentanz, and more. With respect to our art, we hope to continue designing album covers for bands in those genres that explore death and darkness."

Corvis: "Thank you for your time. It certainly has been a pleasure."
Michael: "Likewise! I appreciate the opportunity."

Goth Music

Goth music creates a fine blend of Paganism, (or Satanism) with vampirism and fetish-style for a powerful sound. This dark art form shares the same roots regardless of each band's sense of composition and attitude. The aspect of mixing Goth aesthetics with an orchestral sound offers something unique and seductive—such is the music that Joseph Vargo (also interviewed earlier in the chapter "Gothic Art") creates with his band NOX ARCANA.

Corvis: "Many people who are familiar with you as an artist may not know you are an accomplished musician as well. Can you explain a bit about how you got involved in Nox Arcana?"
Joseph Vargo: "As far as music is concerned, I had been in a few different rock bands throughout the years, but in 1998 I began working with a local musician named Ed Douglas and created the concept and Gothic identity for the band Midnight Syndicate. Aside from horror film soundtracks, there really weren't any bands producing dark symphonic music with haunting melodies, so I decided to fund and head the project. Besides being the producer and director for the project, I created the concept and cover art for the CD

Born of the Night. The CD title and various tracks were named after my most popular works of art. I also wrote several poetic verses and did the vocal work for the narratives.

"The band garnered critical acclaim, and we worked together on a second CD, but after two very successful albums we parted ways over artistic differences. They went off into a more fantasy-themed direction, and I returned to creating the dark style of Gothic music that we had originally done.

"In 2003, I began working with William Piotrowski and together we formed a new band, Nox Arcana. Later that year, we released our first CD, *Darklore Manor,* a Gothic soundtrack based upon a legendary haunted mansion near Salem, Mass. The music is a mixture of ghostly melodies, sinister orchestrations and Gothic chanting. With Nox Arcana, William and I collaborate on every aspect of the music and I'm much more involved with the compositions. Our latest CD, *Necronomicon* is a musical opus based on the forbidden book of black magic rituals from H.P. Lovecraft's Cthulhu mythos.

"Our upcoming release, *Winter's Knight,* is a ghostly symphony for the winter holiday season. I've always wanted darker music for that time of year, and I thought others would too. In addition to several original songs to celebrate the Solstice, we've also recorded a few traditional medieval carols, giving them a darker spin. The CD will also feature guest vocalists for some of the pieces."

Contrary to the idea that all dark music is evil, the Chicago-based Metal/Industrial band **URN** are actually comprised of a mix of many religions, as explained to me by author and vocalist Michelle Belanger and guitarist/ manager Dominic St. Charles, who founded the Goth/Ethereal band Sacrosanct with Michelle and another schoolmate, Barry Tessman.

Dominic refined and channeled into URN, building from some of the songs they previously wrote together. I had the pleasure of meeting all of them after show in Indianapolis during the writing of this book. We spoke about ritual in music and how it is received by fellow bandmates who follow different paths.

Corvis: "One of the song's I found most moving was 'House of Glass.' That one and most of the rest have a deep resonance. I think it has a deep energy vibe that reaches out to people. What do you think is the connection between music, energy and psychically with people?"

Michelle: "Well, first of all in URN we've got a wide variety of traditions represented in the players. We have an agnostic on the drums, we've got a Celtic Pagan, our bassist Rhiobann, and Mistress Sophia on keyboard is Pagan, a psy-vamp and she practices Dragon Magic. You've got me, and Dominic St. Charles is Catholic. We went to college together. He's played in the Electric Hellfire Club, he knows and has played with someone pretty high in the Temple of Set, and he knows all these Left Hand Path people, and he happily gets along with all of us.

"A lot goes into the words of our songs, it's very emotional, very powerful, and we put that emotional resonance into the song, into the music of the song. So when we create the song, we go over the song, not just in how it sounds, but how it feels, and very aware of the energy of the song. Most performers are, and I don't know if they take it to a metaphysical level or not, but we do. A couple of the songs are like ritual, 'Shadowdancer,' 'Firechild,' are Mistress Sophia wrote both of those, she wrote them as rituals with that kind of energy. The same goes for 'Angels Are Weeping,' for me it's a spell of awakening... kind of look into themselves, to become aquatinted with their darker side. That they deny in themselves. And we work magic on stage, very consciously so. The other thing is, putting energy out; its very much a give and take. If the audience absorbs the energy of the music, they get hyped, and the more they do, the more it spirals and builds from there. For myself and Mistress Sophia, we approach the whole performance as a ritual."

Corvis: "How did you meet, and what is the glue that holds you together coming from such differing backgrounds?"
Dominic: "The band mostly came together being friends that frequented the same places ranging from the underground nightclubs of Chicago and Milwaukee to Renaissance Fairs. The chemistry or 'glue' that binds us is sometimes found in that despite each and everyone of us a very different individual from the other, it is that common bond of coming from a broken or turbulent home that has lead us to seek solace with others who have traveled the same path.

"We've come to view each other as a team and or strengths balance or weaknesses. Musically, we all gravitate towards more darker forms of expression and that usually manifest in our own songs as well."

Corvis: "What do you feel is the bond between you and the listener?"
Michelle: "It's actually varied. We're all reaching out in some respects to an audience that slightly converges. I get the psy-vamps, the Goths and the Pagan folk; Sophia gets the Pagans.

"A lot of the songs Dominic writes are about childhood pain. You'll see Catholic references in it. An older fella who is a neighbor of mine listened and said, 'Your guy's Catholic roots are showing.' It's actually hitting a wide audience. Really what we do is try to reach out to people, to make the emotion real. That is what will make people connect to the

Michelle Bellanger
Photo by Pendragon Studios

emotion that comes out in the songs, no matter the tradition they're coming from. Symbols in the song, the emotion is there, people will be able to connect to it."

Corvis: "So you would say its cathartic, as a release for some of you, a ritual for the others?"
Michelle: "It is, for some. A little bit of both. Definitely for me, putting so much of me out there is not only energizes me, but exorcises inner demons. It's a great way to blow off steam."

Rhioban: "Plus the amount of energy you can get from a crowd, you can do amazing rituals…while you're playing. You know, if you've had a bad day, things getting really screwed up in your life, sometimes it's really good to go up on stage and use that energy in a positive way, karma, whatever you want to call it, funnel it out or back into somebody you know who needs it.
Michelle: "Actually, our drummer Rich's son is very sick and he has a 33% chance of living from something he inherited; a genetic defect. One of the things we were aiming for tonight, out of it, healing towards his eight year old whose mortally ill."

Corvis: "Like advanced Reiki?"
Michelle: "Yeah, a group of us, we all connect with the music, regardless of what tradition we're in. A common taking of energy there, spin it back there. Other times, for me, I shunt it right off, like an 'awakening'. Getting more people to be aware. Getting people in touch with themselves, transforming the world in healing. It bloody well needs it!"

Corvis: "Has becoming successful altered anyone's report with people in their lives for the better? Or has it changed?"

Dominic: "Success, by my definition, is looking at where you are now as to where you came from. URN has enjoyed a modicum of success as a band and we are staring to gain more momentum on the national and international levels, but we feel we still have a great more of growing to do and we know we have a lot of work in front of us as well. As a result, we don't view ourselves as 'major rock stars' by any means, more as good friends and that has been approach to other people and will most likely be that way for the future as well."

Corvis: "Do you find a sense of unity from fans that maybe comes from being able to relate through the emotions in the songs?"
Dominic: "We've had a great number of people come to us and express how the lyrics of some of our songs have touched them in a positive matter. As an original artist, I can't think of any higher compliment that you can receive. We do try to put a great deal of emotion into our songs as we're not a cerebral band in our approach to songwriting and performing.

"We do tend to focus on subjects and emotions on the darker side. Some of songs such as 'House of Glass' and 'Father Dearest,' deal with the anger and rejection of parents who disapproved of the people we are. Some deal with depression such as 'Etched in Stone,' dealing with the loss of a loved one. Some deal with inner battle such as 'Liar in Waiting,' and the struggle to overcome them. Of course, we do occasionally try to balance some these dark emotions with more upbeat songs like 'Little Tin Goddess,' which is more for fun and dancing as we wish for our listeners to enjoy the gamut of emotions we feel, not just all the bad ones."

Dominic St. Charles
Photo by Pendragon Studios

Corvis: "They are very passionate and hauntingly beautiful, stirring

buried feelings in some people. Do you all agree that music is cathartic and can heal?"

Dominic: "Absolutely! A lot of what URN is about is us dealing with the more negative aspects of our personalities, so that we can deal with and integrate them, so we can be more functional in social forums. It allows to deals with all of the hurt, anger, betrayal, depression and learn to see that there is hope in life and it is a gift and a process to become the best people we can be.

"Music, like religion, is very individual. No two people worship the same and two people listen to the same music, or in the same way. That is the beauty of the catharsis as it allows us to realize that we are significant and have the ability to become the people we wish to be."

Vampyres influence ambient music, as do the religious diversities of Paganism and Asatru; and Satanism's alternative ideas give voice to a broad overlap of beliefs. Art imitating life, imagery put to music, it's a never-ending cycle. It is an integral part of each group, no matter one's musical preference, and each has a positive role to provide, should one look close enough.

Death Metal & Black Metal

Death Metal and/or Black Metal are probably the most readily stereotyped and most often crticized forms of music, and are most often affected with a negative public image. Matthew, the founder and lead-singer of the death-metal band, SHROUD, helps to clear up some gray areas and misconceptions about this genre of music.

Corvis: "For people who don't know much about it, what in your opinion... is there a difference between Black Metal and Death Metal, and what is the type of music you perform?"

Matthew: "Well, if one were to read a music magazine, I would call it a cross between Black and Death Metal—a lot of Death Metal tends to focus on political issues, even a horror movie put to music, to some extent. Black Metal is more oriented to left Hand Path magic or

Satanic. I would just call us more LHP, sort of a follower of the dark side, an emphasis on Dark Gods. Our topics will sway a bit. I write all the lyrics, so they are dear to my heart, very spiritual for me."

Shroud

Corvis: "I have heard you were Pagan yourself once, but since have chosen a darker path— has that had an influence in your work?"
Matthew: "Most defiantly an influence on the music. I would consider myself a Pagan—I do have places and needs for lighter Deities in my life. I liked to keep a balance."

Corvis: "There is a need for balance between secular Humanism with spirituality in nature."
Matthew: "I'm right there with you. Shall I say reason to worship something intangible...we walk the earth and drink the water."

Corvis: "Any similarity in the Viking's Nordic traditions with songs in general? The book Lords of Chaos especially the band Mayhem. Do you take any of that into your work or is that more European metal?
Matthew: "Definitely more of a European background. We're not going around burning down churches. One of our local churches burned down and inspired the lyrics for my next CD. I just happened to be driving by and there they were, tearing it down! Musically we may be the like those other bands, but lyrically we don't go down the same routes."

Corvis: "So you don't advocate violence against Christianity?"
Matthew: "No, not at all. We come across as very dark, but our titles say a lot, I keep it simple."

Corvis: "A lot of people have the opinion that the LHP we follow has an outright war against Christians. I see it is a backlash, a response against repression. Do you agree?"

Matthew: "I totally agree. I feel that going back to when Led Zeppelin lost fans because they thought Jimmy was a Satanist, when he was an O.T.O. member. I've been into Crowley's teachings a lot, and if I joined any organization like the Church of Satan, it would be the O.T.O."

Corvis: "Would that be a reference to your bands group? The rams head in a pentacle?"

Matthew: "Part of that is. Part of it is me being an Aries. On the Awakening the Ancients album cover we have a ram on one side of a pyramid and a scorpion on the other. That signifies another member. Regardless of what people say, astrology has a spiritual influence on our planets. It's not so much the sign, as the element and direction, Aries, fire, etc."

Corvis: "I've heard and appreciate your music's meaning. People who embrace their darkness itself, strongly identify with it. There is a very broad appreciation for looking into your soul, a trait most mainstream people don't do. What do you feel about darker paths being willing to embrace their Shadow versus other paths?"

Matthew: "That's a difficult question to answer. I think that it's a certain open mindedness. Once folks get real about it, about dark culture, it may be more natural, easier to embrace."

Corvis: "Are more people instinctively drawn to it than others? They're makeup, psychologically speaking?"

Matthew: "I would say yes. At first, I myself have always been drawn to darkness. From as far back as I can remember. Comic books and stuff, I liked Darth Vader, Dr. Doom. Keeping that early significance in mind, I'm sure that had an influence."

Corvis: "How do you feel about mainstreams repression of dark subcultures music, art, etc.? Treated as if we have the plague?"

Matthew: "Right, right. From time to time I've felt ostracized. But that's usually from white Witchcrafters. I've been able to get anyone else to understand my views, rather than just reject me. Generally people of dark or light can talk and mutually accept each other's perspectives, a balance."

Corvis: "Magic and nature are balanced. Any aspects put into your music reflecting that, that you put into your songs?"
Matthew: "Yeah, like our next CD has Enochian Key's in the chants with a keyboard. Lust, war, etc. Energies circulated strongly in the studio. The lyrics are spiritually close to me. We are Pagan, we are LHP, whether people are afraid of that, we will convey that. It is our art form."

Corvis: "I wanted to make sure the public will know the good side we have to offer instead of evil and afraid."
Matthew: "People wrongly draw that conclusion. Looking at the teachings of our predecessors, there are folks that worship Lilith, Arcadian dark Goddess's, some have an appreciation for the dark Gods. Finding a good balance is crucial."

Matt's commentary on dark spirituality is echoed by Inkubuss Sukubus band member Tony Mc Kormack, "Despite the blanket denial of Satan, I think a lot of Pagans are interested in Satan because he's such a colorful figure." Their vision of earth-based religion is darker than a lot of Pagans, simply because they approach everything from a branch of faith and music as a way of expressing the darkside of their own personalities.

Another group called ARSENIC describes how normal they are despite their apparent public persona and the type of music they do. As I talked to them, they seemed just like any other group of young adults wanting to have fun without the heavy emphasis on anything in particular. The point here is, although the public might lump them into the same mindset due to a cd cover, they are totally different inside.

Corvis: "Is there any particular message you are trying to get across? Is there any particular ideology?"

Trent: "The music is basically a reflection of what we feel, we're not trying to push an agenda on anybody."

Terry: "It's the anger and the energy of the crowd which we draw on."

Corvis: "What drew you into the music?"

Trent: "We just started playing the local scene in Huntington. Stuff like Nickleback, etc."

Terry: "Yeah, we had a hard time of it when we changed our sound to what we are now. People started treating us different even though most of these people went to school with us."

Trent: "They see us on stage and expect to hear John Cougar Melloncamp and shit. We start to play, they hear us and some freak."

Terry: "He's in his last few years of being a teacher. It's about the music and enjoying it. Everyone says 'Oh you're in it for the money to make millions.' I say 'No, I'd be happy with $40,000 a year, it's not a huge amount.' I just want to play what I enjoy and live on it."

Corvis: "I sympathize, my careers are the same. Art, writing, etc. All creative people share that. What's the difference in Black Metal? Death Metal?"

Trent: "None that I know, really. The wording I guess. My brother's lyrics reflect a lot, mine are of just feelings."

Corvis: "Anything with religious path?"

Terry: "With me it's definitely my views but I'm not pushing it on anyone. We're not trying to convince anyone to do anything."

Corvis: "A lot of people say you sound better in person than on CD, the opposite of some groups."

Arsenic

Trent: "We've improved since our demo a lot. The crowd helps bring it out."

Corvis: "Is the Devil's use as a shock value important at all?"
Trent: "At first, visually I'd say yes. The Judas Priest look was big for us (all spikey arm bands, face paint.)"
Corvis: "Typical European black metal look?"
Trent: "Yeah, especially Trey. He began with a heavy look and our sound reflected that as a sound, but we've changed."

Terry: "We just get up there with no exact presence to put out. It's just us, raw and honest."

Corvis: "Any connection to LaVey's Satanism? A human, I'm a God, etc.?"
Trent: "I would say we all feel that way. It's a given with most bands we've played with. We're not overly religious at all. We feel it's just for us to do well, to excel."

Terry: "Right, no one's going to do anything for you. You have to do it yourself. I believe in what I do, and don't force others to follow what I do. If they do, that's fine."

Corvis: "Your sound may be the same as the church burners who were the Norwegian 'grandfathers' of black metal when you were growing up. Any direct influence at all?"

Trent: "We liked the look and sound, we just don't follow the lyrics, or push any revolution."

Corvis: "You guys are definitely the opposite of the stereotypical morbid 'Devil Worshipper' metal freaks. You're down to Earth with fans."

Terry: "Sure. We're just ourselves, playing what we feel."

Corvis: "Kind of like Ozzy, 'I'm not out to change the world, I don't want the world to change me.'"

Trent: "Exactly. That's it exactly."

Terry: "I agree, right."

Corvis: "It's been great, thanks for talking to me."

Trent: "We appreciate the opportunity to be heard, thanks!"

I contacted DARK HORIZON records, which operates from my hometown supplying cds across the globe to stores and online customers. Its owner Lord Typhus has been featured in *Pit Magazine* and is also the lead singer in bands FOG and TYPHUS. Both Lord Typhus and his bassist Evil Priest were very obliging when approached for an interview.

Corvis: "One of the first questions that come to my mind as I research is, as a distributor of Black and Death Metal in America and abroad, would there be any validity to the claim that these groups are musical terrorists?"

Typhus: "Well, there is that percentage that have taken action like Emperor, Dissection, and others that have actually murdered people for fame. They were the martyrs for a cause. Now it has exploded into a marketable thing."

A New World Order Shall Rise!

Evil Priest: "It's not like it used to be though."

Typhus: "There is a small fraction of extremists that play the music, that live it, and kind of step to the next level, which is actually breaking the law. That handful of individuals made it a fashionable, marketable thing by getting all of us attention. A vehicle for notoriety."

Corvis: "So it's a musical message, content wise?"
Typhus: "Yeah, I'd say so."

Corvis: "Are U.S. musicians using imagery as strictly shock value, opposed to the Norwegians years ago?"
Typhus: "You know, it basically depends on the individual. Because recently a guy in a L.A. band called Soul Evil took an AK-47 and shot up a church sponsored rehab center. Now, I don't go, 'hey, good going,' or anything. On an intelligence level, it wasn't smart because he's in jail to further his cause. But on the other hand, it did help market the music. Again, more people are like, 'what's this black metal about?' It helps us sell so we can make a living. I think it's a fine line, really."

Evil Priest: "It does tend to over saturate the market."

Typhus: "Yeah, groups start popping up all over everywhere because others want to be like that. It's not the route I would go; trading your freedom in exchange for a reputation of burning a church down is pretty stupid."

Evil Priest: "Regardless of what type of group a person belongs to; there are those that even in normal society who breaks laws. Everybody fights for their beliefs; some do it regardless of the music."

Corvis: "There seems to be an ebb and flow to interest in dark themes. Do you see a mirror effect in your end as well? Is there a connection in subcultures?"
Typhus: "I believe so. We have our good months and bad. The scene is saturated with mediocre, but the good always shine through."

Evil Priest: "Fans of the macabre, appreciators of body modification, horror, what have you all do have a connection. It all runs hand in hand. Misanthropy in most forms such as music and art all do. There are a lot of people who are intelligent, who don't go 'ohh, I'm into it because I'm evil, it's cool shit,' they are just puppets in society. They have no self-worth, no place in society. We have buyers in prison, true."

Typhus: "They just follow a trend. That's why I started the record label, because I wanted to take it to take it to a next level. Not to break the law, but bring the music to more people. And granted your gonna hit those who listen who might be an artist, who listen and absorb it, to enhance there art, but, yes you will always have that fringe section that use music as an excuse to break the law. Normal, intelligent people listen to this will not.

"We're not saying take the red pill in the morning, the blue pill in the evening, you know a *Matrix* movie reference. I say, think about things, Have your own identity; I started this label to spread that out. I wanted to be a spokesman for the movement without taking it past any sane boundaries. Someone who is trying to spread this dark message without murdering someone! Despite the fact so many are bound by the shackles of moral society. Even an avid listener of Black Metal will not bend on one knee and kiss the arse of the goat! Patterning your life for yourself is true Satanism. Don' be a sheep."

Corvis: "What would all of you say is positive about of this group in the subcultures? What stands out the most in society or to the listener?"

Typhus: "I think we offer artistic expression. I play in two bands; I think it is a form of aggressive art form, of expression that is not for everyone. I think with the explosion of bands coming out all over the world, finally, like Dimmu Borgir, active Satanist who are actively in the spotlight who are looked upon by movie producers, TV. producers. We want to be recognized as legitimate artists who have a message. We convey a thought Satanic artists spread their political messages, hip hop culture, spreads theirs, its all the same."

Evil Priest: "It's an art form for those with extreme personalities, a voice and way to express a message, as long as they don't sell out for money."

Typhus: "Fans know that, right away, they hear it and know when you're true to heart. We play in Fog, and in Typhus, for our art, and for people to hear our lyrics. Our messages can be negative or positive. If they love us or hate us, at lest they still acknowledge us. That's the first step; all artists want to achieve a level of immortality, to go on. To be captured in time, so to speak. When I'm dead and gone, I hope it doesn't fade and is gone…I think some of the music we have created does have that kind of potency, to withstand the test of time."

To give them credit for honesty, they both admit that fifty-percent of their fans do live the Satanic stereotype. But as Typhus also mentioned later, older fans and musicians have wised up to LaVey's philosophies and have become intellectuals who use their music as a vehicle for mental wake up calls to pull people away from criminal activity.

Marilyn Manson, Trent Reznor, and many others have used music of this nature successfully to combine Goth's cynicism with a love of the macabre to express the angst of their lives. The majority of other music groups also share this mindset with all the other subcultures covered throughout this book. As different as it might sound or appear to people outside the genre, society need not fear the performers or the fans based on their appearances.

It is my hope that when the fires of intolerance and judgment die out it will be replaced with understanding. Until then the dark resonations will continue to reverberate and call out to those drawn to it's siren call, while haunting the subconscious of others who refuse to understand.

FINDING THE LIGHT IN DARKNESS

"What does not kill us makes us stronger."
— *Friedrich Wilhelm Nietzsche*

Darkness Against Child Abuse

Among the vast number of people in this macabre scene exists future professionals of an entirely different type. The Shelter for Darkness is a combined effort of Shadow and Anajeil Villanueva. Their website branches into areas, each one dealing with different but serious issues. The Shelter for Darkness, Darkness Against Child Abuse (DACA), Darkness Against Domestic Violence (DADV), and Darkness Against Drug Abuse (DADA) reach out to people in dark lifestyles, such as Pagan, Goth and Satanism. Any and all are welcomed and embraced, free of prejudice and condemnation. DACA has existed since 1999 and is the best-known outreach program for alternative people and their children.

Places like DACA need your support, to grow and assist others. DACA is not a charity interested in donations, but exists as an awareness and information website, and an online Yahoo! Group, listed in the resources pages at the end of this book. The founders are earning degrees in child abuse counseling and women's studies.

A surprising amount of Pagan friendly groups that exist for abuse support are unfriendly to Goths and Satanists, which is sad, considering they face similar negative treatment from non-Pagan's. Unfortunately until more people in all walks of life see the truth that we are all human with the same wants and needs regardless of our choices in lifestyle, it will continue to remain an uphill battle.

Following is an interview with SHADOW, who describes this organization's special achievements and goals.

Corvis: "When and why was DACA formed when other family counseling groups exist?"

Shadow: "DACA was formed in late 1999 as an organization that understands people who live dark lifestyles. Most of the other organizations out there are geared towards those who are considered 'normal' people or those who are specifically Christian in their spiritual beliefs. Sometimes this leads to many misunderstandings and often leads to a discussion of 'changing' your beliefs instead of finding the best way to resolve the problems at hand. I have even seen people who are seeking help get treated in rather harsh ways because their beliefs are not those of the mainstream."

Corvis: "Just because people in various subcultures live differently than most, is that a justification to turn them away when they need help? Or worse, get accused of being the predator themselves?"

Shadow: "No it is not, however it happens and sometimes it is indirect. Many of the Christian organizations offer help only after you sit in and listen to a sermon or Sunday school teaching. Then you have those who have been told that any belief other than Christianity is automatically 'evil.'

"As someone who is working towards a professional career in child abuse counseling, I see this behavior as a violation of ethics. It is also rather traumatizing for the children involved to see that other people treat their parents in unjust ways simply because their beliefs are different. It doesn't set a good example at all."

Corvis: "Do you think it would come as a shock to the outsider to dark faith paths to see that Goth parents are just like anyone else who just needs help with similar situations?"

Shadow: "I don't think it would be a shock per se but I do think that some councilors would not know exactly how to treat the situation. For instance they may spend more time trying to learn about the parent's lifestyle than trying to solve the problem at hand. This can get everyone side tracked and in the long run, it doesn't help the situation much."

Corvis: "What positive things would you like to inform my readers about that they might be misinformed about?"

Shadow: "I have noticed a 'family friendly' trend emerging in many dark communities. There are more books from Pagan publishers focusing on the Pagan family, including children, and there are many websites now that have sections geared towards children under 13 years of age. I hope that DACA has helped bring some of these changes about, but I can't say for certain how much of an impact we have had."

Corvis: "How would a website or Pagan occult shop be able to assist any of the situations you encounter?"

Shadow: "I would recommend that anyone who offers information for those in the occult or dark lifestyles to know if there are any Pagan friendly layers or councilors in their community. These are people who can offer you help without judging you for your lifestyle or spiritual choices.

"Other situations I encounter are from within the community itself. There are a lot of people offering bad advice on their websites or in chat rooms so I stress to everyone that if they need help, find a professional. If you need medical help, please see your doctor and if you need legal help, seek out a licensed attorney. There are often well meaning people who offer advice, but sometimes their information is incomplete, out of date or misunderstood. So it is always best to have expert opinions and ideas to help you overcome your challenges in life."

TALIA JULIETTE, a beautiful Goth who works as a model and actress, relates her experiences and courage in the face of adversity, as she gives this testimony for the Shelter for Darkness:

"I'm so glad I decided to give a testimony for the Shelter for Darkness or I fear it would have been lost. This is my true story. I do not request pity or words of sympathy, but rather encourage those of you who read it to take what you can from it and gain what you can as it applies to your life perhaps. Be forewarned, this is an intense story. But it is one that I feel/felt needed to be shared.

"Ever look up at the night and think to yourself, 'Gee I wonder. If I died tomorrow, would anyone care? Would anyone even know that I had lived?' I used to all the time. I think everyone has at one time or another. I always thought that I'd be great someday, if only... Famous last words.

"When I was 14 years old, I became engrossed with the darker side of life. I was introduced to 'being a Goth' by a girl named Casey in the 9th grade. She noticed that I had a habit of writing on my hands in a very twisted henna-type style, dressing in darker colors and writing poetry that flooded with emotional turmoil. During a fire drill, she approached me and initiated a conversation that would change my life.

"Aside from already having bi-polar and a tendency of suicidal ideation and even attempts (on many an occasion) I was extremely open to anything that was off the beaten path so to speak. Anything dark and overlooked was romantic and intriguing to me. It has always been this way. So at 18, it didn't surprise me that I found comfort and friendship at the local art theaters where they held midnight showings of the Rocky Horror Picture Show. Those nights were interesting.

"One night, my friend Joshy called me up and told me that he was coming to kidnap me from my house and abscond with me to one such show. It was a Saturday night and I had nothing better to do. So I didn't argue. It is there that I met my ex-fiancé 'DC' and my life really took an interesting turn. DC was a tall Gothic man, with dusty brown hair and stunning blue eyes and a quarkish smile that I adored. He lived in long beach, California and appeared to be well liked. He smoked clove cigarettes and loved to play bass guitar. He also promoted underground music for the local Los Angeles area and appeared to be doing well at it. I, a naive 18 year old girl, fell madly in love and in lust with him, and within 3 months, ran away from home to escape the 'treachery and despair placed upon me by my father' and to 'prove to him how grown up I could be and that I could make it out there in the real world alone.'

"A friend of DC's named MJ introduced me to a man named

Dwayne Walker. He was a producer of independent film and underground art photography, and seemed to have endless connections to the world of adult entertainment. When the idea of starring in porn films was first pitched to me, I was a bit hesitant as most people would be. I had grown up in an orthodox Jewish household and as dark and open-minded, so to speak, as I was, I still had my morals. (that too would change in time.) Dwayne introduced me to a man named Jim Brewer, a local long beach photographer, who introduced me to Reb, owner of Reb's Pretty Girl International, one of two licensed agents in the entire state of California for adult film. I was offered a roof over my head and the ability to make an endless supply of money so long as I wanted, provided that I do one scene for him to sell a month. (Not with him. He was a very good guy. I have a great respect for him. He hired male talent to do the scenes with). I was running out of money and needed to survive. I accepted.

"It wasn't too long after that I got some bad news. I had ovarian cysts that prevented me from working as often as I needed to maintain a certain level of lifestyle that I wanted. But that didn't stop me. I was convinced that I needed to support that and myself no matter what, I needed to make the money so that I was in control. DC tried to find work, but it was hard for him, especially being as how we moved so often. We tried to settle down but it just never seemed to work out. I specifically remember coming home after a trip to San Francisco to find our apartment had been vandalized by a room mate's tweeker friends and our altar burned to a crisp, along with some of our sacred items of worship, missing. I think that is when I truly began to lose it. For about 6 months afterwards, we bounced around from hotel to hotel, trying to maintain some level of consistency in a world gone to hell. It seemed impossible. I just wanted to scream. DC had found his niche in life and was to be in a band based in Orange County. I couldn't keep up. He was always gone, and when he was home, I was gone. I could see my relationship crumbling before my eyes and there wasn't a damn thing I could do about it.

"It was around March of 2003 that I met a man late one night in an Internet café in Hollywood that would royally mess my world up and change everything forever. His name was T and he was a beautiful man, also with long blondish brown hair and sparkling blue eyes. He made me promises wonderful romantic ideations and wild nights of passionate indulgences, which I so desperately wanted. He also seemed to want to be around me and was kind and caring. It seemed as though it were a dream and he was just too perfect. Almost too perfect. Almost was right. He was into methamphetamines and other sorts of drugs. He lived his life on the streets of Hollywood and I took it upon myself to try and save him from himself. I now realize that I couldn't have done it no matter how much I wanted to. But at that time, I was still a cocky 19 year old stuck up bratty up and coming porn star who thought she could conquer the world and save It from its falling disgrace with the flick of the wrist, and the flash of the camera, and with the green pieces of paper with dead presidents on it, she was going to lead him to his salvation.

"It was not long after that we moved back to Las Vegas, NV, where my mother had her home. I needed help, being as how the industry was just not working in my favor. She had money and I knew it. So did he. He and I started out living in hotels, as I had done the prior year. It wasn't a new thing for me. I thought it made me a 'free spirit.' It just made me broke.

"In August of 2003 I decided that I was not willing to pay good money just to watch him have a good time. My self-esteem had already taken a nose dive by that point and I just wanted to see what it was that he loved so much and found so entrancing about the drugs. In a sense, I just wanted to fit in. I knew it was harmful, and I had heard of its addictive nature, but I never imagined it would ever affect me that way. I was so wrong.

"The next eight months were spent on a one way roller coaster ride to hell spiraling down so fast I didn't know which end was up. A pattern of lies and abuse followed, as well as major trouble with the law. My health had gone from bad to worse, as I grew more and more depressed with every wisp of smoke that entered my lungs. It got to the point where I wanted to die and one day, I decided to attempt to take my life. I had gotten so spun out of my mind that I began to hallucinate and I convinced myself that T was cheating on me. Just a few days prior, he had hit me for the first time and knocked me unconscious. He claimed that I was not paying attention to him or my health and was just sitting around on the computer bullshitting. He had put his foot through the monitor and slammed it up against a wall. I became so depressed, angry and scared that I ran outside, up two flights of stairs and off the second-story balcony, hoping to hit my head on the concrete or snap my neck in the process. I didn't. Luckily. You would think that would have been my wake up call. Instead, I just became more depressed. I figured, hell, I couldn't even kill myself. I must truly be worthless. After all, day after day, my T called me all sorts of names, and pointed out every flaw. I didn't leave him though because I still thought that maybe one day he'd realize that he was hurting me and would love me again as he had promised so long ago. It was not long before I was hardcore addicted to the meth, and began stealing money from my mother to get it. T had convinced me that my mother was the devil and had stolen $7000 from me. In my heart I knew it want true, but I didn't care. The drugs numbed me.

"In October of 2003, T got into trouble big time with the law. Our friend had gotten us a hotel room in T's name under a stolen credit card. Nine cop cars showed up and hauled him off to jail. I was crushed. I stayed with a man who was of the shadiest sorts, until I made enough money to bail T out. Once he was out, we moved hotels, bouncing from one to another, until I had run my bank account dry. I over-drafted about $4000 worth of checks to make sure that t and I had a roof over our heads for a few weeks, food to eat and drugs to smoke. One night, I realized I couldn't write any more checks in the area and the hotel was not going to accept a check either. I had exhausted my resources and I was fixing to be on the streets again. I turned to escorting. A man approached me and asked me if I had considered trying that approach. He explained the similarities between porn and escorting and to my tweeked out mind it made sense. He took me back to his place, saying he was going to go over the details with me there and raped me. When T found out, he was furious. Not at me, at him. He told me he wanted to take me back to

Kansas where he grew up and take care of me as originally planned. Free of drugs, and free of my old life. It was exactly what I wanted to hear and I bought into it.

"Once in Kansas, the patterns of abuse only got worse. Now, we were on his grounds. Afraid of being alone in the dead of winter in snow covered Kansas; I did everything He asked of me, and more. I became an escort full time jumping from agency to agency. He just took more and more of my money, investing it into meth and a new drug introduced to me: cocaine. I liked cocaine. It numbed everything. It gave me the artificial energy of meth, yet I could feel no pain, and go to sleep in a few hours if I wanted to. T became increasingly violent and even sent me to the ER a few times. I didn't leave because I wanted him to kill me.

"One day I was sitting alone in my hotel room, and I switched the television onto the Sci-Fi Channel. I saw before me, 5 people, two of whom reminded me very much of my exes, who I loved very much, interacting and socializing with normal or at least society standard 'normal' people. They themselves weren't perfect, and neither were the people they were interacting with. But they all seemed to have a general respect for one another in a way I longed for so much in my own life. I became instantly entranced. This show, this television program, was a metaphor for my own mad life. I could easily identify with each of the characters on it and for some reason, I felt at peace watching It. It was so soothing to my soul. I didn't understand why, but I knew that I wanted to achieve some sort of peace and acceptance within my own life as well. The show was called Mad Mad House.

"For once, I had found something that I could identify with in my chaotic hell of a life. I would watch the witch Fiona, and remember my own spiritual beliefs. It inspired me to have faith again. I would watch the modern primitive Art, and the naturist Avocado, (who looks a hell of a lot like an old friend of mine named max who I attended poetry night with in Los Angeles as a young teenager) and remember the beauty of my own body, now emaciated and malnourished, a skeleton of 79 lbs. I realized what I was doing to my body and how much I wanted to stop. I watched Iya Ta'Shiya, the

voodoo priestess, and the references to her history and African ancestry, and thought how similar it was to my Jewish history in a way, and that made me think of my family. My Israeli father, and my mother and now 11-year-old brother. And how much I missed them. And then of course there was the vampire Don. His eloquence, sense of humor and style as well as intellect and ingenuity made me remember my own lifestyle prior to the drugs. How beautiful and romantic the dark lifestyle could be when lived correct. He reminded me of all the beauty and people I had once lived in the company of, and I realized that I wanted to achieve it again.

"On April 10, 2004, T hit me for the last time; I took my last puff off the crack pipe, set it down and stood my ground. I was going home. I called his mom, who in turn called the cops to come and get me the hell out. I went, gratefully. I am now almost 90 days into my recovery and have graduated my rehab program respectively. In the fall, I hope to attend a local community college and get my life back on track. I have made it and I cannot help but attribute some of my survival to that show. To those of you in reading this, ponder the following: you never know just how you will influence those around you. If a silly TV program could save my life, imagine what physical actions people do. —*Talia Juliette*

The following is a journal entry by DRAGAN (interviewed earlier in the chapter "Vampires Among Us"). I am reprinting it here, for I feel it encompasses all of us in these communities, at one time or another.

"Sometimes Life is a Bitch... and that black hole at the end of a barrel... seems like the best place in the world to be... but something always pulls you back... Inner strength... A reason that makes you stay... No matter how drunk you are... how loaded on Coke... you always remember that part of you that still loves something... and something that wants to keep going... something that no matter HOW bad things get... it is worth living for... My reason... was that I knew some where... some one else was thinking the same thing... someone sat under the stars wishing they had someone there... I knew that I could make someone happy... I could make someone proud... someone could give me the love... that I always needed... My inner strength... that thought... kept me going long enough to find the Person that would give me a reason to live... a Person that loves me... that is proud of me.. As I know many of you have been in the same situation... what is YOUR inner strength... leave a comment...and if you read this and don't know what it is... you don't know why you carry on... remember this. YOU are on a road... of life... and somewhere on that road it is bound to rain... and even though you think it will rain all the time... you will never know... if you stop walking... so keep at it... stay on your path... push through the rain... someone will be waiting for you when you get out." —*Dragan*

All of us face pain. Each of us struggles to overcome the looming shadow of guilt, self-denial, or trauma that has shaped us over the years. There comes a time when reality must be faced, and it is my strong assertion that these subcultures offer a profound way of releasing ourselves in a positive manner. Being an artist and author, I have used my experiences to shape my thoughts and feelings to create visions of darkness containing hope and beauty, which hopefully stir the minds of my audience. Culled from years of ridicule from schoolmates, strangers passing me by in adulthood who act similarly, I absorb the pain and redirect it in a healthy manner. Looking back on over a dozen foster homes, moving around the country with an alcoholic parent and hating school because it was a source of abuse, I now realize, had I not risen above these times by reading fiction or being introspective and quietly creative, I may never have become who I am now. Nor would I have met the multitude of like-minded people who I call friends. Reflection puts things into prospective, as long as we accept our Shadow with honesty.

A case in point: I refused to have anything to do with my father until I was 25 years old, and then it was too late. I received a call that he fell asleep while smoking and drinking. A lit cigarette dropped into the laundry basket caused his death from smoke inhalation while sleeping. I still have a piece of wood from his house to remind me that we need to live life to its fullest, because sometimes you don't get a second chance to say 'I'm sorry.' It's been seven years, and I recently stopped beating myself up over the fact that I was angry with him for not being there for me while growing up. I'd rather remember him as "Rockin' Robbie," as his friends called him.

Yes, my life has been full of pain, with many tragic incidents, but I survived and am all the stronger for it.

I leave you with a poem written by my friend Talia, who sums up the feelings that are shared by a vast number of the individuals I have met while writing this book.

We all need to be heard, and understood

I walk alone
on a star crossed night
looking up I wonder
have I done right

Where is my life
what is this place
among the darkness
where I feel safe

The shadows hide me
away from truth
away from all that hides me
away from you

There's no need
to lie now
I've already died inside
In my own twisted insanity

I lay here
not dead, not alive
although I already feel
dead inside

Your arms provide no comfort
in these darkened times
I no longer need you
to wipe tears from my eyes

Of all the grief and all the pain
I've felt in this world
it comforts me alone
to just know that I am real...

—Talia Juliett

AFTERWORD

"All my life I've searched for the middle of the road,
not realizing I was standing on it."
— Corvis Nocturnum

Far too often, society makes us question our feelings, our desires, and the human need to express oneself openly, especially at our most crucial years—at a time when these aspects of human experience should be encouraged. Later in life, we encounter various subcultures, whose accoutrements seem to resonate with some of our early repressions, and we undergo a period of awakening. It can be difficult, not only to fully embrace one, but to combine several together. "How can I be a Goth and a Witch?" or "How can I be a Satanist and be into BDSM?" It's at first frustrating when society makes us think we need to fit into neat little self-contained boxes, even while trying to break out of the self-limiting labels to which we are confined. Obviously in time it becomes easier to integrate a multitude of facets together. What becomes clear is that most, if not all, of the subcultures covered in this book overlap, having been shaped by the effects of shared philosophies. In doing so, individuals within these subcultures come to share an appreciation for similar ideals, and eventually form larger communities.

The combination of parts that define our unique makeup is like a puzzle that creates a complete picture. The answer lies in not focusing on the lines of the picture, but in stepping back and letting the lines blur until all you see is that one image that we've become.

I have learned some important things about myself during the course of writing this book. A friend helped me understand that we all need to trust our own instincts on what's right—they will rarely lead you astray. But always try to be objective about your perceptions and experiences. We each are in control—our Will shapes everything, including the direction our lives go in. That which brings some of us to darker paths does not come from some "evil" outside influence; the people we meet along the way are just fellow travelers, and sometimes guides. As John Coughlin,

Michelle Belanger, and others have echoed, those who might seem the most outwardly disturbing are in fact the most mentally well-adjusted. As Carl Jung wrote, "To become conscious of [our Shadow] involves recognizing the dark aspects of the personality as present and real."

Life consists of layers, each peeling back to reveal something deeper and more unexpected. How we answer the many challenges life throws at us, profoundly shapes our concept of "Self." Most often, the deepest part of our psyche, the divine part, the Satanic "Self," already knows what our place is, and what we want. And the minute you lay aside your worries about what others want you to do, what you're expected to do, and just act for yourself, you'll be on the right path. Ironically, we often tend to create our own biggest roadblocks—no one else has so much control of our destiny.

True permanent healing comes from accepting ourselves as we are. I have become stronger through accepting myself, by meditation, having a Satanic backbone, and enjoying a blending of all aspects of myself. I am a realistic humanist owing my joys and losses to my own actions. I perceive the world and its inhabitants without buying into false illusions, and I treat everyone in my path as a potential friend until given good cause not to. Being in tune with my inner gifts, while respecting the Earth and it's seasonal cycles, creating art and enjoying the works of my like-minded acquaintances, I express the dark beauty within myself. I refuse to conform to society's standards, which would force me to deny the real *me.*

My purpose for writing this book was both to explain the history and truths behind so many different types of misunderstood people, and as a way to solidify my own sense of "Self." It has been a wonderful experience that gave me the chance to meet a variety of intelligent and gifted people. I wish to take this opportunity to thank them all collectively.

To you my reader, hopefully I have educated, entertained, and given you an enjoyable visit into our dark world, whether you are just beginning to explore it, or were already in it's midst.

Embrace your darkness, and welcome.

Dark blessing,
Corvis Nocturnm

⊰ About the Author ⊱

Nocturnum resides in Indiana and is the co-proprietor of Spirit Healing Corp. and Pandora's Box. He is an ordained minister of the Universal Life Church, registered member of the Church of Satan, 2nd Degree Usui Reiki Practitioner, Psychometrist and currently holds the office of Vice President of The Fort Wayne Pagan Alliance, an all-faith-tolerant organization. He has authored many articles and has acted as director for the local Pagan Pride Day on quite a few occasions. His artwork appears on the cover of *Dark Horizon Records Catalog*, and is featured in Julie Strain's book *Nightmare On Pinup Street*.

Corvis welcomes commentary via email at:
CorvisNocturnum@yahoo.com

His artwork may be viewed at:
www.angelfire.com/in4/darkartistv

His online articles may be read at:
www.angelfire.com/dragon2/corvisnocturnum

RESOURCES

SHOPPING

Alchemy Gothic
(fine quality pewter)
www.alchemyGothic.com

In Dark Decorum
(Gothic shopping in the UK)
www.indarkdecorum.com

Buzz-Works
(gargoyles and home décor)
www.buzz-works.com

Ipso Facto
(Goth fashion and merchandise)
www.ipso-facto.com

Church of Satan Emporium
(LaVey books & merchandise)
www.cosemporium.com

Kambriel
(custom Gothic fashions)
www.kambriel.com

Coffin Case Co.
(guitar, gun, tattoo cases)
www.coffincase.com

Lip Service
(Goth & fetish wear)
www.lip-service.com

Dark Candles
(colored and scented candles)
www.darkcandles.com

Morticia
(Fog Images Photography)
www.fogimages.deviantart.com

Eternal Love
(medieval clothing)
www.eternallove.com

Monolith Graphics
(Gothic artwork by Joseph Vargo)
www.monolithgraphics.com

Pandora's Box
(a division of Spirit Healing, but darker)
www.angelfire.com/in4/dancingwind/Pandora_sBox.html

Spirit Healing Corp.
(magic, spiritual, Pagan supplies)
www.angelfire.com/moon/spirithealing

MUSIC

Arsenic
illdiefree@yahoo.com
(260) 356-4971

Cryptic
www.crypticweb.net

Fog / Typhus
Dark Horizon Records
6453 W. Jefferson Blvd. #666
Fort Wayne, IN 46804
(260) 422-3268
www.darkhorizon666.com

Nox Arcana
www.noxarcana.com

Shroud / IAE Records
1303 Maple Ave.
Fort Wayne, IN 46807
www.shroudmetal.com

URN
Lost Antiquities Music
PO Box 09116
Chicago, IL 60609
www.urncentral.com

Satanic Radio
www.satanismtoday.net
www.freethoughtradio.com
www.radiofreesatan.com

MAGAZINES

Gothic/Vampire

Bite Me!
www.bitememagazine.com

Dark Realms
monolithgraphics.com/darkrealms.html

Gothic Beauty
www.gothicbeauty.com

Gothic Revue
www.gothicrevue.com

Vampire
www.vampire-magazine.com

BDSM / Fetish

Marquis
www.marquis.de

Skin Two
www.skintwo.com

Consent
www.consentmag.com

Whiplash
www.whiplash.ca

BOOK PUBLISHERS

Pagan / Occult / Magic

Feral House Publishing
www.feralhousepublishing.com

Llewellyn Publishing
www.llewellyn.com

New Page Books
www.newpagebooks.com

Red Wheel/Weiser Books
www.redwheelweiser.com

Satanic

Hell's Kitchen Productions
P.O. Box 499, Radio City Station
New York, NY 10101

Monolithic Productions
PO Box 229, 410 Bank Street
Ottawa, Ontario K2P-1Y8 Canada

Purging Talon Publishing
Reverend Matt Paradise
www.purgingtalon.com

COMMUNITY

Art Aguirre
(Modern Primitive, *Mad Mad House*)
Church of Steel:
Body Piercing and Tattoo
826 Broadway
San Diego, CA 92101
www.churchofsteel.com

Michelle Belanger
(author and psychic vampire)
www.michellebelanger.com

Bianca Beauchamp
(fetish model)
www.biancabeauchamp.com

John Coughlin
(author)
www.waningmoon.com

Dragan Dracul
(founder of Clutch Arcane)
www.dragandracul.tripod.com/clutcharcane

Don Henrie
(Vampire, *Mad Mad House*)
www.vampiredon.net

Talia Juliette
(Gothic model)
www.taliajuliette.com

Konstantinos
(author)
www.konstantinos.com

Martin Perrault
(fetish photographer)
www.martinperreault.com

ORGANIZATIONS

Bloodlines International www.bloodlinesint.com
Created as a way to unite vampires, donors, weres, witches and those who support us from coast to coast and from the street to the internet.

Church of Satan
Founded by Anton LaVey
www.churchofsatan.com

Darkness Embraced www.darkness-embraced.com
A dedicated to the creatures of the night, the vampire. Here, you will find extensive amounts of information on vampire myth, legends, real vampires of modern day society.

First Church of Satan
Founded by John and Lillee Allee
www.churchofsatan.org

House Kheperu www.kheperu.org
An eclectic spiritual society dedicated to balance, education, and transformation. We see ourselves as a wisdom tradition, and our function in the community is to research and safeguard metaphysical knowledge as well as to pass this on to those who may benefit from it.

Sanguinarium, Ordo Strigoi VII
www.vampyrealmanac.com

Spellbound
Online resource, links and information
www.angelfire.com/moon/willow4/index.htm

Shelter For Darkness www.shelterfordarkness.com
Darkness Against Child Abuse, Darkness Against Domestic Violence, Darkness Against Drug Abuse, founded by Shadow and Anajeil Villanueva

Temple of Set
www.xeper.org

The Temple of the Vampire www.vampiretemple.com
An international church devoted to the Vampire religion, legally registered with the U.S. federal government since 1989.

RECOMMENDED READING

Magic   *Gothic Grimoire* by Konstantinos
Occult   *Out of the Shadows* by John J. Coughlin
Wiccan   *Nocturnal Witchcraft* by Konstantinos
             Summoning Spirits by Konstantinos
             Speaking with the Dead by Konstantinos
             The Wiccan Bible by A.J. Drew

Vampire *The Origins of Pranic Vampyrism* by Father Sebastian
             Piercing the Darkness by Katherine Ramsland
             The Psychic Vampire Codex by Michelle Bellanger
             The Science of Vampiress by Katherine Ramsland
             Tales From The Dark Tower by Joseph Vargo
             "V" Vampyre Book by Father Sebastian

Satanism *The Black Flame*, the International Forum of the Church of Satan
             The Church of Satan by Blanche Barton, a detailed history of the Church
             The Cloven Hoof, the official Bulletin and Tribunal of the Church of Satan
             The Devil's Notebook. Satan Speaks! by Anton Szandor LaVey
             Might is Right by Ragnar Redbeard, with a forward by Anton LaVey
             Satan Wants You by Arthur Lyons, published by Mysterious Press (1988)
             The Satanic Witch, with a new forward by High Priestess Nadramia
             and revised afterward by Magistra Blanche Barton
             The Secret Life of A Satanist by Blanche Barton

Books by *Lucifer Rising,* Gavin Baddeley's History of Satanism, with extensive coverage of
Church   the contemporary scene featuring interviews with prominent Satanists such as
of Satan Anton LaVey, Boyd Rice, Blanche Barton, Peter H. Gilmore, and Coop, as well as
members interviews with Satanic bands The Electric Hellfire Club, Acheron, Blood Axis,
             King Diamond, and many more.
             Lord of Chaos, Michael Moynihan and Didrik Søderlind's definitive chronicle of
             the Satanic Metal Underground and how it came to be, featuring interviews with
             members of these bands as well as many commentators on the subject.

BDSM   *Different Loving: A Complete Exploration of the World of Sexual Dominance
             and Submission* by William Brame, Gloria Brame and Jon Jacobs
             Slavecraft: Roadmaps for Erotic Servitude by A Grateful Slave with Guy Baldwin
             *Screw the Roses, Send Me the Thorns: The Romance and Sexual Sorcery of
             Sadomasochism* by Philip Miller, Molly Devon

 ORDERING

To order an additional copy of this book.
Send check or money order for $17.95 plus $3.00 postage per book.
Send payment along with your name and address to:

Eric Vernor
P.O. Box 11496
Fort Wayne, IN 46858-1496

Please allow at least 2 weeks for checks to clear prior to shipping.
Use the order form below -or- include <u>all</u> info on your own paper.

Please send me (#) _____ *of* EMBRACING THE DARKNESS

_____

name

_____

street address or p.o. box

_____

city, state, zip

_____

email or phone (in the event we need to contact you regarding your order)

Spirit Healing
& Pandora's Box

*For all your magical, spiritual
and pagan supplies.*

*If you find yourself in the Fort Wayne area,
feel free to stop by and visit with us.*

SPIRIT HEALING & PANDORA'S BOX
1430 West Main Street
Fort Wayne, IN 46808

Or visit us online at:

PANDORA'S BOX
www.angelfire.com/in4/dancingwind/Pandora_sBox.html

SPIRIT HEALING
www.angelfire.com/moon/spirithealing